Second Language Acquisition and Linguistic Theory

"There's a moment. . . ."
Oh, Bear.

Second Language Acquisition and Linguistic Theory

Edited by

John Archibald
University of Calgary

Copyright © Blackwell Publishers Ltd 2000. Editorial arrangement and introduction copyright © John Archibald 2000.

First published 2000

2 4 6 8 10 9 7 5 3 1

Blackwell Publishers Inc.
350 Main Street
Malden, Massachusetts 02148
USA

Blackwell Publishers Ltd
108 Cowley Road
Oxford OX4 1JF
UK

Library of Congress Cataloging-in-Publication Data

Second language acquisition and linguistic theory / edited by John
  Archibald.
     p. cm.
  Includes bibliographical references and index.
    ISBN 0–631–20591–8 (alk. paper). — ISBN 0–631–20592–6 (pbk. :
alk. paper)
    1. Second language acquisition. I. Archibald, John.
  P118.2.S425 2000
  401′.93—dc21   99–16612
                                            CIP

British Library Cataloguing in Publication Data

A CIP catalogue record for this book is available from the British Library.

Typeset in 10½ on 13pt Sabon
by Graphicraft Limited, Hong Kong
Printed in Great Britain by MPG Books, Bodmin, Cornwall

This book is printed on acid-free paper.

Contents

Contributors

John Archibald is a Professor of Linguistics at the University of Calgary. He specializes in research on the acquisition of phonology in both first and second languages. He has been involved in the authoring or editing of six books on linguistics and language acquisition, most recently *Second Language Phonology* (John Benjamins, 1998) and (co-edited with William O'Grady) the fourth edition of *Contemporary Linguistic Analysis* (Prentice-Hall, in press).

Cynthia Brown is an Assistant Professor of Linguistics at the University of Delaware. Her research focuses on the acquisition of phonological systems by young children and the impact of phonological acquisition on the development and organization of the speech perception system. In addition, her research examines the role that phonological representations play in the on-line processing of native and non-native speech sounds by adults and she has conducted several studies investigating the second language acquisition of English sound contrasts by speakers of Japanese, Mandarin, and Korean.

Alan Juffs is Associate Professor of Linguistics at the University of Pittsburgh. His research interests include the semantics–syntax interface and constraint-based approaches to second language processing.

Donna Lardiere is Associate Professor of Applied and Theoretical Linguistics at Georgetown University. Her research has primarily focused on the relationship between morphology and syntax in second language acquisition, and the role of morphology in formulating theories about access to Universal Grammar in SLA. She lives in Washington, D.C.

Gary Libben is Professor of Linguistics at the University of Alberta, Canada. His research has focused on the role of morphology in lexical processing and has examined differences among languages and subject populations. In his research publications, Dr Libben has also advanced new techniques for the investigation of both on-line and off-line lexical processing by native speakers, aphasics, bilinguals, and second language learners.

Bonnie D. Schwartz is a Reader in the Department of Linguistics and English Language at the University of Durham. She specializes in first and second language acquisition of syntax, in addition to research in Germanic syntax. She has published widely in a variety of journals.

Rex A. Sprouse is an Associate Professor of Germanic Studies at Indiana University. Within the field of second language acquisition, his primary research interests lie in the roles of Universal Grammar and transfer. Much of his current research is devoted to the development of the Full Transfer/ Full Access model (with Bonnie D. Schwartz, University of Durham) and to exploring the syntax–semantics interface in Interlanguage (with Laurent Dekydtspotter, Indiana University). He is also interested in the syntax of Germanic, Romance, and Celtic languages.

Lydia White is Professor of Linguistics at McGill University. She was one of the first researchers to argue for a role for Universal Grammar in L2 acquisition and she has published extensively in this area. She is on the editorial boards of several journals and she is co-editor of the book series Language Acquisition and Language Disorders, published by John Benjamins.

Martha Young-Scholten is a senior lecturer at the University of Durham. Her research revolves around the adult second language acquisition of phonology and morpho-syntax and the implications of such research for classroom teaching. These areas, as well as language and literacy and first language acquisition in exceptional circumstances, are the focus of her teaching.

Acknowledgments

I would like to thank the following people for helping to put this collection together: Susan Bennett, Naomi Bolotin, Susanne Carroll, Ton Dijkstra, Lynn Eubank, Eithne Guilfoyle, Michael Harrington, Murray Munro, Wayne O'Neil, Joe Pater, Keren Rice, Betsy Ritter, and Sara Thomas Rosen. I would also like to thank Anthony Grahame, the copy-editor of this project, for his careful reading of the text, as well as Steve Smith and Beth Remmes at Blackwell Publishers for their help and guidance. Jana Carson proofread the entire text.

Introduction

As its title may well suggest, this collection is concerned with many aspects of second language grammars. Over the years, the amount of research in different sub-fields of second language acquisition research has made it difficult for scholars to keep abreast of all the current literature. This collection is designed to deal with that difficulty (admittedly with the limitation of considering work undertaken within the formalist, generative tradition of grammar). A grammar, then, is taken to be the representation of knowledge that individuals have of their language within a particular domain.

Investigating the properties of these grammars is not simple. Throughout the book, we will see how a number of tools can be brought to bear on the problem: perception studies, processing studies, and the traditional arsenal of linguistic theory.

In this collection, I have brought together chapters that look at knowledge of phonological segments, syllable structure, morphology, syntax, and semantics. There is also a chapter that deals with what processing studies tell us about the storage of second language grammars.

Cynthia Brown, "The interrelation between speech perception and phonological acquisition from infant to adult," develops a model of speech perception, couched within current phonological theory, that accounts for the influence of the native grammar in both infant and adult speech perception. This model accounts for the differential success that speakers of different first languages have in acquiring a given non-native contrast.

Martha Young-Scholten and John Archibald, "Second language syllable structure," also contrast first and second language acquisition of phonological structure focusing on the differing repair strategies (e.g., deletion versus epenthesis) employed by the two populations. They discuss the influence of such factors as elicitation task, written input, and first language feature geometry that may influence the second language syllable structure. They conclude that, as in other domains, while it may be possible to reset existing structures, it may prove to be difficult if not impossible to trigger new structure that is not present in the first language.

Donna Lardiere, "Mapping features to forms in second language acquisition," examines the relationship of morphological form to syntactic competence in second language acquisition. Within current generative models, the featural properties associated with functional categories are presumed to drive syntactic movement via feature-checking computations. She argues that the features thought to be responsible for UG-constrained operations such as subject raising, nominative case licensing, verb raising, etc. are present and fully specified in the L2 grammar despite deficient morphological affixation. This suggests that syntactic and morphological development are autonomous (though related by a mapping procedure) in second language development.

Lydia White, "Second language acquisition: from initial to final state," addresses three broad themes: (1) theories about the L2 initial state and the kind of grammatical knowledge that the L2 learner starts out with, (2) theories about stages of development, the nature of the stages, and the kind of grammar development that takes place, and (3) theories about the final state or ultimate attainment possible in L2 acquisition. She demonstrates that L2 learners can acquire subtle and abstract properties of the L2 which are not obviously present in the L1 and which are underdetermined by the L2 input. This suggests that interlanguage grammars can be pushed in new directions whether the more abstract underlying principles come from UG, or the L1, or both.

Bonnie D. Schwartz and Rex A. Sprouse, "When syntactic theories evolve: consequences for L2 acquisition research," note that the leading question animating generative research on second language acquisition is whether interlanguage grammars fall within the boundaries set by UG, and if they do not, what their formal properties are. In this chapter, they illustrate how the revisions in linguistic theory can fundamentally affect the conclusions drawn in generative L2 acquisition research. By stepping back from the technicalities of theory, researchers must determine if they have uncovered genuine poverty-of-the-stimulus effects, and whether they see convergent developmental paths among speakers of typologically distinct L1's. Such practice illuminates the etiology and epistemological status of interlanguage grammars.

Alan Juffs, "An overview of the second language acquisition of links between verb semantics and morpho-syntax," provides us with an overview of the research on the place of verb semantics in syntactic theory, as well as a discussion of how second language learners come to acquire the knowledge of mapping from the lexicon to morpho-syntax. He addresses such phenomena as the dative alternation, the locative alternation, and the causative/inchoative alternation. He shows strong evidence for the influence of L1 effects in this domain, however, advanced learners seem able to recover from overgeneralizations by relying on positive evidence from verbs which share the same semantic conflation class.

Gary Libben, "Representation and processing in the second language lexicon: the homogeneity hypothesis," addresses the question of how words are represented in the bilingual lexicon and how they are accessed in language production and comprehension. He argues that monolinguals, bilinguals, and second language learners possess the same kinds of lexical representations and employ the same kinds of processes in the activation of words in the mental lexicon. Thus, lexical knowledge can be represented in a single lexical architecture and there is no need to postulate individual lexicons for individual languages.

It should be obvious by now that the scope of this collection is sweeping. I hope that its breadth will be of use to second language acquisition researchers who would like to catch up on what has been going on outside their area of specialization. The collection could also serve as a textbook for senior undergraduate or graduate courses on second language acquisition and linguistic theory.

John Archibald
Calgary, March 1999

1

The Interrelation between Speech Perception and Phonological Acquisition from Infant to Adult*

Cynthia Brown

Introduction

The acquisition of a second language (L2) is clearly *somehow* different from that of a first language (L1): adult second language learners rarely (if ever) achieve the same native competence that children do learning their first language and, conversely, children never experience the degree of difficulty that L2 learners do.[1] This disparity between L2 and L1 acquisition is perhaps most apparent with respect to the acquisition of a second phonological system. Whereas children consistently achieve native competence across the full range of subtle and complex phonological properties of their language,

* Portions of this research were previously presented at the 1994 Boston University Conference on Language Acquisition, the 1994 Second Language Research Forum, and the 1996 Pacific Second Language Research Forum; this chapter is a revised version of chapter four of Brown (1997). Several people have contributed to the completion of this research: I am grateful to Joseph Tomei and John Matthews for lending their voices for experimental stimuli, to Masanobu Ueda for his assistance with the DAT equipment at Hokkaido University, to Dongdong Chen for recruiting Chinese subjects in Montreal, Canada, to Takako Kawasaki for recruiting Japanese subjects in Montreal, Canada and to Michie Namita for recruiting Korean and Chinese subjects in Sapporo, Japan. I would also like to thank Heather Goad and Lydia White for their guidance throughout the course of conducting this research. Finally, this research could not have been completed without the generous contribution of John Matthews to the design and presentation of these studies. The experimental research was supported by SSHRC research grant #410920047 to Lydia White; materials used in stimuli preparation for the picture test reported here were adapted from the Bilingual Aphasia Test (Paradis and Libben, 1987).

second language learners often have extraordinary difficulty mastering the pronunciation and intonation patterns of their L2. This lack of success is often taken as evidence that Universal Grammar (UG) does not operate in second language acquisition; but, perhaps there is another explanation. As White (1989) points out, other factors, in addition to UG, are necessary for successful first and, presumably, second language acquisition (for example, sufficient input and various learning mechanisms). An intriguing line of research suggests that the failure of some L2 learners to attain a native-like competence is attributable to these other factors, rather than to the non-operation of UG.

One such factor that distinguishes second language acquisition from first language acquisition is the fact that the second language learner comes to the task of acquisition already knowing a language. Most current theories of second language acquisition do, in fact, assume that the native language of the learner plays a role in acquisition. Although researchers generally agree that the learner's existing linguistic knowledge exerts some influence on the acquisition process, there is considerable debate as to precisely *what* role the native language plays (e.g., Bley-Vroman's *Fundamental Difference Hypothesis*, 1989, versus White's *Transfer Hypothesis*, 1988; see also papers in Schwartz and Eubank, 1996, on the L2 initial state). Moreover, existing research suggests that the influence of the native grammar is not absolute: some aspects of the L1 seem to prevent successful acquisition of particular L2 structures, whereas other properties of the L2 are acquired with little or no interference from the native grammar (Schwartz, in press). The challenge for second language theory now is to provide a principled explanation for the presence or absence of L1 influence, that is, what determines "partial influence".

Building on the insights of prior phonological research, this chapter develops a model of speech perception, couched within current phonological theory, that accounts for the influence of the native grammar in both infant and adult speech perception. More specifically, by utilizing the theory of Feature Geometry, the proposed model demonstrates how the monotonic acquisition of phonological structure by young children restricts their sensitivity to particular non-native contrasts and how the continued operation of this existing phonological structure in adult speech perception constrains which non-native contrasts adult learners will be sensitive to in the L2 input and, therefore, are capable of acquiring. By forging a link between infant speech perception and phonological acquisition, this research lays the foundation for a unified theoretical account of the interrelation between phonological acquisition and speech perception in children and adults. It also offers an explanation for why learners perceive L2 sounds in terms of their native phonemic categories; by isolating and characterizing those phonological properties of the L1 that impinge upon L2 acquisition, this research identifies why and how this equivalence classification takes place. Finally, by demonstrating how the L1 grammar can both facilitate and hinder acquisition, these findings provide an answer to one of the questions currently central to second language acquisition theory: what determines partial L1 influence? The model outlined in this chapter accounts for the differential success that speakers of different L1s have in acquiring a given non-native contrast; it also accounts for the differential success that speakers with the same L1 have in acquiring various non-native contrasts. Furthermore, the experimental studies reported here demonstrate how the existing phonological system may block accurate perception of the input, thereby preventing the acquisition of novel segmental representations; it also establishes the circumstances in which the native grammar actually facilitates perception of non-native contrasts, demonstrating that when there is sufficient intake to the acquisition device, novel segmental representations can be successfully acquired.

We will begin by reviewing some of the previous research that has been conducted on the L2 acquisition of segments in order to set the context for the present research program and see why a new analysis is needed. Next, the relevant aspects of phonological theory will be laid out and explained. This will be followed by an examination of the development of the native phonological and perceptual systems, which will then lead us to a theory of phonological interference. After the implications of this theory for second language acquisition are laid out, the results of three experimental studies which test this theory will be reported and discussed. The chapter concludes by considering some of the implications of these experimental data for the theory of phonological interference developed here as well as our theory of second language acquisition.

Historical Context and Theoretical Background

Previous L2 phonological research

Although previous L2 phonological research has addressed the question of *whether* the native language plays a role (e.g., Briere, 1966; Flege, 1981; Wode, 1978, 1992), it has not attempted to answer the question of *why* the native language influences L2 acquisition, nor has it formally articulated the mechanisms by which the native grammar influences this acquisition. Using the tools of current phonological theory, we are now in a position to develop a theory of L2 phonological interference which includes a principled explanation for the existence of L1 influence in some instances and its absence in others, as well as a description of the mechanism(s) by which this influence is exerted.

Conducting research in applied areas such as acquisition requires one to strike a delicate balance between (at least) two continually developing theories: our theory of acquisition and our theory of grammar. In the case of

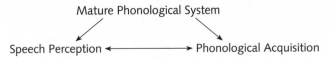

Figure 1.1   Interrelation between speech perception, phonological acquisition and the mature system

L2 phonological acquisition, we must integrate insights from the theory of second language acquisition and current phonological theory. Advances in one of these usually requires us to reinterpret implications of the other in light of these new developments and to recast our theoretical models and experimental hypotheses. Similarly, failure of our acquisition models to correctly account for some aspect of the data force us to consider whether it is the acquisition theory or the linguistic theory underlying our model which is inadequate and needs to be modified. This complex bi-directional relationship often leads to a non-linear flow of progress in acquisition research. We are now once again at a point of reinterpretation, forced by the limitations of current models to reformulate our theory of L2 phoneme acquisition in terms of shifts within both the theory of segmental representation and the theory of second language acquisition.

Successful acquisition of phonological representations requires accurate perception of phonemic contrasts in the input; it is therefore clear that a comprehensive model of L2 phoneme acquisition must integrate not only a theory of second language acquisition and a theory of phonological representation, but also a theory of speech perception. Thus, it is not enough to ask only how the existing phonological system affects acquisition of L2 segments; we must consider all of the relationships illustrated in figure 1.1.

The majority of research on L2 phonological acquisition has investigated the relationship between the mature phonological system and phonological acquisition. But, the interrelation of these factors raises three additional issues that an adequate theory of L2 phoneme acquisition must explain: (1) how does the mature phonological system affect speech perception? (2) how does speech perception affect phonological acquisition? and (conversely) (3) how does phonological acquisition affect speech perception? By isolating the specific research questions addressed by previous L2 phoneme research and highlighting the particular theory of acquisition and/or theory of phonological representation assumed by each approach, we will see why a new analysis is needed.

The earliest systematic approach to the acquisition of L2 segments was undertaken within the contrastive analysis framework, the prevailing theory of second language acquisition of the time (Lado, 1957; Lehn and Slager, 1959; Stockwell and Bowen, 1965). The primary question addressed by this research was how the L1 influenced the acquisition of L2 segments, where acquisition was measured by the learner's ability to produce those segments.

This approach, however, was unable to account for aspects of the observed acquisition data. In particular, it incorrectly predicted that an L2 learner would have the same degree of difficulty with any and all of the L2 sounds not present in the L1 inventory, when, in fact, learners' performance on different L2 segments in experimental conditions ranges from native-like levels of accuracy to chance performance (see Munro, Flege and MacKay, 1996, for a detailed discussion of this point). This approach also failed to explain why learners with different L1s would substitute different L1 sounds for a given L2 sound (e.g., Japanese speakers substitute [s] for [θ] but Russian speakers substitute [t], despite the fact that these L1s contain both /s/ and /t/ – Hancin-Bhatt, 1994a). These shortcomings, and in fact the most significant limitation of this approach, were due not to its comparison of L1 and L2 inventories, but rather to the level of phonological representation at which the languages where compared: these researchers took the phoneme to be the relevant unit of analysis.

Influenced by developments in generative phonology (and publication of Chomsky and Halle's *The Sound Pattern of English*, 1968), the next wave of research on L2 phoneme acquisition focused their analyses on the differences and similarities in distinctive features between the L1 and L2 (Michaels, 1973, 1974; Ritchie, 1968). According to this line of research, difficulty with particular L2 sounds could be explained in terms of featural differences between the L1 and L2, combined with the learner's perceptual biases. This line of research constituted an advance over the previous contrastive analysis approach in that its focus on the distinctive feature as the relevant unit for comparing the L1 and L2 provided language-internal evidence for differential substitutions. Moreover, it represented the first attempt to address the issue of how the mature phonological system might affect speech perception and how that, in turn, might affect phonological acquisition; however, it did not attempt to formally articulate this L1–L2 perceptual mapping, nor did these researchers provide any experimental evidence for their claims about how the native grammar influenced perception.

In the 1970s and 1980s, several perceptual studies conducted with native speakers and language learners provided the necessary experimental evidence, demonstrating that phonemes are indeed generally perceived in terms of the speaker's native categories (Abramson and Lisker, 1970; Miyawaki, Strange, Verbrugge, Liberman, Jenkins and Fujimura, 1975; Werker and Tees, 1984b; Williams, 1977). Since that time, three models have been proposed to explain how L2 sounds are mapped onto L1 sounds. The first model we will consider restricts itself to the relationship between the mature phonological system and speech perception; it does not address how phonological acquisition relates to these two factors. Best (1993, 1994) has developed the Perceptual Assimilation Model (PAM) to explain the role that a speaker's L1 phonological system plays in the perception of non-native sounds. According to this model, non-native sounds are assimilated to a listener's native categories on the basis of their respective articulatory similarities (more specifically, the spatial proximity of constriction location and active articulators); the degree to which a non-native contrast can be assimilated to native categories determines how well (if at all) a listener will be able to perceive that non-native contrast. While Best's proposal is based on, and supported by, experimental perceptual data, it lacks precise objective criteria for determining how non-native contrasts will be assimilated into native categories. Thus, although the PAM describes the role that a speaker's L1 phonological system plays in the perception of non-native sounds, it does not provide an explanation for why or precisely how this mapping occurs. Moreover, Best's model, concerned primarily with the role of the L1 in the perception of *foreign* sounds, is essentially static; that is, it does not include any means by which the existing L1 phonemic system might be altered by exposure to non-native segmental contrasts and, therefore, does not directly address the acquisition of novel segments.

One model that does address the issue of L2 segment acquisition is the Speech Learning Model (SLM), developed by Flege (1991, 1992, 1995). The SLM attempts to explain how speech perception affects phonological acquisition by distinguishing two kinds of sounds: "new" and "similar". New sounds are those that are not identified with any L1 sound, while similar sounds are those perceived to be the same as certain L1 sounds. Flege suggests that although the phonetic systems used in production and perception remain adaptive over the life span and reorganize in response to sounds in the L2 input, a process of "equivalence classification" hinders or prevents the establishment of new phonetic categories for similar sounds. However, this model does not include a theory-based proposal as to how L2 sounds are equated with L1 sounds; although equivalence classification is stated in probabilistic terms, allowing for the eventual development of L2 categories, there is no concrete proposal for how or when this takes place. Thus, these two models, the PAM and the SLM, attempt to elucidate the interrelation between the mature phonological system, speech perception and L2 phonological acquisition. However, despite their claim that there is an underlying mechanism that maps L2 sounds onto L1 categories, they fail to articulate the nature of that mechanism or adequately formalize the perceptual mapping process.

The most extensive model of speech perception–phonological acquisition interaction to be proposed thus far is Hancin-Bhatt's Feature Competition Model (FCM) (1994a, b). Expanding on the earlier work by Ritchie (1968) and Michaels (1973) described above, this model assumes that the features utilized in a grammar differ with respect to their "prominence": features (and feature patterns) used more frequently in the language's phonology will be more prominent than less frequently used features. Those features that are more prominent in the L1 system will tend to have a greater influence on learners' perception of new L2 sounds; that is, the feature prominences in the L1 will guide how L2 sounds are mapped onto existing L1 categories. Thus, like the PAM and SLM, the FCM assumes that L2 sounds are assimilated to L1 categories, yet this model goes one step further by providing an algorithm for determining feature prominence and, thereby, generating testable predictions for differential perception and substitution of interdentals across learners with different L1s. Furthermore, it is the first comprehensive model to investigate both the relationship between the mature phonological system and speech perception and the relationship between speech perception and the acquisition of L2 phonemic representations. Thus, this model addresses two of the three relationships indicated in (1) above; it also provides a more formal articulation of the L1–L2 perceptual mapping. However, to date its scope has been limited to the study of interdental substitutions; it is not clear whether this model can account for substitutions of other types of segments cross-linguistically or whether it can account for differential difficulty that speakers of a single L1 encounter in the acquisition of various L2 segments. Most importantly, though, the FCM does not address the reciprocal relation between perception and acquisition, namely how (L1) phonological acquisition affects speech perception.

So, while we are moving closer and closer to a formalization of the influence that the mature phonological system has on speech perception (and the consequence of this for L2 acquisition), we still do not understand how the interrelation between speech perception and phonological knowledge originates; therefore, we fail to capture the essential nature of the phonological transfer mechanism. Investigating the development of speech perception and phonological acquisition in young children will enable us to explain why the mature phonological system exerts such a profound influence in adult speech perception; moreover, utilizing the tools of current phonological theory will allow us to articulate the L1–L2 perceptual mapping mechanism more precisely, as well as allow us to explain how the new phonemic categories develop in the L2 learner (i.e., how the relationships in figure 1.1 change over time).

Phonological theory and the representation of phonemes

Whereas previous research on L1 phonological interference primarily considered the phonemic categories of a language, phonological theory within the generative framework assumes that phonemes themselves have an internal structure. Thus, one way current phonological theory provides greater insight into the phenomenon of L1 influence is the distinction made between phonological representations and the components that comprise those representations. L2 phonological researchers now have an additional tool of analysis: the internal sub-components of phonemes constitute a further level of linguistic knowledge which may impinge upon L2 acquisition. However, these components (i.e., distinctive features) are not simply unordered bundles, as was assumed in the SPE framework (and theories of L2 phoneme acquisition couched within this framework). Instead, the distinctive features are

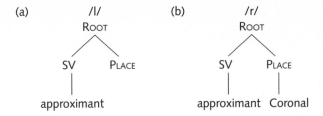

Figure 1.2 Segmental representations for phonemes that are contrastive in a language (English /l/ vs. /r/)

themselves structured – an advancement which has implications for our theory of speech perception and phonological acquisition. Since an understanding of the internal structure of phonemes is necessary for the subsequent discussion of phonological interference, we will begin with a brief review of the relevant aspects of the theory of segmental representation assumed here.[2]

According to the theory of Feature Geometry, phonemes consist of distinctive features which are organized into a systematic hierarchy of constituents (Clements, 1985; Sagey, 1986).[3] Each phoneme has a unique structural representation (i.e., feature geometry) that distinguishes it from other segments in an inventory. Much of the work in phonological theory, as in linguistic theory in general, has been guided by the presumption that redundant information (defined as that information that can be predicted or easily supplied by derivation, e.g., syllable structure) is absent from underlying representations (Chomsky and Halle, 1968). Within Feature Geometry this principle is also extended to segmental representations.

One such theory of underspecification is Minimally Contrastive Underspecification. According to this position, a segmental representation contains only the information needed to contrast it from all other segments in the system; any further specification will be provided by a system of phonetic implementation (Avery and Rice, 1989; cf. Archangeli, 1984, 1988, on Radical Underspecification). Thus, the precise representation of a segment will depend entirely upon which segments it contrasts with in the particular inventory. For example, in English, where the lateral approximant /l/ and central approximant /r/ are contrastive, /l/ may be represented as (a) in figure 1.2 while /r/ may be represented as (b), omitting irrelevant structure (Piggott, 1993; Brown, 1993b, 1995).[4]

The fact that these segments have different representations reflects the fact that they are contrastive phonemes in the language; the presence of [coronal] in the representation of only one of them is sufficient to distinguish these segments in the grammar.

Conversely, when these two segments are not contrastive in a language, they will not have distinct representations. For example, in Japanese, both [l] and [ɾ] are freely varying allophones of a single phoneme, so there will be

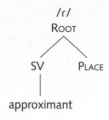

Figure 1.3   Segmental representation of Japanese /r/

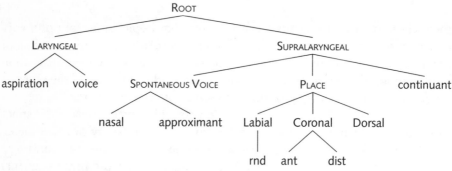

Note: rnd = round, ant = anterior, dist = distributed

Figure 1.4   A model of Feature Geometry

only one underlying representation for these two surface segments. This is given in figure 1.3.

Despite the fact that this Japanese segment is realized as a coronal, in accordance with our theory of underspecification, it is not specified for the feature [coronal] because it does not contrast with any other coronal approximants.[5] The phonetic realization of this segment as an [l] or an [ɾ] (which, unlike the English /r/, is a flap) varies freely (International Phonetic Association, 1979; Vance, 1987). Thus, in this way a speaker's knowledge of which sounds in his or her language are contrastive is represented by distinctive segmental representations.

The full set of features manipulated in the world's languages and their dependency relations can be represented in terms of a single, universal Feature Geometry. This universal geometry is given in figure 1.4 for illustration.[6]

This Feature Geometry is contained in the phonological component of Universal Grammar, the innate language faculty ascribed to the child by generative theorists. Like a syntactic principle or parameter, this geometry constrains the acquisition process and provides the learner with information about what phonemic oppositions are possible in natural languages.

Thus, while no one language manipulates all components of this universal Feature Geometry, every phoneme in the world's languages can be represented in terms of the features and structural relations present in this geometry. Two structural relations between features – constituency and dependency – are particularly important and must be captured in *any* theory of segments. Dependency is a structural relationship between features, such that the presence of a dependent node (or feature) in the representation of a segment entails the presence of its superordinate node in that representation. For example, in the model in figure 1.4, the feature [anterior] is a dependent of the Coronal node and all representations specified for [anterior] will also contain the Coronal node. Constituency refers to the structural relation that holds among features that are dominated by a common node in the geometry. Since phonological processes manipulate constituents of segmental structure, the features of a constituent all pattern together in the phonological operations of a grammar. Again, considering figure 1.4, a phonological process that manipulates the Coronal node will also affect the [anterior] and [distributed] features.

Languages will differ with respect to their phoneme inventories and, hence, with respect to the set of phonological features they manipulate. However, the organization of those features, as given by the universal Feature Geometry, will be the same in every language. The learner's task is to determine which of the phonological features contained in this universal geometry are used to contrast phonemes in the language he or she is learning and to construct the appropriate representations. In the remainder of this chapter, we will consider whether L2 learners can acquire non-native segmental representations as well as how, and to what extent, the native phonological system influences this process.

A Theory of Phonological Interference

In developing a theory of L1 influence, one of the issues we must address is *why* the L1 grammar exerts this influence. With respect to phonological interference, the relevant question is why foreign sounds are perceived in terms of the learner's native sound categories. In order to fully understand why the phonological system affects perception in this way, we must examine the genetic development of these systems, as well as any interdependence between them. Studying the development of the L1 system will offer us insight into its operation in mature speakers; in addition, an understanding of how phonological knowledge is acquired in L1 acquisition will enable us to determine what conditions are necessary for successful L2 acquisition.

L1 phoneme acquisition

Since segments are distinguished in a grammar by their internal feature geometries, acquisition of a phonemic contrast involves the acquisition of the relevant structure (i.e., distinctive features) that differentiates those two phonemes (Rice and Avery, 1995, based on Jakobson, 1941). The child is able to contrast the two phonemes in his or her grammar once that phonological structure has been acquired and a representation has been constructed. Brown and Matthews (1993, 1997) demonstrate experimentally that children's ability to differentiate phonemes phonologically develops gradually over time and in a systematic order that is consistent across children (see also Barton, 1980; Edwards, 1974; Garnica, 1973; Shvachkin, 1948, for related studies). Based on these results, they argue that UG provides the child's emerging grammar with a minimal amount of segmental structure (in fact, only those portions of the feature geometry that are universal) which is subsequently expanded over the course of acquisition until the adult feature geometry for the particular language is attained.

The systematic order of acquisition results from the hypothesized acquisition process and the nature of Feature Geometry itself; the child will only elaborate the feature geometry in his or her grammar in ways that are consistent with the hierarchical organization of features in UG. Specifically, the particular dependency and constituency relations that are encoded in the feature geometry in UG will be respected in the geometry posited by the child. For example, the presence of a dependent feature in a representation entails the presence of that feature's superordinate node. By extension, superordinate structure must be posited in the child's feature geometry before dependent structure can be elaborated. As a result, children will phonologically distinguish those segments that require less structure to differentiate before distinguishing those segments that require highly articulated structure. Thus, phonological structure is added to the child's grammar in a uniform, step-by-step fashion.

This step-by-step elaboration of the child's feature geometry in his or her grammar is driven by the child's detection of contrastive use of segments in the input (Jakobson, 1941; Rice and Avery, 1995). Once a child notices that two segments are used contrastively (i.e., are distinct phonemes), the phonological structure that differentiates the two segments is added to his or her grammar. If the child never perceives contrastive use of two segments (because, for example, they are allophones of a single phoneme in that language), the structure that differentiates them will never be posited. Therefore, the mere *presence* of two contrastive segments in the input (while necessary) is not sufficient to trigger acquisition; the learner must *detect* the contrast in the input.

Infant speech perception

In order for a learner to detect that two sounds are used contrastively, the learner must be able to discriminate the two sounds perceptually. Hence, proper development of the phonological system is dependent on properties of the speech perception mechanism. Given the fact that a child may be born into any language environment, it is imperative that he or she be equipped with adequate cognitive machinery to perceive (or, at the very least, be pre-disposed to perceive) the whole range of possible phonetic contrasts (cf. Burnham, 1986). Researchers have, in fact, demonstrated that infants as young as one month old are able to acoustically discriminate not only the sounds of the ambient language but many non-native contrasts as well (Eilers, Gavin and Oller, 1982; Eimas, Siqueland, Jusczyk and Vigorito, 1971; Streeter, 1976; Trehub, 1976; see Mehler, 1985, for a review).

Since the detection of contrasts in the input is crucial for the acquisition of phonemic representations, we need to consider how this capacity changes (if at all) as the child develops. In particular, whether or not an L2 learner has the capacity to perceive a non-native contrast will be a factor in determining if he or she will be able to construct the phonological representations necessary to distinguish the two segments phonologically. It is now well established that the ability to acoustically discriminate non-native contrasts decreases rapidly in infancy with exposure to a specific language, until the child is able to discriminate only those contrasts present in the language being acquired (see Werker and Polka, 1993, for a review of studies that establish this obser-vation). In a series of studies, Janet Werker and her colleagues demonstrate that the decline in the ability to acoustically discriminate non-native con-trasts occurs within the first year of life (Werker, Gilbert, Humphrey and Tees, 1981; Werker and LaLonde, 1988; Werker and Tees, 1984a, b; and also Best and McRoberts, 1989; Best, 1994).[7] What is particularly fascinat-ing is that this decline in perceptual capacity does not appear to be tempor-ally uniform for all non-native contrasts. Experimental results indicate that perceptual sensitivity to certain non-native contrasts is lost before sensitivity to others, suggesting that loss of perceptual sensitivity to non-native con-trasts is gradual and proceeds in a systematic order. An explanation for this decline in speech perception abilities, in particular one that integrates the role of linguistic experience, is still needed.[8] Both Werker and Best have tentat-ively suggested that the decline in the ability to discriminate some non-native contrasts may reflect the first stage of phonological development in the child, though neither is specific as to which aspect of the developing phonology might be responsible for this change. In the following section, I examine some findings from infant speech perception research and suggest a causal link between the development of a learner's feature geometry and the sub-sequent decline in perceptual capabilities. Establishing such a link will have important consequences for the acquisition of a second phonological system.

The role of the L1 phonological system in speech perception

If we consider the findings from the infant speech perception research together with the research on phonological acquisition, an interesting parallelism emerges. We see that infants' perceptual capacities gradually "*degrade*" from

all potential contrasts to only native contrasts (with some interesting exceptions), while their ability to discriminate segments phonologically gradually
improves from no contrasts to only native contrasts. An exhaustive comparison of the stages of phonological and perceptual development is not
feasible at this point, due to the limited number of non-native contrasts that
have been investigated thus far. However, an examination of the data that
we do have available suggests an intriguing possibility. According to Brown
and Matthews, children first phonologically differentiate labials from velars,
followed by labials from coronals. They do not distinguish segments that
require a coronal node, such as /l/ and /r/, until relatively late. So, the node
that distinguishes velar segments from other places of articulation is posited
by the child before the node to distinguish among coronal segments is posited.
Measuring auditory perception, Werker found the mirror order, with the
perception of contrasts involving velars declining before contrasts involving
coronals. Based on this convergence of the learner's perceptual and phonological capacities on the set of native sounds, Brown (1993a, 1998) proposes
that there is a causal link between the learner's phonological development
and the concomitant decline in his or her ability to acoustically discriminate
non-native sounds.[9]

According to Brown's proposal, the acquisition of phonological structure
(more specifically, the elaboration of feature geometry) in the child's grammar
imposes upon his or her perceptual system the specific boundaries within
which phonemic categories are perceived. In other words, the degradation of
the perceptual capacities and the increase in the ability to distinguish sounds
phonologically are the result of the same internal mechanism, namely the
construction of phonological representations. This layer of phonological structure subsequently mediates between the acoustic signal and the linguistic
processing system.

If we are correct in postulating that the acquisition of a phonological
system determines the course of speech perception development, then it is
reasonable to assume that the phonological system continues to constrain
speech perception in adults. Mediating between the acoustic signal and the
linguistic system, the phonological structure of the native grammar can be
viewed as a filter that funnels acoustically distinct stimuli into a single phonemic category. This results in the well-documented phenomenon of categorical
speech perception, whereby speakers of a language are able to easily distinguish members of different native phonemic categories and relatively unable
to distinguish members of the same native phonemic category (Abramson
and Lisker, 1970; Mattingly, Liberman, Syrdal and Halwes, 1971; Miller
and Eimas, 1977; Pisoni, 1973; Repp, 1984). In other words, the mature
speaker perceives the sounds of his or her native language, filtered through
the existing phonological system, as distinct segments.

The hypothesis that the acoustic signal and phonological categories are
mediated by a level of feature organization is quite intuitive given the fact

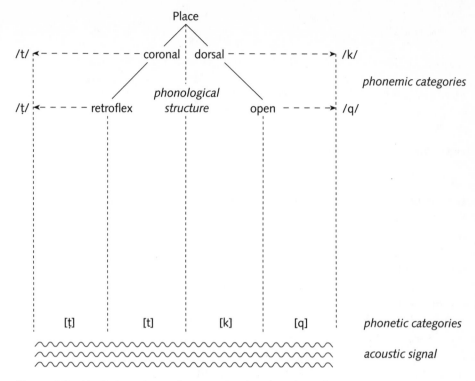

Figure 1.5   Mediation of speech perception by phonological structure

that the acoustic signal cannot be characterized in terms of abstract categories, such as a phoneme, but does correlate to properties of the gesture (e.g.,
place of articulation features correspond to spectral peaks in release bursts
and to formant frequencies). The schematized diagram in figure 1.5 (taken
from Brown, 1993a, 1998) illustrates the role of the intervening layer of
phonological structure and how this level, in effect, funnels the acoustic signal
into the phonemic categories of the speaker's language. The feature geometry
depicted is from a hypothetical language in which /t/, /ʈ/, /q/ and /k/ are
distinct phonemes; we will only consider the Coronal and Dorsal nodes (and
their dependents) of the geometry.

Starting from the bottom of the diagram, the acoustic signal is first broken
down into phonetic categories. At this level, the acoustic signals for an alveolar
[t] and a retroflex [ʈ] remain distinct. These stimuli then pass to the second
level which consists of a speaker's feature geometry. This phonological structure serves to further categorize the phonetic stimuli into phonemic categories which are then fed into the language processor. Because this language
exploits a dependent feature of the Coronal node, the phonetic signals for [t]
and [ʈ] are channeled into the distinct phonemic categories /t/ and /ʈ/. The
acoustic signals for [q] and [k] are processed in the same way. This model of

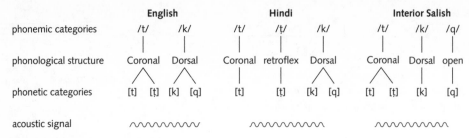

Figure 1.6　Cross-language speech perception

speech perception is supported by research by Werker and Logan (1985), who found evidence for three distinct levels of processing: depending on the length of the interval placed between the stimuli (and hence on the memory load required to perform the task), subjects exhibit perception at either the auditory, phonetic, or phonemic level. In particular, these researchers showed that, under certain conditions, English speakers are able to acoustically discriminate the Hindi /t–ṭ/ contrast more accurately than predicted by chance.

According to the model in figure 1.5, the acoustic signal will first be divided into distinct phonetic categories, which are only subsequently categorized into native phonemic categories. Thus, regardless of the phonological system of a speaker, non-native contrasts are distinct at some level and may be discriminated under certain controlled conditions, as Werker and Logan have demonstrated. In other words, the "loss" of sensitivity observed in young infants is not really a loss at all, but rather is the result of perceptual reorganization – reorganization, I would like to suggest, that reflects the hierarchical organization of the feature geometry in the speaker's grammar.

Figure 1.6 illustrates, in slightly more abstract terms, how the speech perception of English, Hindi and Interior Salish (Nthlakampx) speakers differs from one another.

In English, the Coronal node serves to distinguish coronals from non-coronals (e.g., /t/ vs. /p/), but no distinction is made within the coronal place of articulation (e.g., /t/ vs. /ṭ/). Thus, the English feature geometry does not contain the feature [retroflex]. As a result, (all) coronal sounds, regardless of their distinct acoustic signals, are perceived as a single phonemic category. Likewise, English makes no phonemic distinction between velar and uvular sounds; therefore, the Dorsal node has no dependents and velar and uvular sounds will be perceived as the English phoneme /k/. The feature geometry of Hindi also lacks the dorsal dependent [open], so that perception of [k] and [q] as /k/ is the same as for English speakers. Unlike English, however, the Hindi feature geometry contains both the Coronal node and its dependent [retroflex]. Thus, all coronal sounds will not be funneled into one phonemic category; the two features in the geometry ensure that /t/ and /ṭ/ will be perceived as distinct phonemes. In Interior Salish, the situation is just the reverse: /k/ and /q/ are perceived as distinct phonemes (due to the presence of the feature [open] as a dependent of the Dorsal node) while the acoustic signals for /t/ and /ṭ/ are perceived as the single phoneme /t/ (due to the absence of Coronal node dependents).

That the native system operates in this way is not accidental: perceiving speech in terms of phonemic categories undoubtedly aids processing and facilitates comprehension of the linguistic signal. Native speakers are continually faced with variable realizations of segments, due to coarticulation, sloppy articulation or inter-speaker variability. By filtering out this irrelevant "noise" in the acoustic signal, the memory load put on the auditory system is greatly reduced and processing can proceed more quickly. Those variations in the acoustic signal that do not contribute to differences in meaning are simply not perceived by the listener. Yet, although categorical perception aids processing of one's native language, it can be a barrier to correctly perceiving and processing a foreign language: variation in the acoustic signal which is filtered out by the native phonological system (i.e., is treated as *intra*-category variation) may, in fact, contribute to differences in meaning in the foreign language (i.e., actually constitute *inter*-category variation). Thus, the influence of the mature phonological system on the perception of foreign sounds is an artifact of how speech perception functions in general. To summarize thus far, I have suggested that a learner's developing feature geometry causes the gradual decline in the ability to acoustically discriminate non-native contrasts and then continues to mediate between the acoustic signal and the linguistic processing system. The next section outlines the predictions this proposal makes for L2 acquisition of phonology.

Implications for L2 phonological acquisition

Establishing a link between a learner's phonological development and his or her speech perception has important implications for the acquisition of non-native contrasts by second language learners. In particular, this proposal suggests that the learner's native grammar constrains which non-native contrasts he or she will accurately perceive and, therefore, limits which non-native contrasts that learner will successfully acquire.

A speaker's phonological knowledge consists of phonemic representations as well as the features that comprise those representations. The position that the features exist in grammar (somewhere) independent of the segments they define is an assumption at this point in the discussion; however, we will see experimental support for this claim in experiment 3 below. A priori, either of these levels of knowledge (i.e., featural or segmental) could potentially impinge upon the L2 acquisition process. According to the theory of phonological interference outlined here, however, it is the *features* contained in the learner's native grammar, not the phonological representations themselves, which constrain perception. The prediction of this position is that if a speaker's grammar lacks the feature that differentiates a given phonological contrast, then he or she will be unable to accurately perceive that contrast; conversely, the presence of the contrasting feature in the native grammar will facilitate perception of that non-native contrast, regardless of whether the particular segment is part of the inventory. That is, despite a lack of acoustic, phonetic or phonemic experience with a *particular* non-native contrast, a speaker's experience perceiving native phonemic contrasts along an acoustic dimension defined by a given underlying feature (for example, voicing) permits him or her to accurately discriminate *any* non-native contrast that differs along that same dimension. (This *is* a strong claim, but one I would like to maintain until empirical data force me to a weaker position.) Thus, perception of certain non-native contrasts is possible by virtue of the fact that the phonological feature that underlies that particular acoustic dimension exists independently in the learner's native grammar.[10]

This position does not, however, entail that the phonological categories themselves play no role whatsoever in perception; while it is claimed that it is the features that determine the perceptual sensitivities (and that guide the mapping of the acoustic signal onto perceptual categories), it is still the existing phoneme categories which the incoming acoustic stimuli are sorted into, at least initially. As we will see from the experimental studies reported below, the effects of the L1 phonological categories will be most apparent in the initial stages of acquisition, before new L2 categories have been established. Nevertheless, it is the features of the L1 which ultimately enable or prevent the construction of these new L2 categories.

If the native phonological system affects perception of non-native contrasts in this way, either preventing or facilitating accurate perception, what are the consequences for the acquisition of these contrasts by L2 learners? Recall from our discussion of L1 phoneme acquisition, that acquisition of the relevant phonological structure is triggered by the learner's detection that the two sounds are used contrastively in the language (i.e., that they correspond to separate phonemes). For example, if the learner is to acquire the phonological structure required to differentiate /l/ and /r/ in his or her grammar, then he or she must notice that minimal pairs, such as *right* and *light*, are distinct words. In short, accurate perception of a phonemic contrast is necessary for successful acquisition of that contrast. It follows, then, that L2 learners will acquire only those non-native phonemic contrasts that they perceive as distinct sounds. If an L2 learner detects that two segments are used contrastively in the foreign language, then acquisition of the novel representations will be triggered.[11] On the other hand, if a contrast between two foreign sounds is not perceived (i.e., both sounds are perceived as belonging to the same phonological category), then acquisition will not be triggered and the L2 learner will fail to distinguish those segments in his or her interlanguage grammar. Put slightly differently, if the L2 input continues to be (inaccurately) mapped to L1 representations, there will be no impetus for acquisition.

Experimental Evidence

The following three experimental studies investigate how the grammars of Japanese speakers, Korean speakers and Mandarin Chinese speakers affect their acquisition of English contrasts and whether, given the necessary conditions, novel segmental representations can be constructed. These studies were designed to explore three related issues: the acquisition of a range of phonemic contrasts by a single group of speakers (experiment 1), the acquisition of a particular contrast across different groups of speakers (experiment 2) and whether the nature of L1 phonological influence changes over the course of L2 development (experiment 3). As the studies examine the acquisition of different subsets of English contrasts, the representations of all of the segments under investigation, as well as the phonological properties of the three L1s, will be discussed together, prior to the description of the individual experiments.

Contrasts investigated

The English /l–r/, /b–v/, /p–f/, /f–v/ and /s–θ/ contrasts were chosen to test the proposed model of phonological interference because these pairs are not contrastive in Japanese, Korean or Chinese; furthermore, since these contrasts are distinguished by different phonological features, each contrast could potentially cause a differing degree of difficulty for these groups of learners (both with respect to the various contrasts and with respect to the various L1 groups). The internal structure of each pair is given in figure 1.7; note that these representations are for the segments as they occur in English, a language in which they are contrastive. The phonological feature that distinguishes each contrast is given to the right (the superordinate SUPRALARYNGEAL and LARYNGEAL components are not relevant for this discussion and have been omitted for ease of exposition).

The representations in figure 1.7 are what the learner must acquire in order to distinguish these phonemes in his or her interlanguage grammar. The important thing to note is that each pair of phonemes is minimally differentiated by the presence of a single phonological feature. Without this contrasting feature in the representation of one of the sounds, the two segments will not be distinguished in the learner's interlanguage grammar. The /l–r/ contrast is distinguished by the feature [coronal], the /b–v/ and /p–f/ contrasts by the feature [continuant], while the /f–v/ and /s–θ/ contrasts are distinguished by the features [voice] and [distributed], respectively. Whether an L2 learner will successfully acquire each of these contrasts depends entirely on the presence or absence of the contrasting feature in his or her native grammar.

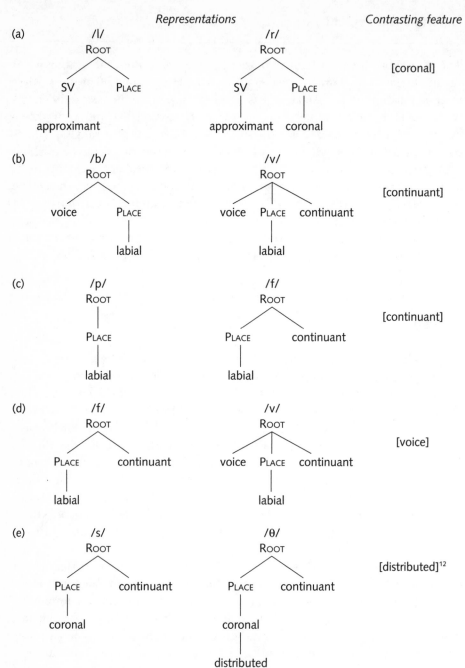

Figure 1.7   Representation of contrasts under investigation

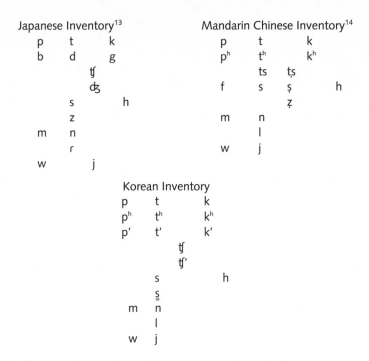

Figure 1.8 Phoneme inventories of L1 groups under investigation

Phonological properties of Japanese, Korean, and Mandarin Chinese

Let us now examine the consonant phoneme inventories of Japanese, Korean and Chinese, given in figure 1.8, in order to ascertain whether the features that distinguish the English contrasts are contained in the mental grammar of these speakers (from Maddieson, 1984, and Vance, 1987). From this, we see that each of the five non-native contrasts we are interested in has a slightly different status *vis-à-vis* the inventories; the status of these contrasts is summarized in table 1.1.

It should be noted that "corresponds to a native segment" means here that the surface realization of a given segment (in Japanese, Chinese or Korean) could reasonably be assumed to be a surface realization corresponding to the underlying representation of an English phoneme. For example, while Japanese does not contain a labiodental fricative (/f/), the Japanese bilabial fricative ([Φ]) can be considered to "correspond" to the underlying representation of the labiodental fricative given in figure 1.7 (c). Thus, while Japanese, Chinese or Korean may not have a given English segment in its inventory, it may contain a very similar sound that could potentially factor into the acquisition of that English segment. For example, considering the Japanese bilabial fricative [Φ] again, the Japanese speaker may successfully perceive the English /p–f/ contrast by virtue of the fact that both English sounds can be categorized

Table 1.1   Status of English contrasts in Japanese, Chinese and Korean

	English Contrasts				
	/b/ vs. /v/	/p/ vs. /f/	/f/ vs. /v/	/s/ vs. /θ/	/r/ vs. /l/
Status in Japanese Inventory					
is a native segment	√	√		√	
corresponds to a native segment		√[15]	√		√[16]
does not correspond to a native segment	√		√	√	√
Status in Chinese Inventory					
is a native segment		√		√	√
corresponds to a native segment	√	√	√		
does not correspond to a native segment	√			√	√
Status in Korean Inventory					
is a native segment		√		√	√
corresponds to a native segment	√				
does not correspond to a native segment	√	√	√	√	√ √[17]

as different segments in the Japanese mental grammar (i.e., English /p/ will be funneled into the Japanese category /p/ and English /f/ will be funneled into the Japanese category [Φ]). In other words, even though a particular learner might not have the exact surface segment in his or her native language grammar, having a native segment that "corresponds to" the non-native segment may be advantageous in the acquisition of the non-native contrast. Notice that, with respect to phoneme inventories, the status of these English contrasts is similar for Chinese and Korean, which would lead us to expect to find comparable patterns of acquisition across these two groups of learners, if it is the phonemes of the L1 which constrain perception.

We can also use the consonant phoneme inventories in figure 1.8, along with our theory of underspecification, to determine which phonological features are used contrastively in these three languages; the adult feature geometries in figure 1.9 illustrate which features are manipulated.

The phonological features that we are interested in (i.e., the ones that differentiate the English contrasts at hand) appear bolded and underlined. For our immediate purposes, it is only the *features* (and not the entire adult *feature geometry* given in figure 1.9) that are relevant for determining whether a non-native contrast will be acquired. Nevertheless, I have included the entire adult geometry to underscore the claim made in this chapter that the full geometry is, in fact, a property of the speaker's mental grammar and, as such, reflects the organization of the perceptual system. Recall that it is this feature geometry that will operate during the process of speech perception

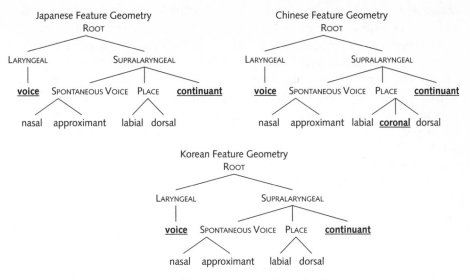

Figure 1.9 Feature inventories of L1 groups under investigation

to map the incoming continuous stimuli onto discrete perceptual categories (e.g., refer back to figure 1.5).

Notice that the features [continuant], which distinguishes the /b–v/ and /p–f/ contrasts, and [voice], which distinguishes the /f–v/ contrast, are present in the grammar of all of the three languages. Even though /b/, /v/, /f/ and /p/ are themselves not contrastive in these languages, other native segments differentiated by these particular features are contrastive. For example, the feature [continuant] is required in the Japanese grammar to differentiate native stop–continuant contrasts, such as the /t–s/ and /d–z/ contrasts, while the feature [voice] is present in the grammar in order to represent native voicing contrasts, such as /t–d/ or /s–z/. Thus, the feature that distinguishes /b–v/, /p–f/ and /f–v/ exists in the grammar for independent reasons.

However, the feature that distinguishes the /l–r/ contrast ([coronal]) is present only in the Chinese grammar (to distinguish the native alveolar /s/ and the retroflex /ʂ/); [coronal] is not present in the Japanese or Korean grammar as there are no consonants in either language that are distinguished from each other by this feature.[18] Finally, the feature that distinguishes the /s–θ/ contrast ([distributed]) is not utilized in any of the three grammars. Thus, in terms of features (as opposed to segments), Korean is more similar to Japanese than either is to Chinese.

Predictions

Recall that according to the theory of phonological interference being pursued here, it is the status of the contrasting *feature(s)* in the learner's native grammar (i.e., presence or absence) that determines the perception and subsequent acquisition of non-native contrasts. Of particular interest is the difference between the acquisition of a non-native contrast when the second language learner's native grammar does NOT contain the feature that distinguishes the segments and the acquisition of a non-native contrast when the learner's native grammar DOES contain the distinguishing feature. Taking Japanese learners of English as an example, three of the contrasts under consideration, /b–v/, /p–f/ and /f–v/, are distinguished by a feature present in the Japanese grammar, whereas /l–r/ and /s–θ/ are not. Thus, we would expect the former three contrasts to pattern together in acquisition, to the exclusion of the latter two.

More specifically, since perception of a non-native contrast is facilitated by the presence of the relevant feature in the learner's grammar, Japanese speakers should accurately perceive that /b/, /v/, /p/ and /f/ are distinct segments. This is by virtue of the fact that the feature [continuant] operates in the mental grammar of Japanese speakers, functioning to sort acoustic stimuli that differ along this dimension. Likewise, Japanese speakers should accurately perceive /f/ and /v/ as distinct segments, in this case, because the feature [voice] exists in their grammar. Since accurate perception of these two non-native contrasts is facilitated by the learner's native grammar, the learner will detect that these sounds are contrastive in English and acquisition of phonological representations for these segments will be triggered. On the other hand, since perception of a non-native contrast is blocked by the absence of the relevant feature from the learner's grammar, Japanese speakers will be unable to accurately perceive a contrast between /l/ and /r/ or between /s/ and /θ/. Lacking the features [coronal] and [distributed], the phonological system of the Japanese speaker's grammar will funnel the distinct acoustic stimuli for /l/ and /r/ into one perceptual category and for /s/ and /θ/ into another. Consequently, Japanese speakers will perceive instances of /l/ and /r/ as the same sound (likewise for /s/ and /θ/). Unable to perceive that they are distinct segments, the learner will not detect contrastive use of these sounds and, as a result, novel representations will not be acquired; consequently, these segments will not be distinguished in the learner's interlanguage grammar.[19]

A summary of these predictions for the acquisition of the English contrasts by Japanese, Korean, and Chinese learners is given in table 1.2. In addition to whether each language contains the relevant feature for a particular non-native contrast (and the resulting prediction for perception and acquisition), information regarding the segments themselves is also included: in particular, whether both members of the English contrast correspond to distinct segments in the L1 system (and could thus potentially be discriminated by the learner on the basis of those L1 categories). This information enables us to directly compare the predictions made by the "feature hypothesis" advocated here and the alternative "phoneme hypothesis" in which accurate perception and acquisition of non-native contrasts are thought to derive from the status

Table 1.2 Predictions for acquisition of English contrasts

English Contrasts	Japanese speakers			Chinese speakers			Korean speakers		
	Correspond to distinct segments in the L1	L1 grammar contains relevant feature	Learners will perceive & acquire	Correspond to distinct segments in the L1	L1 grammar contains relevant feature	Learners will perceive & acquire	Correspond to distinct segments in the L1	L1 grammar contains relevant feature	Learners will perceive & acquire
/b/ vs. /v/	No	continuant	Yes	No	continuant	Yes	No	continuant	Yes
/p/ vs. /f/	Yes	continuant	Yes	Yes	continuant	Yes	No	continuant	Yes
/f/ vs. /v/	No	voice	Yes	No	voice	Yes	No	voice	Yes
/s/ vs. /θ/	No		No	No		No	No		No
/l/ vs. /r/	No		No	No	coronal	Yes	No		No

of the *segments* themselves. In this regard, the most informative cases (i.e., the cases where the two hypotheses make opposite predictions) are the English /f–v/ contrast for all three language groups, the /l–r/ contrast for the Chinese speakers versus the Japanese speakers and the Korean speakers, the /p–f/ contrast for the Korean speakers versus the Japanese speakers and the Chinese speakers, and the /b–v/ contrast versus the /l–r/ contrast for the Japanese and Korean speakers.

Three Experimental Studies

Three experimental studies that test the predictions in table 1.2 are reported in the following section. We will find ample evidence that the critical factor predicting success is indeed the status of the L1 features, not the L1 segments.

Experiment 1

Experiment 1 was designed to test whether the theory of phonological interference outlined in this chapter could accurately account for variation in the acquisition of several different contrasts by learners with the same L1.[20]

Subjects

The experimental group consisted of 15 Japanese speakers, ranging in age from 20 to 32 years, who had learned English as their only second language. Each of these subjects was raised in Japan and had come to North America to study in an undergraduate or graduate program at McGill University in Montreal, Canada, where the testing was conducted. The control group consisted of 15 monolingual native speakers of English, who ranged in age from 15 years to 54 years. Their background information is summarized in table 1.3.

Contrasts investigated and hypotheses

The experimental contrasts were /l–r/, /b–v/ and /f–v/. A native contrast, /p–b/, was also included, as a control item for statistical comparison with the

Table 1.3 Experiment 1: Subject information

Group	Mean age at testing	Mean age of exposure	Mean years studied	Mean years in N. America
Japanese	24.5	9	8	3.5
Controls	25	–	–	–

non-native contrasts. As outlined above, our hypothesis is that the Japanese speakers will accurately perceive the /b–v/ and /f–v/ contrasts, but not the /l–r/ contrast. Moreover, they should perceive these two non-native contrasts and the native /p–b/ contrast equally well. Again, successful acquisition of these two non-native contrasts, to the exclusion of /l–r/, is predicted to follow.

Tasks and materials

An AX Discrimination task was used to assess the subjects' ability to acoustically discriminate (i.e., perceive) the English contrasts. In this task, subjects hear a minimal pair (one item containing, for example, an /l/ and the other item containing an /r/ in onset position) and are asked to indicate whether the words are the same or different (e.g., *rip / lip*).[21] The items used in the test were natural tokens of real English monosyllabic words. These tokens were spoken by a man with a standard American English accent and taped so that the stimuli were identical for every subject.

Two types of foils were also included in the test materials. One foil type, which consisted of native contrasts, was included as a means of checking that poor performance on the task was not due to difficulty with the task itself; any difficulty with the task would be reflected in poor performance on the native contrasts as well as the non-native contrasts. This native-contrast foil comprised 25 percent of the entire stimuli set (i.e., equal to the number of stimuli for each experimental contrast). A second type of foil, which consisted of identical pairs of words, was included to detect any response biases. Since each experimental minimal pair differs with respect to some consonant, the correct response for every trial is that the words are different. This set of foils ensured that any response bias or strategy toward responding that all of the pairs were different would result in inaccurate performance. If a subject responded that these same-word stimuli were different, his or her data were discarded. This type of foil comprised 20 percent of the stimuli for each individual contrast (i.e., three of the stimuli for each contrast were same-word and 12 were different-word).

The second aspect investigated is whether those subjects who can acoustically discriminate the non-native contrast are able to acquire the phonological structure necessary to distinguish the two sounds phonologically. Based on the arguments in Brown and Matthews (1997), data from comprehension tasks are assumed to be a more accurate indication of the learner's underlying competence than production abilities. Since production involves several peripheral mechanisms, such as motor control, relying on production data may lead us to underestimate or (particularly in the case of adults) overestimate the learner's underlying phonological competence. Several researchers have, in fact, demonstrated that L2 learners may be able to accurately produce a non-native contrast even though the same learners are unable to distinguish the two sounds perceptually (Brière, 1966; Flege, Takagi and Mann, 1995;

Goto, 1971; Sheldon and Strange, 1982).[22] Thus, if we rely on production data we may falsely attribute more segmental structure to a learner's underlying phonological competence than he or she actually has. On the other hand, some L2 learners are more like young children in that they are unable to correctly produce a novel contrast despite their ability to perceive and accurately distinguish that contrast phonologically in comprehension, in which case we would underestimate the learner's competence. Of course, this is not to deny the operation of peripheral mechanisms in comprehension (it too is performance), nor would I claim that comprehension can be equated with underlying competence. However, it is reasonable to assume that performance on comprehension tasks (where all context has been removed and the subject must access his or her mental representations in order to perform the task) provides a more accurate picture of grammatical competence than does performance on production tasks and is, therefore, to be preferred.

Subjects were given a Forced Choice Picture Selection task (modified from Brown and Matthews, 1993, 1997), in which the subject is presented with two pictures and a verbal cue that corresponds to one of the pictures.[23] For example, the subject would see a picture of a *rake* on the left side of the page and a picture of a *lake* on the right side. At the same time, the subject would hear the word *lake*. The subject's task is to indicate which of the pictures the verbal cue names. In order to successfully complete this task, the learner must refer to his or her internal phonological representations of the pictured objects and determine which lexical representation corresponds to the verbal stimulus. If the subject's lexical representations of the pictured objects are identical (i.e., if they do not have the necessary phonological structure to contrast /l/ and /r/), then he or she will be unable to determine to which picture the verbal cue corresponds and should perform the task with chance accuracy. Successful completion of this task indicates that the subject has acquired the non-native contrast. The monosyllabic words used in this task were the same as those used in the AX Discrimination task. Both tasks were administered on the same day, with a short break between tasks.

Results and discussion

For the auditory discrimination task, a response that the two words in the minimal pair were "different" was counted as correct and a "same" response was counted as an error. Performance scores on each of the contrasts were tabulated separately for statistical analysis. The graph in figure 1.10 reports the mean performance scores of both groups on each of the contrasts.

From the Japanese subjects' near perfect performance on the native /p–b/ pairs, it is clear that the task itself does not pose any difficulty for the learners. Thus, performance on the non-native contrasts can be interpreted to reflect properties of the speakers' interlanguage grammar. As can readily be seen from the graph in figure 1.10, the Japanese speakers were significantly poorer

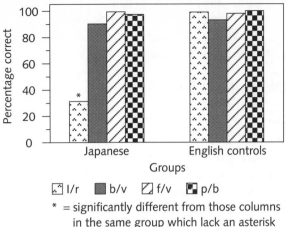

Figure 1.10 Experiment 1: Overall auditory performance by group

than the English controls at discriminating the /l–r/ contrast [t (28) = −16.16, p = .0001]. Yet, there was no statistical difference between the two groups in their ability to perceive the other contrasts; the Japanese speakers discriminated each of these English contrasts as accurately as the native controls [/b–v/ contrast: t (28) = −1.28, p = .21; /f–v/ contrast: t (28) = 1.87, p = .08; /p–b/ contrast: t (28) = −1.46, p = .15]. The Japanese speakers' performance on the /b–v/ and /f–v/ contrasts is quite striking: despite the fact that these are both non-native contrasts, they are very good (in fact, native-like) at discriminating each of them.[24] This suggests that these subjects perceived /b/, /v/ and /f/ as distinct speech sounds.

In order to evaluate performance on each contrast relative to the other contrasts, additional analyses were carried out separately on the two groups.[25] Beginning with the Japanese group, we find that their performance on the /l–r/ contrast is significantly worse than their performance on the other three contrasts [F (14, 45) = 119.85, p = .0001]; however, their performance on the other three contrasts (/b–v/, /f–v/, /p–b/) was not significantly different from one another. Thus, the Japanese speakers are unable to discriminate /l/ from /r/, perceiving them, instead, as a single category.

One might be tempted to surmise that the Japanese speakers are unable to discriminate the /l–r/ contrast precisely because they have allophonic experience with these segments: given the allophonic variation in the native language, we could imagine that these speakers have been "trained" to ignore these variations (recognizing them both as instantiations of the same underlying phoneme). Under this account, the allophonic exposure, rather than the absence of the contrasting feature, would be responsible for their lack of perceptual sensitivity to this contrast. However, this allophonic explanation cannot be correct because /b/ also varies allophonically in Japanese, with the voiced bilabial fricative [β], which shares acoustic and phonological properties with English /v/ (Kawakami, 1977).[26] Thus, if allophonic variation were the cause of the learners' inability to accurately perceive certain non-native contrasts, we would (incorrectly) expect perception of the /l–r/ and /b–v/ contrasts to be similarly impaired, which, as we see in this experiment, is certainly not the case.

In contrast to /l–r/, though, not only do the Japanese speakers perceive the non-native /b–v/ and /f–v/ contrasts with native-like accuracy, as predicted, but they perceive them equally well. This is what we would expect, given that they are both distinguished by a feature in the Japanese grammar. Note that uniform performance is not predicted if the aspect of the native grammar responsible for filtering non-native sounds is the phonemic representations themselves (rather than the features). Recall from table 1.1, that the members of the /b–v/ and /f–v/ contrasts have a different status vis-à-vis the Japanese phoneme inventory. Hence, if the phonemic representations constrain perception, we might expect differential perception of these two pairs, since the segment /b/, but not /f/, occurs in Japanese.

Moreover, that these non-native contrasts are discriminated as well as the native /p–b/ contrast suggests that perception of non-native sounds operates in the same manner as perception of native sounds. Although the native controls' performance on the /b–v/ contrast appears to be depressed relative to the other contrasts, there is, in fact, no statistical difference between the four contrasts [$F (14, 45) = 1.44$, $p = .25$]. Thus, we can regard the Japanese speakers' performance, in light of the native speaker data, as a true reflection of their perceptual capabilities.

To summarize, then, we have found a difference in the Japanese speakers' ability to perceive non-native contrasts, depending on whether the feature that distinguishes a given contrast exists in their grammar: the /l–r/ contrast (whose contrasting feature is absent from the Japanese grammar) is not accurately perceived, whereas the /b–v/ and /f–v/ contrasts (whose contrasting features are contained in the Japanese grammar) are accurately perceived, in a native-like manner (with respect both to the English controls and to the native Japanese contrast).

For the picture identification task, selection of the target picture was counted as a correct response, and selection of the contrast picture was counted as an error. The groups' overall performances are compared in figure 1.11.

Near perfect performance was attained by the Japanese group on the control items in this task. As in the auditory task, the Japanese speakers were significantly poorer than the English controls at differentiating the /l–r/ contrast [$t (28) = -9.73$, $p = .0001$]. There was, however, no statistical difference between the two groups in their ability to discriminate the other contrasts [/b–v/ contrast, $t (28) = -1.8$, $p = .08$; /f–v/ contrast, $t (28) = -.32$, $p = .75$; /p–b/ contrast, $t (28) = -1.27$, $p = .22$]. When shown two pictures that constituted a minimal pair (e.g., rake, lake), the Japanese subjects were unable to correctly choose the one that corresponded to the verbal cue. Yet

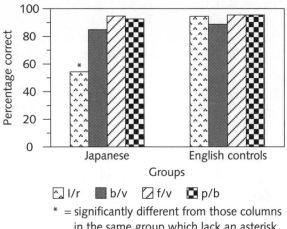

Figure 1.11   Experiment 1: Overall picture performance by group

these subjects performed this task with native-like accuracy when the pair of pictures differed by /b–v/ (e.g., *boat*, *vote*) or /f–v/ (e.g., *fan*, *van*).

Let us now compare performance on each of the contrasts relative to each other. In this analysis, too, the Japanese speakers' performance on the /l–r/ contrast was significantly worse than performance on the other three contrasts, while performance on the /b–v/, /f–v/ and /p–b/ contrasts was uniform [F (14, 45) = 57.65, p = .0001]. This pattern of performance is confirmed by an examination of individual scores. Looking at the native controls, their mean performance on each of the contrasts was not significantly different from each other [F (14, 45) = 1.56, p = .21]. Thus, as with the auditory task, the performance of the Japanese subjects can be taken to accurately reflect their underlying phonological competence.

Although the performance of the Japanese subjects on the /l–r/ contrast was lower than their performance on the other contrasts, their accuracy rate (almost 60 percent) would seem to indicate that these learners have some knowledge of the /l–r/ contrast. However, in order to correctly interpret these results, it is necessary to consider the expected baseline performance on this task, that is, what chance performance would be. Suppose that a learner has no phonological knowledge of the /l–r/ contrast and is, therefore, unable to distinguish /l/ from /r/ in lexical representations. When that subject is presented with two pictures and a single verbal cue, he or she simply will be unable to decide which picture corresponds to the cue (i.e., since the representation for both items is the same, both correspond to the verbal cue). With a choice between two pictures, this subject has a 50 percent chance of choosing the correct one, just by guessing.[27] The observed performance, then, at 60 percent, is not significantly different from chance. We can infer with reasonable confidence from the Japanese speakers' performance on this task, that /l/ and /r/ are not differentiated in their grammars. Performance on the other contrasts, on the other hand, indicates that both the /b–v/ and /f–v/ contrasts are differentiated. In other words, the phonological structure that represents the /b–v/ and /f–v/ contrasts has successfully been acquired by these learners.

The hypothesis guiding this experiment was that perception of non-native contrasts is constrained by the phonological features manipulated in the native grammar of the learner. This led us to predict that Japanese learners of English would accurately perceive the /b–v/ and /f–v/ contrasts, as these two pairs are differentiated by features already present in the Japanese grammar, but that accurate perception of the /l–r/ contrast would be blocked by the absence of the relevant feature from the Japanese grammar. Each of these predictions was borne out by the data. The Japanese speakers' inability to perceive /l/ and /r/ as distinct phonemes can be understood as a direct consequence of the influence of the native grammar on the operation of the speech perception mechanism. The Japanese speakers' perception of /b/, /f/ and /v/ as distinct phonemes likewise provides experimental support for the model of phonological interference outlined in this chapter. In a similar vein, since acquisition of a phonemic contrast is dependent upon accurate perception of that contrast, we predicted that Japanese learners would successfully acquire the /b–v/ and /f–v/ contrasts, but would fail to acquire the /l–r/ contrast. These predictions, too, were confirmed by the data. The Japanese learners successfully acquired only those non-native contrasts which they accurately perceived. The finding that Japanese speakers do not accurately perceive the difference between /l/ and /r/ is not particularly surprising, given the large body of literature that reports this observation (Goto, 1971; Miyawaki et al., 1975; Sheldon and Strange, 1982; Strange and Dittmann, 1984; Yamada, 1995). However, this current research is the first to also examine and compare Japanese speakers' perception of additional English contrasts; it is also the first to investigate these speakers' acquisition of the /l/ and /r/ feature geometric representations.

The theory of phonological interference that has been tested in experiment 1 has correctly accounted for differences in Japanese learners' abilities to acquire different English phonemic contrasts. The theory further predicts that speakers of different L1s which differ in the features that they utilize will exhibit differing success rates of acquiring various contrasts. The following experiment tests whether this model of phonological interference can account for *cross-language* differences in L2 phonological acquisition.

Experiment 2

The purpose of this experiment was to examine differences in the acquisition of English contrasts by speakers of different native languages, and to replicate the findings in experiment 1 for Japanese speakers.

Table 1.4 Experiment 2: Subject information

Group	Mean age at testing	Mean age of exposure	Mean years studied
Japanese	20.3	11.8	8
Chinese	30.7	12.6	10.4
Korean	30	12.8	9.9
Controls	34.3	–	–

Subjects

A total of 51 subjects, divided into one control group and three experimental groups, participated in this study. One experimental group consisted of 15 undergraduate Japanese speakers who were learning English at Hokkaido University, Sapporo, Japan and had never lived in an English-speaking country. The second experimental group consisted of 15 native Mandarin Chinese speakers who were enrolled in graduate programs at Hokkaido University (and, therefore, were proficient in Japanese). Eleven native speakers of Korean (also proficient in Japanese) comprised the final experimental group; these subjects were also graduate students at Hokkaido University. Neither the Chinese native speakers nor Korean native speakers were enrolled in English classes at the time of testing. The control group consisted of ten native monolingual speakers of American and British English, who teach English at universities in Sapporo, Japan. Table 1.4 summarizes the background information for each of the four groups.

Contrasts investigated and hypotheses

Acquisition of the following contrasts was investigated: /p–f/, /f–v/, /s–θ/ and /l–r/, with the /p–t/ contrast (a native contrast for all groups) serving as a control item. Speakers of Chinese, Korean, and Japanese were chosen for comparison because the grammars of these languages differ in interesting, theoretically relevant ways. In particular, when we compare the status of English contrasts in L1 phoneme inventories (table 1.1), Chinese and Korean appear to be more similar to one another, which might lead us to expect that speakers of these two languages would have the same difficulty (or success) acquiring the English contrasts under investigation. However, when the features employed in each of these grammars are compared (table 1.2), Korean and Japanese are more similar to one another. Thus, examining acquisition by all three groups should provide evidence as to which level of phonological knowledge is responsible for L1 interference. To briefly review the predictions set out in table 1.2, according to the theory of phonological interference adopted in this study, speakers of all three languages should accurately perceive and have successfully acquired the /p–f/ and /f–v/ contrasts since each of the L1 grammars utilizes the contrasting features ([continuant] and [voice], respectively) to distinguish native segments. Likewise, as the three L1 grammars lack the feature that contrasts /s/ and /θ/ ([distributed]), we predict that these two segments will be perceived (inaccurately) as a single category by speakers of all three languages; unable to hear a contrast between the two segments, they will also fail to acquire the feature geometric structure necessary to distinguish them phonologically in their interlanguage grammars. Finally, the three language groups should differ with respect to their ability to perceive and acquire the /l–r/ contrast: Chinese speakers, whose L1 contains the feature [coronal], will accurately perceive and, therefore, acquire this contrast; whereas, the adult feature geometry of Japanese speakers and Korean speakers will fail to sort the acoustic signal for these two sounds into distinct perceptual categories and their acquisition of the novel segmental representations will be prevented.

Tasks and materials

Phonological competence was assessed with the same Forced Choice Selection task used in experiment 1 above. A 4IAX Discrimination task, rather than an AX task, was used to assess perception in this study. In the 4IAX task, each trial consists of two pairs of words (Pisoni, 1971); in one of those pairs, the two words will be different (i.e., a minimal pair), and the other pair of words will be the same (e.g., *ra/ra, ra/la*). The subject's task is to indicate which of the two pairs of words is different. This task is becoming increasingly employed in speech perception research, since the AX task has been argued to bias the subject to respond "same" when discrimination is difficult (Beddor and Gottfried, 1995). The 4IAX task avoids this response bias since the subject knows that one of the pairs is, in fact, different and must simply determine which one.

The stimuli for this task, again in contrast to experiment 1, were nonwords in order to prevent the subjects' perception from being influenced by their familiarity with particular lexical items (Yamada, Kobayashi and Tohkura, in press). The "same" pairs consisted of two instances of a CV (consonant–vowel) syllable whose onset consonants were members of the same phonemic and phonetic category (e.g., aspirated [pʰa]), but which were not physically identical. Thus, subjects could not accurately choose the "same" pair (and thereby determine the "different" pair) simply by comparing physical objects and attending to non-linguistic acoustic variations, such as amplitude or speed. The "different" pairs consisted of two CV syllables whose onset consonants were members of different phonemic categories. Given these type of stimuli, accurate performance on this task requires the learner to filter out irrelevant variations across the segments and respond to higher-order phonological information. Stimuli were recorded by a male speaker of standard American English onto a Sony DAT Workstation and then arranged temporally by computer to create uniform intervals of 1000 milliseconds between members of a pair, 1800 millisecond intervals between pairs in a trial and 3000 millisecond intervals between trials. These time intervals were chosen following Werker and Logan (1985) to ensure phonemic processing of the stimuli.

Results and discussion

For each 4IAX trial, selection of the pair whose members were from different phonemic categories was counted as correct and selection of the pair whose members were from the same phonemic category was counted as an error. The mean performance scores of all groups on each of the contrasts are reported in figure 1.12.

The comparison that we are primarily interested in here is between the performance of the three language groups on particular/individual contrasts. As can be seen from the graph, the Japanese and Korean speakers are not as good as the Chinese speakers at discriminating the /l–r/ contrast. Statistical analyses reveal two distinct perceptual patterns: the Chinese speakers' performance is not significantly different from the native controls' performance, while the performance of the Japanese and Korean speakers is significantly worse than the Chinese speakers and native controls, but they are not significantly different from each other [F (3, 47) = 16.39, p = .0001]. As we saw in experiment 1, the Japanese speakers are unable to distinguish spoken tokens of /l/ and /r/; we see that Korean speakers, too, perceive these segments as a single category (confirming Borden, Gerber and Milsark's 1983 findings), whereas the Chinese speakers have no problem discriminating this contrast.

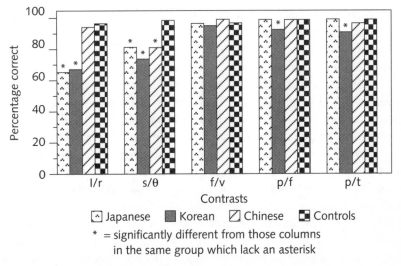

Figure 1.12   Experiment 2: Overall auditory performance by contrast

Turning to the /s–θ/ contrast, we find that the Japanese, Chinese and Korean speakers all discriminated this contrast equally poorly; they are significantly worse than the native controls, but not significantly different from each other [F (3, 47) = 3.8, p = .016]. The acoustic signals for these two sounds are funneled into the same perceptual category by speakers of all three language groups. With respect to the /f–v/ contrast, we also find consistent perform-ance but, in this case, the groups are equally good, and not significantly different from the native controls [F (3, 47) = 1.49, p = .23]. The feature [voice] in the L1 grammar serves to separate, and keep distinct, the acoustic signals for these two sounds as they are processed.[28] Performance on /p–f/, the other non-native contrast that is distinguished by an L1 feature mani-pulated by all three L1s, is roughly uniform for all groups, although we do find a small statistical difference between the experimental groups [F (3, 47) = 2.93, p = .04].

The Japanese and Chinese speakers are able to discriminate these two sounds as accurately as the native controls, though the Korean speakers are significantly worse than both experimental groups and the native controls. However, the Korean speakers' performance, at 90 percent accuracy, is still well above chance and can be considered accurate, albeit not native-like. Finally, all of the groups are able to accurately discriminate the native /p–t/ contrast, though small differences among groups do approach statistical significance [F (3, 47) = 2.6, p = .06]. Once again, the performance of the Korean speakers (91 percent) is a bit lower than the other groups. Given that /p–t/ is a native contrast for these speakers, this result is somewhat surprising and suggests that the Korean speakers' performance on all of the contrasts in this task is slightly depressed. Overall, the performance of the Japanese, Korean and Chinese speakers on the /f–v/ and /p–f/ contrasts is quite remark-able: despite the fact all three languages lack these two contrasts, these learners perceive them with native-like accuracy. Their ability to perceive these con-trasts is particularly striking in light of their inability to discriminate the /s–θ/ contrast. Moreover, the differing ability of the Chinese speakers, on the one hand, and Japanese and Korean speakers, on the other, to accurately perceive the /l–r/ contrast indicates that the ability (or inability) to perceive non-native contrasts is linked to phonological properties of those contrasts and the L1 grammars, not to acoustic properties of the sounds themselves.

Although our main interest in this study is in differences between groups, it is still informative to consider performance on each of the contrasts relative to the others. In order to make such comparisons, additional statistical analyses were carried out separately for each group. It should be kept in mind that baseline performance on the 4IAX task is different than on the AX task. Recall that in the AX task the subject's decision is whether the two words are the same or different. If a subject cannot hear a difference between two sounds, then he or she will respond "same". In this case, performance would theoretically be 0 percent accuracy. In other words, given the influence of the native grammar, the probability of responding "same" or responding "different" is not 50 percent. In contrast, the subject's decision in the 4IAX task is which pair of sounds is different. If the subject's L1 grammar causes him or her to hear both pairs of words as being the same, the choice is still between "first pair" and "second pair" and the probability of randomly choosing either one is 50 percent. Thus, an inability to perceive a contrast in the AX task would result in 0 percent accuracy, whereas an inability to perceive a contrast in the 4IAX task would result in 50 percent accuracy. A consequence of this is that comparing performance on the 4IAX task across different phonemic contrasts is more difficult since differences between performance on contrasts that are perceived accurately and those that are not will be smaller (50 percent–100 percent; cf. AX task: 0 percent–100 percent); for the same reason, scores from the two tasks cannot be directly compared.

Starting with the Chinese group, we find they are equally good at discriminating the /p–f/, /f–v/ and /l–r/ contrasts, and with the same accuracy with which they distinguish their native /p–t/ contrast; they discriminate all of these contrasts significantly better than they do the /s–θ/ contrast [F (14, 60) = 8.55, p = .0001]. This is what we would expect, given that the former non-native contrasts are distinguished by a feature contained in the Chinese grammar, whereas the latter is not. The Japanese group, too, discriminate the /p–f/ and /f–v/ contrast with the same accuracy that they discriminate their native contrast, and they are significantly better at perceiving these contrasts than they are the /s–θ/ or /l–r/ contrasts [F (14, 60) = 29.78, p = .0001]. These speakers do not, however, perceive the /s–θ/ and /l–r/ contrasts equally poorly; their discrimination of /l–r/ is worse than their discrimination of /s–θ/. It appears that, even though the acoustic signals for both sets of sounds will each be funneled into their respective category and perceived as the same sound, in a temporally adjacent presentation, the Japanese speakers are able to distinguish /s/ and /θ/ (but not /l/ and /r/) with higher accuracy than would be predicted by chance (possible reasons for this difference are discussed below). We find a similar pattern with the Korean speakers: /l/ and /r/ are discriminated less accurately than /s/ and /θ/ and performance on both of these contrasts is significantly worse than on the other contrasts [F (10, 44) = 9.06, p = .0001].

The most important thing to note from these perceptual data is that Japanese speakers and Korean speakers differ from Chinese speakers in their ability to discriminate /l/ and /r/. This difference between the language groups might seem surprising given that all three languages lack this phonemic contrast. However, it can be properly understood as a direct consequence of the influence of the phonological features in their respective native grammars: the presence of the feature [coronal] in the grammar of Chinese speakers ensures that acoustic stimuli which differ on this dimension will be perceived as distinct, whereas the absence of the feature from the Japanese and Korean grammars causes the acoustic signal for these two sounds to be funneled into

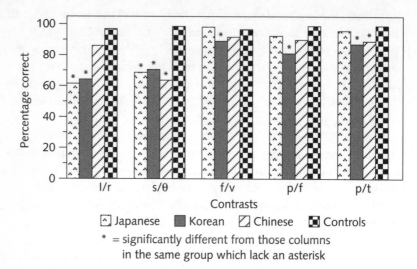

Figure 1.13   Experiment 2: Overall picture performance by contrast

a single perceptual category. The three language groups do not differ in their ability to accurately discriminate those contrasts which are distinguished by a feature that exists in all three L1s or in their inability to perceive those contrasts which are distinguished by a feature not utilized in their native grammars.

Figure 1.13 compares the groups' overall performance on the picture selection task. With respect to the /l–r/ contrast, we find that, as in the auditory task, the Chinese speakers perform more accurately than the Korean speakers and the Japanese speakers [F (3, 47) = 21.35, p = .0001]; in fact, they perform as well as the native controls. Chinese speakers have no problem choosing between two pictures that constitute a minimal /l–r/ pair, indicating that these two phonemes have distinct representations in their interlanguage grammars. The Japanese and Korean speakers, however, were significantly worse on this contrast than the Chinese speakers and native controls, though not different from each other; thus, neither of these two groups of speakers distinguishes /l/ and /r/ phonologically.

All three groups of learners were unable to perform this task accurately when the lexical items differed by /s–θ/; there was no difference between experimental groups, and their performance was significantly lower than the controls' performance [F (3, 47) = 11.53, p = .0001]. This indicates that a new segmental representation for /θ/ has not been acquired by the learners, as we predicted, so /s/ and /θ/ are represented by the same geometric structure in their interlanguage grammars. In contrast, lexical items containing /f/ and /v/ are distinguished phonologically by all three groups of learners, as indicated by their high performance levels, though the Korean speakers' performance, at 89 percent accuracy, is slightly worse than the native controls' performance

[F (3, 47) = 3.21, p = .03]. Similarly, on the /p–f/ contrast, the Japanese and Chinese speakers are as accurate as the controls, while the performance of the Korean speakers, though significantly lower, is still well above chance (83 percent) [F (3, 47) = 5.9, p = .002]. With respect to the native /p–t/ contrast, all language groups distinguish /p/ and /t/ in their interlanguage grammars. Japanese speakers distinguished these two sounds in a native-like fashion; however, both the Chinese and Korean speakers were just slightly less accurate than the native speakers [F (3, 47) = 3.22, p = .03]. Overall, then, we see that the learners in all three groups have distinct segmental representations for /p/, /f/ and /v/, while the Chinese speakers also have distinct representations for /l/ and /r/, and none of the learners have distinct representations for /s/ and /θ/. Let's now compare performance on the different contrasts by each group individually to confirm these acquisition patterns.

A separate analysis of the Chinese group reveals that the /s–θ/ contrast is distinguished much more poorly than the other contrasts, including the native /p–t/ contrast [F (14, 60) = 13.4, p = .0001]; the /l–r/, /p–f/ and /f–v/ contrasts, however, are distinguished equally well and as accurately as the native /p–t/ contrast. This means that /l/, /r/, /p/, /f/ and /v/ each have a distinct segmental representation in the Chinese speakers' interlanguage grammars; /s/ and /θ/, on the other hand, will correspond to the same phonological structure and, therefore, will not be distinguished in these learners' interlanguage grammars.

Analysis of the Japanese data also confirms two distinct acquisition patterns [F (14, 60) = 34.99, p = .0001]. These learners represent the /p–f/ and /f–v/ contrasts in their interlanguage grammars in the same way that they represent the native /p–t/ contrast; there is no statistical difference between their (equally good) performance on these three types of contrasts. There is also no difference in their (in)ability to phonologically distinguish the /l–r/ and /s–θ/ contrasts: they are equally poor. This finding is especially interesting, given the difference we found between these two contrasts on the auditory discrimination task. Despite the slight advantage in perceiving /s/ and /θ/, it is not sufficient to trigger acquisition. Neither the segmental representation for /l/ nor for /θ/ has been acquired by these learners.

Finally, we turn to the Korean group, who have the identical pattern of acquisition as the Japanese speakers: the /l–r/ and /s–θ/ contrasts are not distinguished in lexical items, whereas the /p–f/ and /f–v/ contrasts are [F (10, 44) = 12.8, p = .0001]. In fact, although we saw above that the performance of the Korean speakers was slightly depressed on the /p–f/ contrast relative to the other language groups, it is not significantly different from their performance on their native contrast. Thus, it appears that whatever is causing the lower performance on the non-native contrast is not due to the non-native nature of the contrast, but rather to some more general performance factor. Nevertheless, additional studies examining Korean speakers' auditory and phonological discrimination are clearly required to establish their perceptual and linguistic abilities conclusively.

In summary, this experiment was conducted in order to determine whether our theory of phonological interference could account for the acquisition of English phonemes by speakers of different languages. Assuming that perception of non-native contrasts is constrained by the phonological features manipulated in the learner's native grammar and that languages differ as to the features they manipulate, we would expect learners with different L1s to differ in their ability to acquire particular non-native contrasts. Japanese, Korean, and Chinese differ in just this way.[29] Specifically, the grammar of Chinese contains the feature [coronal], whereas the grammars of Japanese and Korean lack this feature. Given this, speakers of Japanese and Korean, on the one hand, and Chinese, on the other, should differ in their ability to acquire the /l–r/ contrast, which relies on the feature [coronal]. This is, indeed, what we found. Chinese speakers accurately perceive this contrast and, therefore, successfully acquire it. Japanese and Korean speakers are unable to acquire this contrast since they do not perceive /l/ and /r/ as different segments.

These three groups were fairly evenly matched for age of exposure, education and years spent studying English. Therefore, we can be confident that the differential performance of these groups stems from their respective L1s. Simply comparing the phoneme inventories of these three languages, however, does not allow us to explain why Chinese speakers accurately perceive and acquire the /l–r/ contrast, but that both the Japanese and Korean speakers do not. By the same token, it is only by considering the features utilized by the L1s that we can adequately explain why all three language groups were able to perceive and acquire the /p–f/ and /f–v/ contrasts, which are distinguished by features that exist in Japanese, Chinese, and Korean.

Likewise, the absence of the relevant feature from all three L1s accounts for their uniform inability to acquire the /s–θ/ contrast. Thus, the differential abilities of the Japanese and Chinese speakers lends support to our theory of phonological interference: not only can we account for disparate acquisition of non-native contrasts by speakers of a single language, we can also explain disparate acquisition of a particular non-native contrast by speakers of different languages.[30]

Now that we have seen how the native grammar can affect perception and acquisition of non-native contrasts, a question that naturally arises is whether the native grammar always constrains phonological acquisition in this way or whether its effect changes over time, as the learner progresses. The Japanese learners tested in experiment 1 were relatively advanced, living in North America and receiving abundant natural English input. Since these learners had already acquired two of the three non-native contrasts, we found no evidence for any stages of acquisition. The learners tested in experiment 2 had never lived in an English-speaking environment and were receiving minimal to no aural English input at the time of testing; but, although these learners were not always as accurate as the native speaker controls on those contrasts they had acquired, we still did not observe distinct stages of acquisition. Since the first two experiments were not longitudinal and also did not compare learners with differing levels of L2 proficiency, we have no data to determine whether there is any change in learners' perceptual capacities. Does perception of non-native contrasts improve over time? Is there any effect of increased linguistic input? Is there evidence for stages of acquisition? These questions were addressed in the following experiment, which investigated the acquisition of English contrasts by low proficiency and higher proficiency Japanese learners of English.

Experiment 3

This experiment was conducted in order to determine whether the influence of the native grammar on the perception of non-native contrasts changes over time as the L2 learner progresses.

Subjects

The subjects for this experiment were 35 native speakers of Japanese and 10 native speakers of English. The control group comprised American, British, and Canadian English teachers at Hokkaido University and Hokkai Gakuen University, in Sapporo, Japan. The Japanese subjects were learning English as a foreign language at Hokkaido University and had never lived in an English-speaking country. Based on teacher interview assessment of their overall proficiency in English, the Japanese speakers were divided into two experimental groups: Low-level (n = 20) and High-level (n = 15). The relevant background data are given in table 1.5.

Contrasts investigated and hypotheses

Two experimental contrasts were tested in this experiment, /l–r/ and /b–v/; the native /p–b/ contrast was also included as a control item. If perception and acquisition of non-native contrasts is constrained by the features of the native grammar, then, since both beginner Japanese learners of English and

Table 1.5 Experiment 3: Subject information

Group	Mean age at testing	Mean age of exposure	Mean years studied
Low-level	19	11.7	7.6
High-level	24.5	12	11.5
Controls	35	–	–

more advanced Japanese learners of English have the same native grammar, they should both be able to perceive the /b–v/ contrast, yet unable to perceive the /l–r/ contrast.

Tasks and materials

The tasks and materials used in this experiment were the same as those used in experiment 1; an AX Discrimination task was used to assess perception and a Forced Choice Picture Selection task was used to assess phonological competence.

Results and discussion

On the auditory discrimination task, a response that the two words in the minimal pair were "different" was counted as correct and a "same" response was counted as an error. Performance scores on each of the contrasts were tabulated separately for statistical analysis. Figure 1.14 reports the mean performance scores on each of the contrasts for each group.

From both the Low-level and High-level groups' near perfect performance on the control items (i.e., native /p–b/ pairs), it is clear that the task itself does not pose any difficulty for the learners. Furthermore, the control group performed as expected, accurately discriminating each of the three contrasts, with no significant difference between contrasts [F (9, 20) = 1.09, p = .36].

As figure 1.14 illustrates, both groups of Japanese speakers were significantly worse than the English controls at discriminating the /l–r/ contrast [F (2, 44) = 74.49, p = .0001]. However, there was no difference between the Low-level and High-level groups in their ability to discriminate this contrast; learners in both groups were unable to perceive the difference between /l/ and

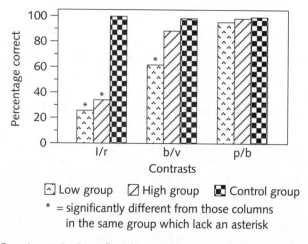

Figure 1.14 Experiment 3: Overall auditory performance by contrast

/r/. Thus, an increase in English proficiency does not appear to affect perception of this non-native contrast. Accurate perception is blocked by the native grammar in the earliest stages of acquisition and continues to prevent perception even as the learner progresses.

The situation is slightly different with respect to the other non-native contrast. While the learners in the Low-level group were not as accurate at discriminating the /b–v/ contrast as the learners in the High-level group, there was no difference between the High-level and the control groups' performance on this contrast [F (2, 44) = 9.79, p = .0003]. Thus, there was improvement in the Japanese speakers' ability to perceive this non-native contrast. We must keep in mind, though, that the Low-level group's somewhat poorer ability to discriminate /b/ and /v/ is still much better than either Japanese group's ability to distinguish /l/ from /r/. Finally, there was no statistical difference between the three groups in their ability to perceive the native /p–b/ contrast: all Japanese speakers discriminated this contrast as well as the native controls did [F (2, 44) = 1.08, p = .35]. In short, whereas the ability to accurately perceive the /l–r/ contrast does not improve over time, the ability to perceive the /b–v/ contrast does improve, from being fairly good to being native-like.

We can now evaluate the relative effect of the native grammar on each of the contrasts at different stages of acquisition by examining the performance of each group individually. Beginning with the Low-level group, we find that their performance on each of the contrasts is significantly different from each other [F (19, 40) = 73.53, p = .001]. That is, performance on the /p–b/ contrast, which is native-like, is better than performance on the /b–v/ contrast, which is better than performance on the /l–r/ contrast. However, there was no difference in the High-level learners' ability to discriminate the /b–v/ and /p–b/ contrasts; both were perceived equally well and more accurately than the /l–r/ contrast [F (14, 30) = 91.75, p = .001]. These data show that at both stages of acquisition, the Japanese speakers are unable to discriminate /l/ and /r/, perceiving them, instead, as members of a single category. However, they differ in their ability to distinguish /b/ from /v/, indicating that the influence of the native grammar is not static, but changes as the learner's interlanguage grammar develops.

To summarize, these data allow us to see the influence of the native grammar at different stages of acquisition. We found that the ability to discriminate the /l–r/ contrast does not change over time, whereas learners do improve in their ability to perceive the /b–v/ contrast. We might be tempted to conclude from this that the influence of the native grammar simply changes over time, constraining perception more tightly in the early stages of acquisition but gradually weakening as the learner's interlanguage grammar develops. However, the situation is a bit more complex. We know that the native grammar influences perception of non-native sounds in two ways: it may either *block* perception or *facilitate* perception, depending on whether the relevant feature

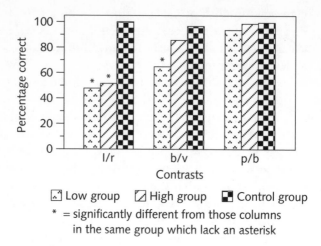

Figure 1.15   Experiment 4: Overall picture performance by contrast

is present or absent in the L1 grammatical system. Looking at the data again, we see that perception of the /l–r/ contrast does not improve; it is only the perception of /b–v/ which improves. Thus, when the relevant feature is absent from the native grammar, as it is in the case of /l–r/, and perception is blocked, the effect of the grammar remains constant. However, if the relevant feature is present in the native grammar, as it is for /b–v/, then the effect of the grammar may change. In other words, the negative influence of the native grammar on perception is absolute, but the positive influence of the native grammar is enhanced as the learner progresses.

For the picture identification task, selection of the target picture was counted as a correct response and selection of the contrast picture was counted as an error. The groups' overall performance is compared in figure 1.15.

Near perfect performance was attained by the Japanese group on the control items in this task. Again, the performance of the control subjects – accurate and with no differences between contrasts – ensures that our task and materials are reliable [F (9, 20) = 2.39, p = .12].

The pattern of performance on this picture task is very similar to that on the auditory task. Both groups of Japanese speakers were significantly worse than the English controls at distinguishing lexical items that differed by /l/ or /r/ [F (2, 44) = 35.20, p = .0001]. Yet, there was no difference between the Low-level and High-level groups in their ability (or inability) to distinguish this contrast; learners in both groups were unable to discriminate /l/ and /r/ phonologically. This indicates that neither the beginner learners nor the more advanced learners have acquired the phonological structure necessary to differentiate these segments in their interlanguage grammars. This is not the case, though, with the /b–v/ contrast. While the learners in the Low-level group were not as accurate as the learners in the High-level group at distinguishing items that differed by /b/ or /v/, there was no difference between the High-level and the control groups' performance on this contrast [F (2, 44) = 5.43, p = .007]. Thus, duplicating the results from the auditory task, the ability to differentiate /b/ and /v/ in one's interlanguage grammar appears to develop over time. This suggests that there are, in fact, stages of phoneme acquisition. With respect to the native /p–b/ contrast, there was no statistical difference between the three groups: all Japanese speakers discriminated this contrast as well as the native controls did [F (2, 44) = 1.94, p = .15].

Looking at each group individually, we find that the performance of the Low-level group on each of the contrasts is significantly different from the others [F (19, 40) = 47.81, p = .0001]. We find the same pattern of perform-ance by the High-level group [F (14, 30) = 31.82, p = .0001]. Both groups are better at distinguishing the /b–v/ contrast than they are the /l–r/ contrast, but they are still not as good at distinguishing the /b–v/ contrast as they are their own native /p–b/ contrast. It is clear from the data that the learners do not differentiate /l/ and /r/ in lexical items (i.e., the same structure is used to represent both segments). It is also clear that they do have distinct repres-entations for /p/ and /b/.

What, then, is the status of the /b–v/ contrast, which seems to fall some-where between the other contrasts; has it been acquired or not? I think the answer to this question is different for the two groups. In the case of the Low-level group, it appears that the new representations have not been acquired. This is not so surprising, given their perception of the /b–v/ contrast, which while quite good is not native-like. It is possible that these learners have not yet detected contrastive use of these segments in English and, as a result, have not yet acquired the new representations. In the case of the High-level group, however, I think we can be confident that they have acquired the new representations. Importantly, their perception of /b–v/ is native-like; thus a necessary condition for proper acquisition has been met. Moreover, their ability to distinguish /b/ and /v/ in this task (although poorer than their ability to distinguish the /p–b/ contrast) is as good as the native speakers' ability to distinguish /b/ and /v/, who undoubtedly differentiate these two sounds in their grammars.[31]

The research question we attempted to answer in this experiment was whether the influence of the native grammar on the perception and acquisi-tion of non-native contrasts changes over time as the L2 learner progresses. The data demonstrate that there is not one answer to this question. The effects of the grammar, either to *block* or to *facilitate* perception and acquisi-tion are differentially altered by the learner's development. If the feature underlying a non-native phonemic contrast is absent from the native gram-mar, then the native phonological system will continue to funnel the distinct acoustic signals for those sounds into a single perceptual category through-out the learner's development; perception of these non-native contrasts will not improve. In this case, the influence of the native grammar is rigid, immut-able by increased exposure to a second language. If, however, the feature underlying a non-native phonemic contrast is present in the native grammar, the capacity of the native phonological system to use this feature in the processing of non-native sounds will be enhanced over the course of the learner's development; perception of these non-native contrasts will improve. In this case, increased exposure to a second language will actually strengthen the facilitative influence of the native grammar.

General Discussion and Conclusions

The goal of the research program presented in this chapter is to develop a comprehensive theory-driven model of L2 phoneme acquisition that accounts for the interrelation between perception and phonological acquisition and explains how and why this interrelation affects L2 phonological acquisition. It was proposed that the monotonic acquisition of feature geometric structure by young children reduces their perceptual sensitivity to particular non-native contrasts and that this adult feature geometry continues to mediate between the acoustic signal and the linguistic processor in adult speech perception, constraining which non-native contrasts adult learners will be sensitive to in the L2 input and, therefore, capable of acquiring. Thus, in order to fully understand why the L1 grammar exerts such a profound influence on the perception and acquisition of non-native phonemic contrasts, it is important that we understand the development of these systems in first language acquisition and their operation in the mature speaker.

Having determined how the interrelation between speech perception and the phonological system originates, we are in a better position to capture the nature of the mechanism that maps the L2 input onto L1 phonological categories; utilizing the tools of Feature Geometry theory enables us to formally articulate this mapping process. The central claim of the theory of phonological interference developed here is that the L1 influence found in L2 phonological acquisition is a consequence of how the speech perception mechanism operates in the native speaker. Based on the proposal that the decline in infants' ability to discriminate non-native contrasts is caused by the acquisition of phonological structure, speech perception in the native speaker will continue to be constrained by phonological properties of his or her native language throughout adulthood; more specifically, all speech sounds (native and non-native) will be perceived in terms of the features exploited by that particular language.

The experimental studies reported above have demonstrated that not all non-native contrasts are created equal: learners with the same L1 have more difficulty perceiving and acquiring some non-native contrasts than they do others; likewise, certain non-native contrasts are easily perceived and acquired by speakers of some languages, while those same contrasts will not be perceived or acquired by speakers of other languages. These differences, both between contrasts and between speakers of different languages, were argued to follow directly from the status of the relevant distinctive feature in the learner's L1 grammar: presence of the contrastive features in the grammar serves to sort the acoustic signal along that particular dimension, mapping the signals for two segments onto distinct phonological categories, whereas absence of the contrastive feature entails that the acoustic signals for the phonemes be mapped onto a single phonological category.

We saw in experiment 1 that Japanese learners' perception and acquisition of various English contrasts differed in exactly this respect: they were able to perceive and, therefore, acquire those contrasts which are distinguished by a feature that their native grammar employs for independent reasons (e.g., /b–v/ and /f–v/), but were unable to perceive that contrast that is distinguished by a feature not utilized in the L1 (e.g., /l–r/). Similarly, experiment 2 provided evidence that Japanese, Korean, and Chinese speakers differ in their acquisition of particular English contrasts just as the model predicts: speakers of all three languages were unable to perceive the /s–θ/ contrast, which relies on a feature absent from all three L1s, yet were able to perceive those contrasts distinguished by features present in all three L1s (i.e., /p–f/ and /f–v/); most importantly, speakers of these three languages differed in their ability to perceive and acquire precisely that contrast, /l–r/, which is distinguished by a feature whose status differs among these languages.

While the discussion of experimental results has not focused on individual differences, some inter-subject variability does exist, and so it is necessary at this point to address how such variability fits into my model. It might seem that the model – with performance so heavily influenced by the speaker's L1 grammar – would allow for no variability between subjects having the same L1 background. In fact, though, we might expect two different kinds of inter-subject variability: "grammar-driven" variability and "test-strategy" variability. "Grammar-driven" variability would be those differences in subjects' performance that directly reflect properties of their interlanguage. This kind of variability will be restricted to those contrasts distinguished by a feature utilized in the L1. Since it is precisely these contrasts that are acquirable, we should find subjects at different stages of development: a learner in the early stages of L2 acquisition will assimilate the non-native segments to native categories to a greater degree (and thus have lower performance) than a more advanced learner whose grammar has developed the novel L2 categories. This situation is indeed what we observed in experiment 3 regarding the /b–v/ contrast – considerable (albeit, not wild) variability across the two levels of Japanese learners. Thus, although my model would predict that all Japanese speakers, for example, will eventually perceive this contrast in a native-like fashion, it does allow, even expect, that these speakers will vary somewhat in their accuracy according to their particular point in development. This "grammar-driven" variability will typically constitute a range of good performance on a task (e.g., 75 percent vs. 96 percent).

The other kind of variability – "test-strategy" variability – we would expect to find for those contrasts that are distinguished by a feature *not* present in the L1. As mentioned previously, in an AX task we would theoretically expect 0 percent accuracy since the L1 grammar funnels both L2 sounds into a single L1 category (i.e., the subject's answer will always be "same"). However, in practice subjects often surmise that some trials will be the same and some will be different and so adopt a strategy of simply guessing between "same" and "different". This strategy results in chance performance of approximately 50 percent. Thus, in the testing situation subjects may respond on the basis of their grammar, they may adopt a guessing strategy, or some combination of both. This would give us accuracy scores ranging from 0 percent to roughly 50 percent. In contrast to the "grammar-driven" variability, this "test-strategy" variability will always fall within the range of poor performance (e.g., 9 percent vs. 33 percent correct). Although "test-strategy" variability is not explicitly predicted to occur by my model it also does not compromise the model, providing that all scores are within chance levels (e.g., we should never find that some Japanese speakers perceive the English /l–r/ contrast with native-like accuracy and that other Japanese speakers do not).

If we expect to find some inter-subject variability for both kinds of non-native contrasts, those distinguished by a feature present in the L1 grammar ("grammar-driven" variability) and those by a feature absent in the L1 grammar ("test-strategy" variability), is there any empirical difference between the two? We can in fact make an interesting prediction regarding these two types of variability. Since "test-strategy" variability does not derive from the subjects' interlanguage, we should find this type *across* all levels of learners; in other words, we should find inter-subject variability for a contrast such as /l–r/ for both beginner and advanced Japanese or Korean learners of English. "Grammar-driven" variability, on the other hand, would be limited to variation *between* the different levels of learners since this type of variability directly reflects properties of the learners' grammars.

One implication of the model I have outlined is that prior to the development of a phonological system, infants should be able to perceive contrasts which they will fail to perceive as adults. With respect to Japanese speakers, if their difficulty discriminating /l/ and /r/ does indeed stem from the interference of their phonological system (rather than to, say, some genetic property of Japanese speakers), then before that system is in place, accurate perception of those sounds should be possible. Japanese infants have, in fact, been shown to perceptually distinguish /l/ from /r/ (Tsushima, Takizawa, Sasaki, Shiraki, Nishi, Kohno, Menyuk, and Best, 1994). Thus, the inability of Japanese speakers to discriminate /l/ and /r/ as adults does indeed appear to be a consequence of language development.[32] Moreover, an early study by Miyawaki et al. (1975) shows that the difficulties Japanese speakers have discriminating /l/ and /r/ are due to specific properties of their perception of *speech*, not to deficiencies in their basic auditory mechanisms. These researchers found that adult Japanese speakers accurately discriminate /l/ and /r/ when they are presented in a "non-speech mode".[33] In other words, Japanese speakers are able to discriminate /l/ and /r/ when the acoustic signal is processed directly by the auditory system, rather than the linguistic module.

We know from first language acquisition research that the development of segmental structure involves the interaction of Universal Grammar and the learner's detection of phonemic contrasts in the input. Thus, successful acquisition of novel phonemes by L2 learners depends not only on the availability of UG, but, importantly, on adequate intake to the language acquisition device. By demonstrating that some L2 learners do not perceive the L2 input correctly (in fact, precisely those learners who are unable to acquire the given contrast), this research strongly suggests that the inability of some L2 learners to acquire novel phonemic contrasts is due to the lack of proper input, rather than the unavailability of UG. Thus, the failure of L2 learners to acquire novel phonemes should not necessarily be taken as evidence that UG is not available in L2 acquisition. In fact, these results demonstrate that if L2 learners are able to perceive a non-native contrast, they are able to acquire that contrast, suggesting that the mechanism for constructing novel segmental representations (which is arguably part of UG) is still operative in L2 acquisition.

These findings fit in nicely with recent trends in second language acquisition theory which suggest that differences in L1 and L2 acquisition (as well as differences across learners in L2 acquisition) stem not from the unavailability of Universal Grammar but rather from the initial state of acquisition (papers in Schwartz and Eubank, 1996). The goal of this new line of research is to define the initial state of L2 acquisition and, thereby, explain the development of the L2 grammar. Differences in L2 acquisition of a particular language that co-vary with learners' native language are now assumed to be a result of the L2 initial state. The research agenda, then, is to define this initial state. Research on the acquisition of syntactic properties of the L2 has been used to support several hypotheses regarding the linguistic content of the initial state (see Schwartz and Eubank, 1996, for Schwartz and Sprouse's *Full Transfer/Full Access Model*, Vainikka and Young-Scholten's *Minimal Tree Hypothesis*, and Eubank's *Weak Transfer Hypothesis*). The findings from experimental research on the L2 acquisition of phonemes seem to be most consistent with Schwartz and Sprouse's hypothesis that the entire L1 system forms the initial basis of L2 acquisition: all of the data indicate that in the earliest stages of L2 acquisition, L2 phonemes are mapped according to the L1 feature geometry onto L1 phonemic categories; only subsequently are new L2 categories acquired.

The claim that the entire L1 phonological system constitutes the initial state for L2 phoneme acquisition raises an interesting question: If the acoustic signal is perceived in terms of the learner's L1 phonemic categories, how can the learner accurately perceive non-native sounds in order for new phonemic categories to be established? In other words, how can the input be mapped by the adult feature geometry onto new L2 categories when those categories don't yet exist? The answer to this question, I believe, depends on whether it is the *phonemes* or the *features* of the L1 which constrain perception. If the acoustic signal is mapped onto L1 phonemes, then it would seem that it is the phonemic level which impinges upon L2 acquisition. Yet, I have argued that it is the featural level which is relevant.

A closer examination of the data from low and high proficiency learners presented in experiment 3 suggests how these two positions might be reconciled. In particular, these data suggest that initially, in the earliest stages of acquisition, the phonemes of the L1 have a profound influence on the perception of non-native contrasts. In an attempt to understand the L2 input, and in the absence of new phonological categories, the L2 input is fitted into the L1 system any way it can be (often by brute force, ignoring variations that the system senses but cannot yet deal with appropriately). For example, the acoustic signals for both /b/ and /v/ will be mapped by Japanese speakers onto the L1 phoneme /b/ and the acoustic signals for /l/ and /r/ will be mapped onto /ɾ/. This will be the initial stage of acquisition and, incidentally, the situation for loanword phonology.[34]

However, despite the initial attempt of the L1 system to accommodate all of the input within L1 structures, portions of the L2 input will not map adequately to the L1 system, as a result of the presence of the relevant contrasting feature. Taking our example again, the English /b/ will map completely onto the Japanese phoneme /b/, but the English /v/ will not map precisely to the Japanese category.[35] Thus, although both are perceived as a single category in the early stages of acquisition, the presence of the feature [continuant] ensures that the acoustic signal for /v/ does not correspond exactly to a Japanese category; this slight mismatch between the L2 input and the L1 structures will cause perceptual reorganization (the beginner learners in experiment 3). Over the course of development, and with increased exposure, a new phonological category will be established; following the establishment of this new category, the original native category will be bypassed entirely in perception, and perception of those contrasts will be native-like (the advanced learners in experiment 3).

If, however, the feature that distinguishes a given non-native contrast is absent from the L1 grammar, then the L2 input will map perfectly onto an existing L1 category and there will be no trigger for acquisition, as was the case with both our beginner and advanced learners for the /l–r/ contrast. Thus, while the input is initially sorted in terms of L1 phonemes, it is the L1 features which guide this mapping process and, therefore, determine to what extent the L2 input can be accommodated by existing phonological structure; in this way the features also constrain which non-native contrasts will be acquired by the learner. This picture receives empirical support from recent research by Matthews and Brown (1998) who, using measures of reaction time, demonstrate that non-native contrasts that are distinguished by an L1 feature are processed differently on-line than those contrasts distinguished by a feature not used by the L1 grammar; they also show that the on-line processing of non-native segments changes over time as novel phonemic categories emerge. This exciting new avenue of research provides additional support for the model of speech perception outlined here and, in particular, for the claim that the organization of feature geometry in a speaker's mental grammar operates in the on-line processing of speech sounds to map the incoming acoustic stimuli onto discrete perceptual categories, giving rise to categorical perception and, thus, making segmentation of the speech stream possible.

Notes

1   Although the term "second language acquisition" (SLA) technically refers to the acquisition of a second language by either an adult or a child, it is typically used to denote acquisition by post-pubescent learners. In this chapter, we will only consider SLA by adults; however, the claims made here may be extended to L2 learners of all ages.

2   Note that the introduction of Optimality Theory (Prince and Smolensky, 1993; McCarthy and Prince, 1993) and the concomitant shift away from concern about the structure of representations, including the internal structure of phonemes, does not negate the insights captured by the theory of Feature Geometry assumed here; any theory must capture the fundamental dependency and constituency relations that exist between phonological features. As it is not the goal of this chapter to argue in favor of Feature Geometry over Optimality Theory, I will only direct the reader to some relevant papers on this issue (see Cole and Kisseberth, 1994; Padgett, 1994; Pulleyblank, 1997; see Brown, 1997: 291–317, for arguments that segment-internal structure must be maintained in underlying representations; these arguments take the form of a demonstration that the type of speech perception results discussed in this chapter cannot be captured easily, or possibly at all, in terms of constraint ranking).

3   I will assume, along with a growing number of researchers, that features are monovalent and that it is the mere presence of a feature in the representation of a segment that designates the active involvement of its corresponding articulator; likewise, the absence of a feature entails that the corresponding articulator is not active for a given segment (e.g., Anderson and Ewen, 1987; Avery and Rice, 1989; van der Hulst, 1989). For example, the voiceless segment /t/ will simply not contain the feature [voice] in its representation (that alone ensures that the vocal cords are not active for this segment), whereas the phoneme /d/ will be specified for the feature [voice].

4   The representations for /l/ and /r/ assumed here differ from standard representations. The phonological feature [lateral] is generally assumed to distinguish laterals from non-laterals, in this case /l/ from /r/. However, Brown (1993b, 1995) argues that [lateral] is not tenable as a phonological feature and that the contrast between /l/ and /r/ is best captured in terms of Place features (see reference for specific theoretical motivation and empirical evidence to support this claim; see also Piggott, 1993, and Spencer, 1984, for this view). Importantly, the representations for /l/ and /r/ given

in figure 1.2 provide an explanation for differential acquisition effects due to a speaker's first language grammar, which is not expected given the standard view of liquids.

5   The Japanese /ɾ/ will be distinguished from other coronal sounds (e.g., /s/) in terms of manner features.

6   This model integrates properties of models proposed by Clements and Hume (1994), Piggott (1992) and Rice and Avery (1991); however, the arguments and findings presented here do not hinge on the correctness of this particular hierarchical organization.

7   Perception research has tended to focus on very young infants (0–14 months) or older children (4–12 years); there is a surprising lack of perceptual data for young children (1–3 years). Thus, while the decline in sensitivity to non-native contrasts has been shown to begin in the first year of life, it has not yet been determined whether this early perceptual reorganization is rigid or remains relatively flexible until the phonological system is firmly in place. For example, it has not yet been determined whether the observed early pattern of perception persists throughout language development or whether a child, if placed in the appropriate language environment once perceptual reorganization has begun, would regain the original sensitivities.

8   See papers in Strange (1995) for reviews of the relevant speech perception data as well as several interesting proposals regarding the relationship between linguistic knowledge and the developing speech perception system.

9   There appears to be a time lag (approximately four to six months) between the age of the perceptual loss and the corresponding phonological development. A possible explanation for this time lag is that there is a confound between lexical development and phonological development, such that segmental representations are integrated into lexical items (which is what Brown and Matthews actually measured) shortly after they are first acquired. If this is indeed the case, acoustic discrimination tasks (specifically, lack of sensitivity) might provide a means of measuring the phonological development of children at even earlier ages than is currently available. This suggests that there may be an inventory of segments that is independent from the lexical items that contain them; this is a possibility that I will leave open for future research.

10 Note that this is true regardless of the actual phonetic realization of a particular contrast. Take, for example, voicing contrasts: although languages may vary as to how they choose to acoustically realize the voicing contrast (i.e., actual Voice Onset Time (VOT) may vary), since the same phonological feature underlies this contrast (i.e., [voice]), the claim is that speakers whose native language exploits this feature will be able to perceive all non-native voicing contrasts. A caveat is necessary here: this claim does not entail that speakers whose L1s contain the feature [voice] will necessarily perceive non-native voicing contrasts with 100 percent accuracy *initially*, nor that their performance will be equally accurate for that contrast in all positions within the syllable; only that there will be a qualitative difference between their perception of such a contrast and a contrast for which their L1 lacks the relevant feature (even initially), and that such a voicing contrast will be *acquirable* for such speakers (and that speakers will attain native-like performance given the appropriate input), even in syllabic positions not allowed in the L1 system.

11 The ability to construct novel segmental representations presumes, of course, that the acquisition device is still operative in L2 acquisition. See White (1989) for arguments regarding the operation of Universal Grammar in L2 acquisition; see Brown (1998) for a discussion of this issue with respect to L2 phonological acquisition.

12 The segments /s/ and /θ/ also differ acoustically in terms of stridency, and some phonologists distinguish them by the feature [strident]; however, following Kenstowicz

(1994: 30), I assume that their phonological representations differ in terms of place features. The predictions for the learners of English will not differ, though, under either analysis, as neither [strident] nor [distributed] is an underlying feature in any of the three languages under investigation.

13 While other segments are realized phonetically in Japanese, such as [Φ], they are derived (i.e., occurring in predictable phonological contexts) and do not, therefore, constitute independent phonemes.

14 The claim that Mandarin Chinese does not contrast /l/ and /r/ phonemically requires some comment. This language contains /l/ and a segment which is transcribed in romanized script as "r"; this transcription gives the impression that there is a contrast between the lateral approximant /l/ and a central approximant /r/. This "r" segment, however, is classified by linguists as a voiced retroflex fricative, /ʐ/. For this study, I follow Maddieson (1984) in treating /ʐ/ as a voiced retroflex fricative and, crucially, not as a retroflex sonorant. But compare Rice (1992) who analyzes this segment as /r/ underlyingly; postulating that it surfaces as a voiceless retroflex fricative [ʂ] in onset position and as rhoticization of the vowel when in coda position [ɚ]. Thus, according to this analysis, /r/ and /l/ do contrast as sonorants in Mandarin. However, it is not clear that this analysis is correct. The coda position in Mandarin is restricted to nasals; thus it is unlikely that the rhoticization of the vowel is from the presence of an approximant in the coda position. Finally, only certain vowels are rhoticized (Chao, 1968; Wu, 1991). This suggests that the rhoticization is a property of the vowel itself, rather than the result of /r/ in the coda position.

15 Japanese contains a bilabial fricative [Φ]; however, this is an allophone of /h/ and is realized before the high back unrounded vowel /ɯ/.

16 Japanese contains one liquid described as a flap [ɾ], which is not identical to the central approximant [r] in English, but is traditionally considered to correspond to English /r/, not /l/. This flap has several variants, which vary freely, one of which is phonetically similar to English [l] (Vance, 1987).

17 In Korean, [ɾ] and [l] are in complementary distribution, with [ɾ] (an apical flap) occurring intervocalically (Jung, 1962).

18 Although there are coronal segments in Japanese (e.g., /t/, /s/, /n/), under a theory of Minimally Contrastive Specification, a feature will only be present in a grammar if that feature is required to contrast segments; accordingly, coronal segments in Japanese will be represented with a bare Place node. However, based on palatal prosody in Japanese mimetics, Mester and Itô (1989) argue that Japanese coronal segments are, in fact, represented with the feature [Coronal]. This specification is proposed in order to account for the fact that all coronal segments *except* /ɾ/ are palatalized (as are non-coronals). By specifying all coronal sounds, other than /ɾ/, with the feature [Coronal], the authors explain why /ɾ/ is not a target of this operation. The same facts, however, can be obtained by assuming (as the authors themselves do to explain why /ɾ/ cannot be geminated) that /ɾ/ is not specified for any Place Node at all, whereas coronal segments are specified for a bare Place Node (with no [Coronal] feature). Lacking a Place Node, /ɾ/ will never be the target of palatalization. This specification would also explain why coronals are the preferred target of this operation, with non-coronals becoming palatalized only in the absence of a coronal: since coronals lack Place features, the palatal morpheme has a free place to dock on these segments, whereas the addition of palatalization to the non-coronal segments creates a less-favored complex structure.

19 While Japanese learners of English receive ample instruction in their language classes regarding the fact that /l/ and /r/ are contrastive in English, this type of explicit input,

due to its very nature, does not feed into the acquisition device and, thus, does not trigger acquisition (Schwartz, 1993).

20 As this study was originally reported in Brown (1993a, 1998) a summary of the methodology and statistical analyses will be given; the reader is referred to the original study for more details.

21 Brown (1993a, 1998) also examines acquisition of the /l–r/ contrast in onset clusters (e.g., glass/grass) and coda position (e.g., ball/bar).

22 Japanese speakers, for example, have been shown to correctly articulate /l/ and /r/, despite their inability to perceive a difference between these two sounds. This is possible since adult learners have a developed motor control system and are able (with practice) to execute the necessary articulations. Once a speaker knows the spelling of a word that contains /l/ or /r/, he or she can accurately produce the correct liquid, thus giving the appearance of having acquired the contrast. To my knowledge, no one has investigated how this knowledge of proper articulation might be encoded into the learner's lexical representation of words. It is not clear whether this knowledge (which is dependent on orthography) is represented in terms of phonological structure.

23 A training book was constructed which included every picture (one to a page) appearing in the experimental test. This book was used to familiarize the subjects with each of the pictures, and corresponding name, to appear in the Picture Selection task. This was done in order to minimize any errors that might be caused by the subjects' unfamiliarity with a particular stimulus item or illustration of an item. The materials used in stimuli preparation for the pictures were adapted from the Bilingual Aphasia Test (Paradis and Libben, 1987).

24 This result is perhaps even more surprising given the tendency of many Japanese learners to substitute /b/ for /v/ in production. But, as pointed out above, there is a well-known dissociation between comprehension and production skills, with comprehension assumed to be a more accurate reflection of the speaker's phonological knowledge.

25 For reasons of space and the goals of this chapter, I will not discuss subjects' individual performances, other than to point out that each of the Japanese subjects (not just the group as a whole) accurately discriminates the non-native /b–v/ and /f–v/ contrasts, but not the /l–r/ contrast. For a more detailed discussion of these individual data, the reader is referred to Brown (1998) in which these subjects' individual performances are analyzed in terms of a standard binomial distribution, showing that the group data are indeed representative of each subject. I will return to how the present model deals with individual differences, more generally, in the concluding section of this chapter.

26 According to Kawakami (1977: 32), the phoneme /b/ is realized as a plosive word-initially, but is often realized as a voiced bilabial fricative word-internally (compare [bareru] "be revealed" with [aβareru] "rampage").

27 Note that baseline performance on the AX Discrimination task is different from the picture task. According to the hypothesis that the Japanese grammar funnels the acoustic signal for both /l/ and /r/ into a single native phonemic category, Japanese speakers should perceive minimal pairs as identical. Thus, we would theoretically expect 0 percent accuracy at discriminating /l/ and /r/. In practice, though, they are able to correctly discriminate pairs more often – perhaps due to variations in duration and amplitude, which were not controlled for in this study. The difference in the subjects' performance on the two tasks (30 percent vs. 60 percent), then, is not indicative of differing abilities to perform each task, but rather reflects the fact that the baseline performance is different for each task.

28   An anonymous reviewer asks how this finding regarding accurate perception of a non-native voicing contrast squares with a previous finding by Jamieson and Morosan (1986) that speakers of Canadian French appear to have difficulty with the English θ/ð voicing contrast, despite the fact that the French grammar contains the feature [voice]. It would indeed be problematic for my proposal if French speakers did have trouble with the English θ/ð voicing contrast. However, a close examination of the Jamieson and Morosan study reveals several factors that undermine this conclusion. First, the stimuli in their study were presented with background cafeteria noise; it is likely that this noise depressed overall perceptual performance, so we cannot conclude that these results indicate that French speakers have any sort of absolute difficulty with the θ/ð contrast. Secondly, there were no native English speaker controls included in the design for comparison; this point is especially important considering that the stimuli were presented with cafeteria noise – we need to know how native speakers would do under these circumstances before we conclude that the French speakers cannot perceive θ/ð. Finally, the subjects were tested on a variety of stimuli spanning the voiceless–voiced continuum: while performance was low on the middle, more ambiguous stimuli (about 50 percent), it is quite good at either end of the continuum (about 80 percent), suggesting an ability to perceive the θ/ð contrast (again it would be useful to have native speaker data on the more ambiguous stimuli for comparison). Jamieson and Morosan's findings are in fact wholly compatible with the model of L1 interference developed here: they show significant improvement in between-category discrimination ability following training (e.g., θ/ð), but no improvement for within-category discrimination (e.g., two instances of θ along the voicing continuum), as well as striking improvement in subjects' ability to correctly identify each segment as voiced or voiceless (e.g., from 48 percent to 96 percent accurate identification). This kind of improvement is exactly what we would expect to find given that the French speakers' L1 grammar contains the feature [voice] – if their grammars lacked this feature the kind of improvement Jamieson and Morosan demonstrate would be impossible. Indeed, we will find a similar pattern of improvement below in experiment 3 where beginner and advanced learners' perception and acquisition of the English /b–v/ contrast are compared.

29   The differential performance of the two language groups also speaks to phonological theory, providing experimental evidence for the representations of /l/ and /r/ assumed in this chapter. According to Brown (1993b, 1995), /l/ and /r/ are distinguished by the presence of Coronal in the representation of /r/. We can interpret the differential performance of the two groups in terms of the presence of this feature in Chinese and the lack of it in Japanese. However, according to Rice and Avery (1991), /l/ and /r/ are differentiated not in terms of place features, but by manner features: /r/ contains a vocalic node whereas /l/ does not. Chinese and Japanese do not differ with respect to this feature, thus Rice and Avery's representations incorrectly predict that Chinese and Japanese speakers should perform similarly.

30   These conclusions are supported by Brown (1998), which compares the auditory and phonological discrimination abilities of Japanese and Chinese speakers living in North America, and Brown (1996), which compares Japanese and Chinese speakers living in Japan.

31   Depressed performance by both the High-level and the native control group on the /b–v/ contrast is likely caused by acoustic properties of this pair of sounds, especially in the environment of high front vowels, which minimize their distinctiveness.

32   Cochrane (1980) demonstrates that preadolescent Japanese children (ages 3–13 years) were no better than adults at perceiving /l–r/ minimal pairs. This finding indicates

that the inability of the Japanese adults to perceive this contrast is a result of a change that occurs very early in language development (i.e., acquisition of phonological structure) and not the result of a more general change that occurs sometime prior to puberty (e.g., lateralization of brain function).

33 In the "non-speech mode," all of the acoustic information that does NOT differentiate the two sounds – namely the first and second formants – was removed from the stimuli, resulting in something that sounds like a high-pitched glissando.

34 Loan words in Japanese are written in katakana, one of the two Japanese syllabary writing systems. When a foreign word containing the segment [v] is borrowed, this segment is traditionally transcribed as one of the kana for [ba], [bi], [be], [bo] or [bu] (i.e., [b] is substituted for [v]). However, within the last five years, a new kana symbol has been introduced by *Monbusho* (Japan's Ministry of Education) to represent the sound [v], ヴ, which is the symbol for the vowel [u], plus a voicing diacritic. Thus, just as it is possible for the learner, who originally maps all L2 sounds onto L1 categories (even those that do not match perfectly), to acquire a new perceptual category for those L2 sounds that do not correspond perfectly to the L1 categories, so too can writing systems be adapted to better represent the original pronunciations of loanwords. Words that were borrowed into Japanese before the introduction of this new symbol for [v] continue to be written as though they contained a [b] (e.g., "boribou" for volleyball), but words that have been borrowed after the introduction of this symbol are written to accurately reflect the language of origin's pronunciation (e.g., "Bon Jovi" for Bon Jovi). It is quite interesting (and not accidental, I think) that a new katakana symbol has been introduced for [v] (an L2 phoneme which Japanese speakers have been shown above to accurately perceive), but not for [l] (an L2 phoneme which these speakers do not accurately perceive). That the writing system has been modified to accommodate [v], but not [l], reflects, I think, the increasing perceptual awareness of Japanese speakers that [v] does not adequately correspond to any native Japanese phonemes.

35 This position predicts that the time required to process English /b/ and /v/ by Japanese speakers, for example, will differ. Since English /b/ maps exactly to the Japanese category, it should be identified as /b/ more quickly than /v/ is identified (as /b/ or /v/).

References

Abramson, A. and Lisker, L. (1970) Discriminability along the voicing continuum: Cross-language tests. *Proceedings of the Sixth International Congress of Phonetic Sciences*, pp. 563–7. Prague: Academia.

Anderson, J. and Ewen, C. (1987) *Principles of Dependency Phonology*. Cambridge: Cambridge University Press.

Archangeli, D. (1988) Aspects of Underspecification Theory. *Phonology* 5(2): 183–207.

—— (1984) *Underspecification in Yawelmani Phonology and Morphology*. Doctoral dissertation. Massachusetts Institute of Technology. [Published 1988, Garland, New York.]

Avery, P. and Rice, K. (1989) Segment structure and coronal underspecification. *Phonology* 6(2): 179–200.

Barton, D. (1980) Phonemic perception in children. In G. Yeni-Komshian, J. Kavanagh and C. Ferguson (eds.), *Child Phonology*, vol. 2, pp. 97–116. New York: Academic Press.

Beddor, P. and Gottfried, T. (1995) Methodological issues in cross-language speech perception research with adults. In W. Strange (ed.), *Speech Perception and Linguistic Experience: Issues in Cross-language Research*, pp. 207–32. Baltimore: York Press.

Best, C. (1994) The emergence of native-language phonological influence in infants: A perceptual assimilation model. In H. Nusbaum, J. Goodman and C. Howard (eds.), *The Transition from Speech Sounds to Spoken Words: The Development of Speech Perception*, pp. 167–224. Cambridge, MA: MIT Press.

—— (1993) Emergence of language-specific constraints in perception of non-native speech: A window on early phonological development. In B. de Boysson-Bardies (ed.), *Developmental Neurocognition: Speech and Face Processing in the First Year of Life*, pp. 289–304. Dordrecht: Kluwer Academic Publishers.

—— and McRoberts, G. (1989) Phonological influences in infants' discrimination of two non-native speech contrasts. Paper presented at the Society for Research in Child Development, Kansas City, Kansas, April 1989.

Bley-Vroman, R. (1989) The logical problem of second language acquisition. In S. Gass and J. Schachter (eds.), *Linguistic Perspectives on Second Language Acquisition*, pp. 41–72. Cambridge: Cambridge University Press.

Borden, G., Gerber, A. and Milsark, G. (1983) Production and perception of the /r/–/l/ contrast in Korean adults learning English. *Language Learning* 33: 499–526.

Brière, E. (1966) An investigation of phonological interferences. *Language* 42: 768–95.

Brown, C. (1998) The role of the L1 grammar in the acquisition of L2 segmental structure. *Second Language Research*.

—— (1997) *The Acquisition of Segmental Structure: Consequences for Speech Perception and Second Language Acquisition*. Unpublished Ph.D. dissertation. McGill University, Montréal, Québec.

—— (1996) English tongues, Japanese ears: A theory of phonological interference. *Language and Culture: Journal of the Institute of Language and Culture Studies* 30: 165–203. Hokkaido University, Sapporo, Japan.

—— (1995) The feature geometry of lateral approximants and lateral fricatives. In van der Hulst, H. and van de Weijer, J. (eds.), *Leiden at Last*, pp. 41–88. University of Leiden, Holland.

—— (1993a) The role of the L1 grammar in the L2 acquisition of segmental structure. *McGill Working Papers in Linguistics* 9: 180–210.

—— (1993b) On the representation of laterality. *McGill Working Papers in Linguistics* 8(2): 109–42.

—— and Matthews, J. (1997) The role of feature geometry in the development of phonemic contrasts. In S. J. Hannahs and M. Young-Scholten (eds.), *Generative Studies in the Acquisition of Phonology*, pp. 67–112. Amsterdam: John Benjamins Publishing Company.

—— and —— (1993) The acquisition of segmental structure. *McGill Working Papers in Linguistics* 9: 46–76.

Burnham, D. (1986) Developmental loss of speech perception: exposure to and experience with a first language. *Applied Psycholinguistics* 7: 207–40.

Chao, Y. R. (1968) *A Grammar of Spoken Chinese*. Berkeley: University of California Press.

Chomsky, N. and Halle, M. (1968) *The Sound Pattern of English*. Cambridge, MA: MIT Press.

Clements, G. N. (1985) The geometry of phonological features. *Phonology Yearbook* 2: 223–50.

—— and Hume, E. (1994) The internal organization of speech sounds. In J. Goldsmith (ed.), *A Handbook in Phonological Theory*, pp. 245–306. Oxford: Blackwell Publishers.

Cochrane, R. (1980) The acquisition of /r/ and /l/ by Japanese children and adults learning English as a second language. *Journal of Multilingual and Multicultural Development* 1: 331–60.

Cole, J. and Kisseberth, C. (1994) An optimal domains theory of harmony. MS., University of Illinois at Urbana-Champaign.

Edwards, M. (1974) Perception and production in child phonology: The testing of four hypotheses. *Journal of Child Language* 2: 205–19.

Eilers, R., Gavin, W. and Oller, D. (1982) Cross-linguistic perception in infancy: Early effects of linguistic experience. *Journal of Child Language* 9: 289–302.

Eimas, P., Siqueland, E., Jusczyk, P. and Vigorito, J. (1971) Speech perception in infants. *Science* 171: 303–6.

Flege, J. (1995) Second language speech learning: Theory, findings, and problems. In W. Strange (ed.), *Speech Perception and Linguistic Experience: Issues in Cross-language Research*, pp. 233–73. Baltimore: York Press.

—— (1992) Speech learning in a second language. In C. A. Ferguson, L. Menn and C. Stoel-Gammon (eds.), *Phonological Development: Models, Research, Implications*. pp. 565–604. Baltimore: York Press.

—— (1991) Perception and production: The relevance of phonetic input to L2 phonological learning. In T. Heubner and C. Ferguson (eds.), *Crosscurrents in Second Language Acquisition and Linguistic Theory*, pp. 249–90. Philadelphia: John Benjamins Publishing Company.

—— (1981) The phonological basis of foreign accent. *TESOL Quarterly* 15: 443–55.

——, Takagi, N. and Mann, V. (1995) Japanese adults can learn to produce English /ɹ/ and /l/ accurately. *Language and Speech* 38: 25–55.

Garnica, O. (1973) The development of phonemic speech perception. In T. Moore (ed.), *Cognitive Development and the Acquisition of Language*, pp. 215–22. New York: Academic Press.

Goto, H. (1971) Auditory perception by normal Japanese adults of the sounds "L" and "R". *Neuropsychologia* 9: 317–23.

Hancin-Bhatt, B. (1994a) *Phonological Transfer in Second Language Perception and Production*. Unpublished Ph.D. dissertation. University of Illinois at Urbana-Champaign.

—— (1994b) Segment transfer: A consequence of a dynamic system. *Second Language Research* 10(3): 241–69.

Hulst, H. van der (1989) Atoms of segmental structure: Components, gestures and dependency. *Phonology* 6: 253–84.

International Phonetic Association (Principles of the) (1979) University College, London: International Phonetic Association.

Jakobson, R. (1941) *Kindersprache, Aphasie und Allgemeine Lautgesätze*. Uppsala: Almqvist and Wiksell. Citations from the English translation, *Child Language, Aphasia and Phonological Universals*, translated by A. Keiler, 1968. The Hague: Mouton.

Jamieson, D. and Morosan, D. (1986) Training non-native speech contrasts in adults: Acquisition of the English /T/–/D/ contrast by francophones. *Perception and Psychophysics* 40: 205–15.

Jung, M.-W. (1962) *A Contrastive Study of English and Korean Segmental Phonemes with Some Suggestions Toward Pedagogical Application*. MS. dissertation, Georgetown University.

Kawakami, S. (1977) *An Outline of Japanese Sounds [Nihongo Onsei Gaisetsu]*. Tokyo: Ouhussha.

Kenstowicz, M. (1994) *Phonology in Generative Grammar*. Oxford: Blackwell Publishers.

Lado, R. (1957) *Linguistics Across Cultures*. Ann Arbor: University of Michigan Press.

Lehn, W. and Slager, W. (1959) A contrastive study of Egyptian Arabic and American English: The segmental phonemes. *Language Learning* 9: 25–33.

Maddieson, I. (1984) *Patterns of Sound*. Cambridge: Cambridge University Press.

Matthews, J. and Brown, C. (1998) Qualitative and quantitative differences in the discrimination of second language speech sounds. *Proceedings of the 22nd Annual Boston University Conference on Language Development*, pp. 499–510. Boston: Cascadilla Press.

Mattingly, I., Liberman, A., Syrdal, A. and Halwes, T. (1971) Discrimination in speech and non-speech modes. *Cognitive Psychology* 2: 131–57.

McCarthy, J. and Prince, A. (1993) Prosodic Morphology I: Constraint Interaction and Satisfaction. MS., University of Massachusetts, Amherst, and Rutgers University, New Brunswick, NJ.

Mehler, J. (1985) Language related dispositions in early infancy. In J. Mehler and R. Fox (eds.), *Neonate Cognition: Beyond the Blooming, Buzzing Confusion*. Hillside, NJ: Erlbaum.

Mester, A. and Itô, J. (1989) Feature predictability and underspecification: Palatal prosody in Japanese mimetics. *Language* 65(2): 258–93.

Michaels, D. (1974) Sound replacements and phonological systems. *Linguistics* 176: 69–81.

—— (1973) Sinhalese sound replacement and feature hierarchies. *Linguistics* 170: 14–22.

Miller, J. and Eimas, P. (1977) Studies on the perception of place and manner of articulation: A comparison of the labial-alveolar and nasal-stop distinctions. *Journal of the Acoustical Society of America* 61: 835–45.

Miyawaki, K., Strange, W., Verbrugge, R., Liberman, A., Jenkins, J. and Fujimura, O. (1975) An effect of linguistic experience: The discrimination of /r/ and /l/ by native speakers of Japanese and English. *Perception & Psychophysics* 18: 331–40.

Munro, M., Flege, J. and MacKay, I. (1996) The effects of age of second language learning on the production of English vowels. *Applied Psycholinguistics* 17: 313–34.

Padgett, J. (1994) Feature classes. In J. Beckman, S. Urbanczyk and L. Walsh (eds.), *Papers in Optimality Theory*, University of Massachusetts Occasional Papers 18: 385–420.

Paradis, M. and Libben, G. (1987) *Assessment of Bilingual Aphasia*. Hillsdale, NJ: Lawrence Erlbaum.

Piggott, G. (1993) The geometry of sonorant features. MS., McGill University, Montreal, Canada.

—— (1992) Variability in Feature Dependency: The case of nasality. *Natural Language and Linguistic Theory* 10: 33–77.

Pisoni, D. (1973) Auditory and phonetic memory codes in the discrimination of consonants and vowels. *Perception and Psychophysics* 13: 253–60.

—— (1971) *On the Nature of Categorical Perception of Speech Sounds*. Unpublished Ph.D. dissertation: The University of Michigan.

Prince, A. and Smolensky, P. (1993) *Optimality Theory: Constraint Interaction in Generative Grammar*, RuCCs Technical Report #2, Rutgers University Center for Cognitive Science, Piscaraway, NJ [in press, Cambridge, MA: MIT Press].

Pulleyblank, D. (1997) Optimality theory and features. In D. Archangeli and D. T. Langendoen (eds.), *Optimality Theory: An Overview*, pp. 59–101. Oxford: Blackwell Publishers.

Repp, B. (1984) Categorical perception: Issues, methods, findings. In N. J. Lass (ed.), *Speech and Language: Advances in Basic Research and Practice*, vol. 10. Orlando: Academic Press.

Rice, K. (1992) On deriving sonority: A structural account of sonority relationships. *Phonology* 9: 61–99.

—— and Avery, P. (1995) Variability in a deterministic model of language acquisition: A theory of segmental acquisition. In J. Archibald (ed.), *Phonological Acquisition and Phonological Theory*, pp. 23–42. Hillsdale, NJ: Lawrence Erlbaum Associates.

—— and —— (1991) On the relationship between laterality and coronality. In C. Paradis and J. F. Prunet (eds.), *Phonetics and Phonology: The Special Status of Coronals*, vol. 2, pp. 101–24. San Diego: Academic Press.

Ritchie, W. (1968) On the explanation of phonic interference. *Language Learning* 18: 183–97.

Sagey, E. (1986) *The Representation of Features and Relations in Non-linear Phonology*, Doctoral dissertation, Massachusetts Institute of Technology, Cambridge, MA.

Schwartz, B. (in press) On two hypotheses of "transfer" in L2A: Minimal trees and absolute L1 influence. In S. Flynn, G. Martohardjono and W. O'Neil (eds.), *The Generative Study of Second Language Acquisition*. Hillsdale, NJ: Lawrence Erlbaum Associates.

—— (1993) On explicit and negative data effecting and affecting *competence* and *linguistic behavior*. *Studies in Second Language Acquisition* 15: 147–63.

—— and Eubank, L. (eds.) (1996) Special issue of *Second Language Research* 12(1).

Sheldon, A. and Strange, W. (1982) The acquisition of /r/ and /l/ by Japanese learners of English: Evidence that speech production can precede speech perception. *Applied Psycholinguistics* 3: 243–61.

Shvachkin, N. Kh. (1948) Razvitiye fonematicheskogo vospriyatiya rechi v rannem vozraste. *Izvestiya Akademii Pedagogicheskikh Nauk RSFSR* 13: 101–32. Citations from the English translation, The development of phonemic speech perception in early childhood. Translated by E. Dernbach and republished (1973) in C. Ferguson and D. Slobin (eds.), *Studies of Child Language Development*, pp. 91–127. New York: Holt, Rinehart and Winston.

Spencer, A. (1984) On eliminating the feature [lateral]. *Journal of Linguistics* 20: 23–43.

Stockwell, R. and Bowen, J. (1965) *The Sounds of English and Spanish*. Chicago: University of Chicago Press.

Strange, W. (ed.) (1995) *Speech Perception and Linguistic Experience: Issues in Cross-language Research*. Baltimore: York Press.

—— and Dittmann, S. (1984) Effects of discrimination training on the perception of /r–l/ by Japanese adults learning English. *Perception and Psychophysics* 36: 131–45.

Streeter, L. (1976) Language perception of 2-month-old infants shows effects of both innate mechanisms and experience. *Nature* 259: 39–41.

Trehub, S. (1976) The discrimination of foreign speech contrasts by infants and adults. *Child Development* 47: 466–72.

Tsushima, T., Takizawa, O., Sasaki, M., Shiraki, S., Nishi, K., Kohno, M., Menyuk, P., and Best, C. (1994) Discrimination of English /r–l/ and /w–y/ by Japanese infants at 6–12 months: Language-specific developmental changes in speech perception abilities. Unpublished manuscript, Boston University.

Vance, T. (1987) *An Introduction to Japanese Phonology*. Albany, NY: State University of New York Press.

Werker, J. and LaLonde, C. (1988) Cross-language speech perception: Initial capabilities and developmental change. *Developmental Psychology* 24: 672–83.

—— and Logan, J. (1985) Cross-language evidence for three factors in speech perception. *Perception and Psychophysics* 37: 35–44.

—— and Polka, L. (1993) Developmental change in speech perception: New challenges and new directions. *Journal of Phonetics* 21: 83–101.

—— and Tees, R. (1984a) Cross-language speech perception: Evidence for perceptual reorganization during the first year of life. *Infant Behavior and Development* 7: 49–63.

—— and —— (1984b) Phonemic and phonetic factors in adult cross-language speech perception. *Journal of the Acoustical Society of America* 75: 1866–78.

——, Gilbert, J., Humphrey, K. and Tees, R. (1981) Developmental aspects of cross-language speech perception. *Child Development* 52: 349–53.

White, L. (1989) *Universal Grammar and Second Language Acquisition.* Amsterdam: John Benjamins Publishing Company.

—— (1988) Universal Grammar and language transfer. In J. Pankhurst, M. Sharwood Smith and P. Van Buren (eds.), *Learnability and Second Languages: A Book of Readings,* pp. 36–60. Dordrecht: Foris.

Williams, L. (1977) The perception of stop consonant voicing by Spanish–English bilinguals. *Perception and Psychophysics* 21: 289–97.

Wode, H. (1992) Categorical perception and segmental coding in the ontogeny of sound systems: A universal approach. In C. Ferguson, L. Menn and C. Stoel-Gammon (eds.), *Phonological Development: Models, Research, Implications,* pp. 605–31. Baltimore: York Press.

—— (1978) The beginnings of L2-phonological acquisition. *IRAL* 16: 109–24.

Wu, Y. (1991) Mandarin suffix [R] revisited. *Proceedings of the 1991 Annual Conference of the Canadian Linguistics Association.* University of Toronto.

Yamada, R. (1995) Age and acquisition of second language speech sounds: Perception of American English /ɹ/ and /l/ by native speakers of Japanese. In W. Strange (ed.), *Speech Perception and Linguistic Experience: Issues in Cross-language Research,* pp. 305–20. Baltimore: York Press.

——, Kobayashi, N. and Tohkura, Y. (in press) Effect of word familiarity on non-native phoneme perception: Identification of English /r/, /l/ and /w/ by native speakers of Japanese. In A. James and J. Leather (eds.), *Second Language Speech.* New York: Mouton de Gruyter.

2

Second Language Syllable Structure

Martha Young-Scholten and John Archibald

1 Introduction

In this chapter, we provide an overview of a number of issues related to how language learners acquire the syllable structure of their second language. It is not just the ability (or lack thereof) to produce an individual segment that results in second language accent; a second language learner must also be able to combine the segments in the sequences demanded by the target language.

Thus, although the aim of this chapter is to examine the development of syllables in a second language in terms of the interaction of the learner's L1 syllable structure with principles of prosodic organization, we begin with a consideration of how children acquire the syllable structure of their first language. We then proceed to review some recent studies on the acquisition of a first language by children, moving on to discuss similar studies on the acquisition of a second language and to consider several as yet unresolved issues. The chapter closes with a detailed look at the interface between segmental features and syllable structure – a possible route to resolving some of these issues.

2 L1 Prosodic Development

2.1 Syllable structure

Because languages such as English and German, which allow initial and final sequences of more than one consonant preceding and following a vowel, figure prominently in studies on the second language acquisition of syllable

structure, we will consider the first language acquisition of these two languages and of Dutch.[1] In doing so, we will address the question of whether
development in the sub-syllabic units onset and rhyme seems to differ.

Let's begin by considering how the very young child might proceed with
the words "tree" and "spoon". That children are operating under a non-
adult system is attested to by the extremely robust findings that words in the
ambient input regularly undergo various sorts of modifications before being
produced by the child. Taking these two words as examples, we find a range
of possibilities regarding what the child might conceivably produce – just in
terms of the consonants involved (vowels, including vowels that might be
inserted to break up consonant clusters, are ignored here).

(1) Possible syllable modifications for "tree" and "spoon"

		tree	spoon
a.	V	[i]	[u]
b.	CV	[ti]	[su]/[pu]
c.	VC		[un]
d.	CVC		[sun]/[pun]
e.	CVCVCV	[tiri]	[sipuni]
f.	$C_1C_x \rightarrow C_1C_y$	[twi]	[swun]
g.	$C_1C_2 \rightarrow V\ C_2\ VC_1$	[tir]	[sup]

The child might simply produce the vowel, as shown in (1a). Alternatively,
the child might produce a so-called universal CV syllable, as in (1b). The
child might omit the initial consonant and just produce the vowel plus the
final consonant, as in (1c), or he or she might retain the initial consonant and
produce a CVC syllable, as shown in (1d). Rather than omit consonants, the
child might instead insert vowels to break up the consonants in the initial
clusters in both words and might add a vowel after the final consonant
in "spoon", yielding two or three CV syllables, as in the examples in (1e).
Another possibility is the production of different consonants (e.g., less marked)
than those in the adult word, as in (1f). Finally, the child might rearrange the
sequence of segments to produce the forms in (1g). But what forms do we
actually find in data from young children?

The literature is replete with studies of child phonologies dating back to
the turn of the century (e.g., Scupin and Scupin, 1907 or Stern and Stern,
1907). Among the robust findings to emerge from the wealth of production
data on first language development is that syllables are routinely simplified
by children as CV sequences. In addition, the well-attested "substitution processes" are related to the position of the segment in the syllable; for example,
children voice obstruents in pre-vocalic position and devoice them in post-
vocalic position. Features other than voicing have also been observed to be
associated with specific positions, e.g., labials with pre-vocalic and velars
with post-vocalic position. More recently, perception data on phonological

development within the first year of life suggests that the input is processed at a prosodic level through the first six months of the child's life (see e.g., Juszcyk, 1997), at least for the languages which have been investigated (primarily English) young children focus on initial consonants, i.e., onsets, rather than on vowels or final consonants, i.e., syllable rhymes. Around the time children start to recognize their first words, between 8 and 10 months, perception experiments reveal that these young language learners have developed a high level of awareness not only of the distribution of phonetic features in the ambient language but also of the phonotactics of the language.

That the consonants preceding and following the vowel in, for example, a CVC sequence have a different status both in adult languages and in children's emerging phonologies is formalized in various hierarchical models of the syllable. Two such models are shown in (2) and (2'), for the words "tree" and "spoon". (2a) shows the standard assumption of onset and rhyme. The rhyme further branches into the sub-syllabic units nucleus (syllable peak) and coda. "X" positions represent timing units; for example two "X" slots represent a long vowel. While the nucleus is obligatory, onsets and codas typically are not obligatory. One of the ways in which languages can vary involves branching of syllabic nodes. The model in (2a) can be further elaborated to represent extra-syllabic segments and syllable appendices, but since the research we will be discussing refers only to the onsets and codas, the model in (2a) will suffice.

(2b) illustrates a moraic model of the syllable (Hayes, 1989) which dispenses with onset and rhyme. This model entails the attachment of initial consonants directly to the syllable node, with all vowels and some final consonants represented as moras (μ). Short vowels are mono-moraic, while long vowels and diphthongs are bimoraic. If a language has a weight-by-position rule (and is quantity-sensitive with respect to stress assignment), the consonant following a long or a short vowel may be moraic. In other words, both open syllables with long vowels or diphthongs, and syllables closed by a consonant attract stress in languages such as English.

(2) "tree"

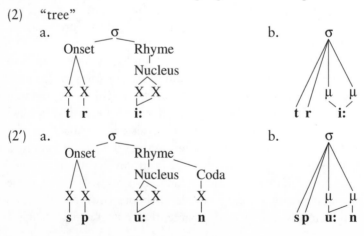

Similar to the child's development of syntax, phonological development also presents a picture in which children know more about phonology than is directly available from the input to which they are exposed; that is, the stimulus is impoverished. The infant perception data mentioned earlier (discussed in Jusczyk, 1997) and the abundance of production data from the child's first few years of life not only show that the child readily detects order in what is rather noisy input, but also reveal that the child's mental representations include from a very young age such abstract entities as phonological features, sub-syllabic constituents, and metrical feet.[2] We thus assume the child initially operates under a system of constraints, templates or parameter settings, which change over time and eventually come to resemble those of the adult language.

The principles and parameters that have been proposed to constrain L1 phonology (and L2 phonology, as we shall see below) include the two most central principles given in (3) and (4) phonology. The onset first principle (Kahn, 1980; Clements and Keyser, 1983) specifies that after vowels are associated with the syllable node, consonants are then exhaustively connected to the onset, in conformity with language-specific phonotactics and with the sonority sequencing principle (see e.g., Selkirk, 1982) shown in (4), which specifies the order in which consonants arrange themselves from the syllable peak to its edges.

(3)   Onset first
      CVCV $\Rightarrow$ CV.CV
      sofa $\Rightarrow$ so.fa   not *sof.a

(4)   Sonority sequencing principle
      stops–fricatives–nasals–liquids–glides **vowels** glides–liquids–nasals–fricatives–stops
      "dentist" $\Rightarrow$ den.tist not *de.ntist

How close in sonority adjacent consonants can be is language-specific and is expressed as the Minimal Sonority Distance Parameter (MSD; see e.g., Broselow and Finer, 1991). The MSD specifies that the least adjacent tautosyllabic consonants can differ by is 5, 4, 3, 2 or 1:

(5)   Minimal Sonority Distance Parameter
      <u>class</u>   <u>value</u>
      stops   1
      fricatives   2
      nasals   3
      liquids   4
      glides   5

Under the MSD, the simplest language is generated by a setting of 5, and allows only single consonant onsets, since no consonants on the sonority scale differ by five. A setting of 4 yields the CV syllables generated by a setting of 5, with the addition of stop–glide onsets. English, with its setting of 3, adds to this both stop–liquid and fricative–glide onsets.

Further syllable structure conditions can be captured by the parameters discussed in Fikkert (1994), shown in (6).

(6) a. minimal onset parameter: are onsets obligatory?
   b. maximal onset parameter: can onsets branch?
   c. nucleus parameter: can the nucleus branch?
   d. coda parameter: are closed syllables allowed?
   e. complex coda parameter: is more than one segment allowed?

A syllable structure algorithm making reference to these principles and parameter settings proceeds in several steps. First, vowels are associated with the nucleus. Next, consonants preceding the nucleus are exhaustively assigned to the onset, in conformity with both the sonority sequencing principle, the MSD parameter value and the values of the parameters shown in (6). Additional consonants preceding and following the nucleus may also be assigned to onset and coda, respectively, in conformity with allowable appendices in that language. The subsequent assignment of stress may then make reference to the composition of the syllable rhyme, if the parameter that states only a certain type of syllable may attract stress is set at "yes". In a quantity-sensitive language such as English or Dutch, stress may be attracted by a long vowel or diphthong in the nucleus, or a single consonant following the vowel, in the coda.

For the young child just setting out to acquire the syllable structure of his or her language, all the parameters shown in (6) will presumably be set at a default or unmarked value, i.e., "no" (although see below). Three recent accounts of prosodic development cast within current linguistic theory provide evidence regarding what happens next. The first is Paula Fikkert's (1994) quasi-longitudinal study of twelve Dutch children aged 1;0 to 2;11. To account for their development of prosodic structure, Fikkert adopts the principles and parameters framework, and through reference to the principles shown above and the parameters given (6), she posits the initial stages shown in (7).

(7) Fikkert's (1994) stages for Dutch

Stage	Onset	Rhyme
I	CV	CV
II	onsetless syllables also permitted	CVC (C = obstruent)
III	CCV	CVC (C = sonorant, but
	where obstruent + sonorant	either V: or V + son.
	(but some children S + obstruent)	

While the child's first stage suggests a setting of "yes" for the minimal onset parameter, by Stage II, in response to the Dutch input, the parameter has been set at "no" under which both CV and VC syllables are allowed. The third stage with respect to the onset involves the branching of this sub-syllabic unit, while the second stage with respect to the rhyme involves establishment of a coda. Of note here is the restriction the child places on type of rhyme at Stage III, indicating that the child's nucleus is still immature, that the child is still figuring out the status of vowel length (i.e., whether the nucleus branches) and the status of sonorant and obstruent consonants in Dutch. Fikkert's Stage III data reveal the variability that has frequently been observed in children's emerging phonologies: some children first develop branching onsets, while other children first append /s/ to a non-branching onset. Interestingly, the latter tack is not predicted by the sonority constraint given in (4): a fricative preceding a stop is disallowed. This, however, is precisely what Dutch (and English, German etc.) permits, pointing to the special status of /s/.[3]

Lleó and Prinz's (1997) study of the acquisition of German based on longitudinal data from five German children aged 1;5–2;2 reveals similar findings. While the authors' main aim was to determine whether affricates such as "pf-" and "kn-" appear at the same time as true consonant clusters such as "pr-" and "kl-" (affricates are earlier) and to compare the German data with similar Spanish data, their findings shed light on the overall development of onsets and codas. Like Fikkert, the data show that CV syllables precede VC syllables. However, unlike Fikkert's children, the German children seem to allow branching rhymes before branching codas, at least when the first element in the cluster is a sonorant consonant.

(8)   Lleó and Prinz's (1997) parameter setting for German
   - simple onsets exist before simple codas: CV > (C)VC
   - the parameter for branching codas is set first (CC = sonorant + obstruent)
   - the parameter for branching onsets is then set, around 1;10

What is clear from both studies is that both consonant composition (especially with respect to sonority) and position play a major role during the development of the syllable: initial and final consonants are not treated in the same manner by children. In quantity-sensitive languages such as Dutch, English and German, children's development shows a gradual increase in sensitivity to the status and composition of the vowels and consonants in the syllable rhyme of the input language.

Demuth and Fee's (1995) account of the acquisition of Dutch and English considers in more depth the nature of the syllable rhyme, integrating an account of the development of syllable structure with an account of the acquisition of stress, as shown in (9).

(9) Demuth and Fee's (1995) stages of prosodic acquisition
    I   Core syllables/subminimal words
          (no length distinction)   CV
    II   Minimal words
                    a. epenthesis   (C)VCV
                    b. closed syllables   (C)VC
                    c. open syllables w/ long Vs   (C)V:
    III   Stress feet
                    a. one stress-foot per word
                    b. two feet per word
    IV   Phonological words
                    extrametrical syllables

In their exploration of the metrical status of children's first CV syllables, the authors reach the conclusion that these early syllables do not yet represent metrical structure. It is only at Stage II that the beginnings of metrical structure are first seen, with three options available to the child: word either contains two syllables, with no length distinction, a single, closed syllable or a single syllable with a long vowel. At this stage it is already apparent that the child is grappling with input from quantity-sensitive languages. Once the child reaches Stages III and IV the data begins to show evidence of adult-like metrical structure in Dutch and English.

What these accounts all illustrate is that children's emerging prosodic structure is constrained by universal principles; children are sensitive to phonological features and to syllable position and are sensitive to the role that both can play with respect to stress. These three views differ from each other in terms of what is claimed to be present at the start of acquisition – apart from the principles of prosodic organization. Demuth and Fee's proposals might be viewed as comparable to Radford's (1995) or Vainikka's (1993/1994) weak continuity account of the acquisition of morpho-syntax, under which children build up structure. Both Fikkert's and Lleó and Prinz's proposals suggest a strong continuity approach (e.g., Wexler, 1994, Hyams, 1992), under which structure is present from the start. Learning then involves setting parameters which are open or set at a default value.

2.2 Epenthesis in L1 acquisition

One robust finding from first language acquisition research is that the insertion of vowels to break up consonant clusters (epenthesis) does not figure prominently in child phonologies. Demuth and Fee's inclusion of epenthesis at Stage II notwithstanding, studies set the frequency of epenthesis in child language at 1–2 percent of words produced (see e.g., Kehoe and Stoel-Gammon's 1997 study of 39 children aged 1;10 to 2;10). This is somewhat puzzling since there is nothing involving the principles or parameters cited thus far that would demote epenthesis. Moreover, epenthesis is widely attested in languages of the world as well as in the developing phonologies of second language learners, as we shall see. Weinberger (1988) cites findings that epenthesis, when it does surface in child phonologies, emerges later than deletion as a syllable simplification process, and deletion ceases by about the age of three. Weinberger attributes the low frequency of epenthesis to the maturation of "recoverability", i.e., to superficial transparency of the underlying representation (as shown in (10)), after the child has figured out its syllable structure.

(10)   Recoverability
      <u>deletion</u>   CVCC→CVC/CV   /list/→[lis]~[li]
          UR not recoverable
      <u>epenthesis</u>   CVCC→CVCCi/CVCiCi   /list/→[list$i$]~[lis$i$ti]
          UR is recoverable

For children who develop their first language earlier than normal, epenthesis has been found to be more frequent. Stoel-Gammon and Dale (1988) studied twelve "early talkers" at the age of 1;8 and found they had a longer mean length of utterance (MLU), a larger phonetic inventory and a larger lexicon, and their syllable modifications consisted of up to 30 percent of (mostly final) epenthesis (paragoge). According to Weinberger, recoverability matures for these children prior to their mastery of syllable structure, resulting in much more epenthesis. An alternative account is given in Young-Scholten (1997); it is not recoverability that matures, but the cognitive capacity associated with storage of early words. This account tallies with Newport's (1990) observation that age is in inverse proportion to the language learners' tendency to omit information from representations. For early talkers, it is cognitive capacity that matures earlier than for other children. Such an explanation would also account for the finding that children much older (e.g., age five) with diagnosed phonological disability rarely epenthesize, preferring cluster reduction and single consonant deletion (Ingram, 1989).

3 L2 Prosodic Development

When looking at second language development, we attempt to determine the role played by the learner's knowledge of a first language, and the role played by the learner's knowledge of the principles and parameters discussed above. When the L1 is not relied on, to what extent do the mechanisms that guided first language acquisition come into play and guide the second language acquisition of syllable structure? If and when the L2 learner goes beyond the L1 syllable structure, is the L2 syllable structure, like that of L1 children, constrained by universal principles? Are adult L2 learners sensitive to sonority and position and to the role that both can play with respect to stress? Three possibilities, similar to those in White (1989) for the acquisition of syntax, are shown in (11).

(11) • UG is "dead", the learner's L1 (and general cognition) play the *only* role (fundamental difference)
  • UG is accessible, but the learner's L1 plays *no* role (full access/no transfer)
  • UG aids acquisition, and the learner starts with his or her L1 (full transfer/full access)

The data currently available present some difficulties in allowing a complete treatment of these issues. Much of the data come from small-scale and case studies, with little data from either longitudinal or large-scale cross-sectional studies. In addition, many studies are of intermediate-level learners living in the target-language country with often considerable exposure to L1-accented input in their native countries. And finally, the data are typically production rather than perception data.[4] Nonetheless, these studies have allowed us to offer the tentative conclusion that second language learners' syllable structures are indeed constrained by prosodic principles.

3.1 L2 syllable acquisition data

As mentioned above, the earliest claim that more than L1-transfer was involved in the second language acquisition of phonology comes from the study of the acquisition of syllables. Tarone's (1980) analysis of the errors made by six intermediate learners in an oral story-telling task pointed to influences other than the learner's L1 at work. While she hypothesized that learners would transfer L1 rules of epenthesis and deletion from their native languages, she concluded that both processes occurred in the learners' emerging interlanguage phonologies, regardless of whether such rules existed in their native languages. As shown in table 2.1, Tarone applied a further metric to determine L1-influence: was the sequence of consonants the learner produced in English possible in the learner's native language? Based on this

Table 2.1 Processes underlying syllable structure errors (Tarone, 1980)

	Number of errors	Errors due to L1-influence	Errors *not* due to to L1-influence	Epenthesis vs. deletion
Korean #1	17	53%	47%	29% vs. 71%
Korean #2	15	73%	27%	20% vs. 80%
Cantonese #1	25	77%	23%	32% vs. 68%
Cantonese #2	29	73%	27%	38% vs. 62%
Portuguese #1	19	84%	16%	80% vs. 20%
Portuguese #2	10	90%	10%	80% vs. 20%

Table 2.2 Access to principles of syllabification

Principle	Study	Findings
Sonority hierarchy	Tropf (1987)	Deletion of consonants in final clusters by Spanish learners of German showed sensitivity to violations by /s/.
Sonority hierarchy	Broselow (1987)	Varying epenthesis patterns in initial clusters produced by Arabic English learners showed sensitivity to violations by /s/.

metric, Tarone concluded that learners sometimes simplified syllables in English that were permissible in their native languages.

The observation that Korean learners applied epenthesis to L1-permissible sequences as in the English word "sack" to produce [sæke] led Tarone to propose that, like children, adult second language learners revert to the universal CV syllable. That these learners' simplifications were CV rather than VC syllables confirms that their knowledge of the basic organizing principles of prosodic structure constrains their developing L2 phonologies. However, without data from the earlier stages of acquisition for these learners, we do not know whether VC was in fact an earlier preference, nor do we know whether they reverted to Demuth and Fee's *sub*minimal word stage at the start of their acquisition of English.[5]

There is a fair amount of research following in Tarone's wake which indeed suggests adult L2 phonologies obey the constraints of UG with respect to prosodic structure. One striking finding is that learners are sensitive to violations by /s/ of the sonority hierarchy. The data show that clusters involving such violations are treated differently from those which do not by adult second language learners. As shown in table 2.2, these are learners whose native languages, Spanish and Arabic, do not even allow tautosyllabic clusters, so this knowledge cannot have come from their native languages. When an /s/ precedes a stop in a syllable onset, or follows a stop in the coda, as in English "stops", this constitutes a (obviously allowable, language-specifically) violation of the sonority sequencing principle, as /s/ is more sonorous than /t/ and /p/ is less sonorous than /s/. In words such as "slide" or "list" there are no sonority violations. Through their patterns of production of such violating and non-violating words in German and English, Tropf's and Broselow's learners demonstrated a clear sensitivity to this violation.[6]

In addition to evidence regarding post-puberty access to principles, there is also evidence, presented in table 2.3, that adult second language learners also reset parameters, either at the target language value or at some intermediate value.

Table 2.3   Parameter resetting

Parameter	Study	Findings
Minimal sonority distance	Broselow and Finer (1991)	Intermediate learners acquired a minimal sonority distance in English smaller than that which obtains in their native Japanese and Korean.
Coda[7]	Young-Scholten (1993)	Advanced learners acquired consonant clusters in L2 German codas impermissible in their native Korean, Spanish and Turkish.

3.2   Ultimate attainment

Given these indications of access to UG by adult learners, we would predict the attainment of native competence to be successful more often than it has frequently been shown to be. Indeed, despite a number of studies which show a clear correlation between age of initial exposure to the second language and eventual attainment, such as Patkowski's (1990), we do find some post-puberty success stories. The three studies presented below in table 2.4, by Ioup, Boustagui, El Tigi and Moselle, in table 2.5, by Bongaerts, Planken and Schils, and in table 2.6, by Neufeld, provide evidence that native or near-native attainment is possible.

What exactly do these studies show? The Ioup et al. study of two learners is convincing, although it could be argued – as Ioup et al. do – that the findings represent exceptional talent. While Bongaerts et al.'s study confirms that not all learners attain equal levels of L2 competence, it is not clear whether their study truly represents post-puberty exposure, given the wealth

Table 2.4   Near-native L2 attainment by adult learners of Arabic (Ioup et al., 1994)

Learner	Exposure	Results	
		accent rating	accent iden.
Julie	Beginning at age 21 resident of Cairo; no formal instruction and no literacy in Arabic.	7/13 rated as native	like native-speakers
Laura	Beginning at age 20 at university, eventually Ph.D. in Arabic, later resident of Cairo.	7/13 rated as native	nearly native

Notes: Non-native subjects: age of initial exposure to Arabic (English L1) 20/21 years old.
Data: spontaneous speech (recipe description); regional accent identification task.
Evaluation: thirteen teachers of Arabic as a foreign language rated Julie and Laura, two other non-native speakers of Arabic and three educated native speakers of the Cairene dialect of Arabic.

Table 2.5 Native L2 attainment by adult learners of English (Bongaerts et al., 1995)

Group (mean age: 32)	group means 1 = very strong accent; 5 = no accent, definitely native
1 Control: five university-educated native speakers of English, without neutral accents	3.94
2 Ten excellent Dutch English speakers, studying/teaching English	4.31
3 Twelve normal Dutch English speakers	2.35

Notes: *Non-native subjects*: age of initial exposure to English (Dutch L1) around 12 years old.
Data: elicited through free speech, reading aloud: words, sentences and story.
Evaluation: by four naive (non-linguists) native English speakers.

Table 2.6 Native L2 attainment by adults in the language laboratory (Neufeld, 1980)

Exposure	Results (1–5 rating system)	
	Chinese	Japanese
18 hours of audio-visual laboratory instruction in Chinese and Japanese	one at "5" mean 3.20	three at "5" mean 3.30

Notes: *Non-native subjects*: 20 English-speaking university students.
Data: ten repeated statements.
Evaluation: by two Chinese, two Japanese judges, with experience teaching these languages.

of (subtitled) English programs on Dutch television. One could, of course, also argue that the similarities between Dutch and English mean there is less to acquire in the first place. But viewed in this way, the issue of why some Dutch learners of English are successful and others not then arises. Neufeld's results are certainly compelling, yet the learners in his study were exposed only to language laboratory lessons covering the segmental and prosodic aspects of these languages and were not actually acquiring them.

3.3 A more detailed examination of L2 syllables

The question then remains: to what extent are adults able to acquire the prosodic structure of an L2?

To explore possible answers, we return to an examination of findings from studies which focus on L1 influence rather than ultimate attainment. Upon closer examination, these studies suggest that development in the syllable onset is more rapid than development in the syllable rhyme. Thus while we find studies showing transfer of an L1 parameter setting with respect to syllable rhymes, as in table 2.7, there has been little evidence presented that parameters are reset, especially at the target language value.

Table 2.7 Transfer of parameter setting: syllable rhymes

Parameter	Study	Findings
Minimal weight	Broselow (1988)	Arabic speakers lengthen the vowel in closed syllables with lax vowels in English: [baas] for "bus".
Metrical stress	Archibald (1993)[8]	Polish, Spanish, Hungarian learners of English reset some parameters.
	Pater (1997)	French learners of English adopt a new parameter setting – but neither that of the L1 nor the L2.
Maximal weight	Broselow and Park (1995)	Korean speakers of English add an epenthetic vowel after closed syllables with long vowels.

One study that suggests syllable rhyme difficulties persist for advanced adult learners is Young-Scholten's (1993) on weightless syllable nuclei and minimal codas. This study examined the L2 acquisition of the non-obligatory personal pronoun clitics in German shown in (12). Unlike their unstressed counterparts (and unlike in English) these forms cannot be derived via rules of reduction or vowel deletion. Gaps exist in the clitic paradigm, with many of the personal pronouns in German lacking a clitic allomorph, due to the rhymal constraint that clitics can consist of at most a single coda consonant or a single lax vowel, unlike monosyllabic German words which minimally contain a long vowel. These pronominal clitics are also subject to syntactic restrictions: they typically follow whatever fills COMP.

(12)   Clitic types in German

Types	Clitics
-CV (V = short, lax, central)	[vʌ] "we" [mʌ] "me" [dʌ] "you" [də] "you" [zə] "she/they"
-C	[ç] "I" [s] "it" [n] "him" [m] "him"
-V (V = short, lax, central)	[ʌ] "her"

The L2 data consisted of elicited imitations of 80 sentences containing clitics and unstressed pronouns by 21 speakers of American English, Turkish, Korean and Spanish (and a control group of ten native German speakers). In table 2.3 it was noted that advanced learners of German from the three non-American groups had acquired German codas. The acquisition of both the sonorant consonant and the reduced vowel clitics by all groups, including the English speakers, tells a different story.

The resistence of these central, unstressed vowels and single, syllabic consonants to acquisition by adult L2 learners might well be compounded by

Table 2.8 Target repetition of clitics and of non-clitic affixes by phonetic type

	Clitics				Affixes	
	[n] [m]	[ʌ] [mʌ]	[dʌ]	[də] [zə]	total schwa	syllabic C in schwa~C alternation
English (n = 9)	14%	9%		7%	64%	38%
Turkish (n = 4)	7%	5%		15%	55%	11%
Korean (n = 5)	7%	1%		6%	36%	7%
Spanish (n = 3)	4%	0		0	17%	21%

their morphological status as clitics. Moreover, such syllables containing such minimal nuclei are marked, much like the devoiced vowels of Japanese. The data do raise the question of whether we can, in fact, conclude that a learner has acquired the syllable structure of that language when only the syllable onset has been mastered. Let's look at some additional evidence to determine whether learners might be treating onsets and rhymes differently.

3.4 Syllable simplification in the onset vs. the rhyme

Recall from section 2.1 the finding that the onset appears to get sorted out prior to the rhyme (at least in Germanic languages). In this section we review L2 acquisition studies which show differential distribution of simplification errors. We find that the frequency of errors as well as the particular strategy employed differ in the onset and rhyme. As shown in table 2.11, the longitudinal data Sato (1984) collected from two Vietnamese boys (aged 10 and 12) acquiring English reveals sustained and considerable difficulty with final, coda clusters when compared with initial, onset clusters. (In the table, the denominator represents the number of non-target forms or errors.) The distribution shown in table 2.9 cannot be explained purely by L1-influence, since Vietnamese hardly allows initial or final clusters, with the exception of initial clusters with "w". Moreover, syllables can end in nasals, glides and voiceless stops.

Table 2.9 Initial vs. final consonant deletion in clusters[1] in L2 English (Sato, 1984)

Learner	Weeks 2 and 3[2]			Weeks 19 and 20			Weeks 36 and 37		
Thanh	initial	1/27	3%	initial	5/64	8%	initial	4/58	15%
	final	46/52	88%	final	87/91	96%	final	69/87	79%
Tai	initial	8/27	30%	initial	1/66	2%	initial	4/102	4%
	final	40/47	85%	final	87/96	91%	final	91/116	78%

Notes:
1 Epenthesis was nearly non-existent throughout the entire data collection.
2 Data collection was begun roughly six months after the learners' arrival in the USA.

Table 2.10 Initial vs. final deletion and epenthesis (Anderson, 1987)

Language	L1 influence?		Syllable-initial		Syllable-final	
	epenthesis	syllables	deletion	epenthesis	deletion	epenthesis
Arabic	yes	C-	0	7.1%	-C 1.4%	0.2%
		-CC			-CC 14.7%	2.7%
					-CCC 16.7%	11.1%
Chinese	no	C-	10.4%	0	-C 20.2%	0.1%
		-C			-CC 46.2%	2%
					-CCC 68.4%	5.3%

While Sato's study uncovered virtually no epenthesis, the data in table 2.10, which come from Anderson's (1987) high intermediate/low advanced adult learners, show rates of epenthesis typical for adult learners (of Egyptian Arabic and Mandarin and Amoy Chinese). What is of interest, however, is that these learners, too, exhibit far greater problems with consonants in the rhyme than in the onset. This again appears to be independent of L1 syllable structure. L1-influence predicts that the Arabic speakers would have greater problems with syllable onsets, since Egyptian Arabic has no initial clusters. And since Egyptian Arabic has final clusters, problems here should be negligible, especially with two-member clusters. However, the data show the reverse to be the case. Chinese learners' L1 syllables show less asymmetry, yet their L2-syllable development shows the same asymmetric pattern, favoring the onset, that the Arabic learners' shows.

Sato's and Anderson's studies both indicate primacy of the CV syllable, giving way to earlier expansion of the onset, followed by an expansion of the rhyme to varying degrees for these second language learners. The two studies reviewed here suggest that when considered separately from the nucleus, the coda itself presents more problems than the onset. Since there are few studies which allow the examination of adult L2 development from initial exposure to final, steady state, the hypothesis that the rhymal difficulties persist remains untested.

At this point, let's take another look at syllable simplification processes to examine whether the route of L2 development parallels that of L1 acquisition. To be precise, what does the rarity of epenthesis in L1 acquisition and its prevalence in adult L2 acquisition indicate?

3.5   Epenthesis in L2 acquisition

While epenthesis is expected to occur – and does – when there is a productive L1 rule which can be adopted in the acquisition of an L2 as in (13a), given that children rarely employ epenthesis, one would expect adults to behave similarly, since they have been shown to do so in other respects, employing deletion, feature changes, etc. However, the data is replete with examples such as those in (13b), (13c) and (13d), where L2 learners at various points in their acquisition employ epenthesis.

(13) a. Broselow (1987): influence of L1 epenthesis

Iraqi Arabic English	Egyptian Arabic English	
chilidren	childiren	"children"
ifloor	filoor	"floor"

   b. Broselow and Park (1995): L1 minimal prosodic weight, realized through epenthesis

	Korean English	English target	
*-s	[bəsɨ]	[bʌs]	"bus"
*-d	[midɨ]	[mɪd]	"mid"
ok -n	[bin]	[bi:n]	"bean"
ok -t	[bit]	[bɪt]	"bit"
ok -t	[bitʰɨ]	[bi:t]	"beat"

   c. Eckman (1981): developmental process

Mandarin English

[zɪp]	"zip"	[rabə]	"rob"
[mɪs]	"miss"	[hizə]	"he's"

   d. Major (1987): influence of L1 epenthesis, with subsequent developmental process

Brazilian Portuguese English

Stage I (L1)	[dogi]	"dog"
Stage II (not L1)	[dogə]/[dok]	

What accounts for the increased frequency with which adult second language learners epenthesize? One idea was mentioned earlier: L2 learners epenthesize more than L1 children because recoverability matures only after syllable structure is acquired, giving epenthesis no chance to surface in L1 acquisition. But not only does this fail to account for the infrequency of epenthesis by older children who still haven't acquired their syllable structure, there is also child L2 research which indicates that maturation of recoverability cannot be involved. For example, as we have already noted above, Sato (1984) found rates of epenthesis by her pre-puberty young Vietnamese learners of English comparable to those very low rates for L1 children. In a cross-sectional study, Riney (1990) found an increase with age, essentially corroborating Sato's epenthesis results for the youngest L2 learners and others' for older learners.

Sine maturation of recoverability prior to age three cannot possibly account for the variability observed here, what might the explanation be? One possibility that has been entertained is that of task type during data collection

Table 2.11   Epenthesis vs. deletion: Vietnamese learners of English (Riney, 1990)

Process	Age at testing	10–12	15–18	20–25	35–55
Final epenthesis		5.6%	16.3%	20.4%	32.4%
Final deletion		10.2%	18.5%	9.6%	6.3%

Note: n = 40; length of residence 1–7 years – cross-sectional design

Table 2.12   Exposure and task type as variables in simplification strategy

Learner's L1 researcher	Input (age)	Task Type(s)	L1 epenthesis?	IL epenthesis?
ARABIC			YES	
Anderson	instructed (adults)	interview		YES and some deletion
PUNJABI; URDU			YES	
Verma et al.	naturalistic (children)	spontaneous data		SOME more final deletion
SPANISH			YES (initial)	
Tropf (L2 German)	naturalistic (adults)	spontaneous data		SOME deletion favored
PORTUGUESE			YES	
Tarone	instructed (adults)	pictures		YES
Major	instructed (adults)	reading		YES with non-L1 final epenthesis
Anderson (also Amoy Chinese)	instructed (adults)	interview		YES
CANTONESE			NO	
Tarone	instructed (adults)	picture description		YES
VIETNAMESE			NO	
Sato	naturalistic (children)	spontaneous data		NO
Riney	naturalistic (age range)	spontaneous data		NO for younger YES for older

(Young-Scholten, 1995, 1997). The use of reading tasks during data collection may well lead to an increase in epenthesis, i.e., the observed frequency is simply an artefact of testing.

The middle column in table 2.12 indeed points to the possibility of task-type influence, with non-L1-based epenthesis occurring when a reading task was used to collect the data (Major, 1987). Of course it is difficult to reach any conclusions on the basis of a single study. Young-Scholten (1995, 1997) and Young-Scholten, Akita and Cross (1999) consider a further possibility: that exposure type influences frequency of epenthesis. Indeed table 2.12 reveals that when learners' primary exposure to the second language is in instructed contexts (with abundant exposure to written texts), learners epenthesize regardless of the status of epenthesis in their L1s.[9] On the other hand, learners whose primary exposure to the L2 involves less interaction with written texts epenthesize less frequently, even when their native language contains rules of epenthesis, as in Verma, Firth and Corrigan's study.

It is the learner's familiarity with the written representations of words in the L2 which increases the likelihood that more phonological information about words will be retained in memory long enough to feed into the formation of underlying representations. A simplification strategy such as epenthesis is employed when the learner's L1 syllable structure continues to constrain his or her interlanguage phonology. Given that literacy co-varies with age, one might expect it to be a factor that promotes epenthesis, in other words, literacy is (at least partly) responsible for the age-based increase. Not mentioned previously is the observation (Oller, 1974) that, although children quite often delete unstressed syllables, adult L2 learners rarely do so. This is a curious observation, as there is no reason to suspect that the difficulty of perceiving unstressed syllables is age-dependent.[10] We would therefore expect to find instances of unstressed syllable deletion in the adult L2 data. That very little has been found is further evidence that exposure to the L2 through written text plays a role in determining which syllable repair strategies are employed by the L2 learner. Still further support for this proposal comes from the finding (e.g., Major, 1987; Weinberger, 1988) that intermediate learners epenthesize more than beginners. If we are correct with respect to the role of literacy, the proficiency-based increase in epenthesis can be attributed to the fact that with more exposure, learners' underlying representations come to contain more information. Literacy simply speeds up this process.

The study by Young-Scholten, Akita, and Cross (1999) sought to experimentally investigate the role of written text both in the formation of lexical representations during learning and in their production during testing. The study involved the manipulation of second language input during the learning such that one sub-group in each of two L1 groups (English and Japanese) looked at only pictures and one sub-group looked at pictures with words written under them while they heard 18 Polish words on a tape. Their post-treatment productions of the Polish words learned revealed that epenthesis was promoted both through exposure to the written representations of these words during learning and subsequently during testing.

In one sense literate second language learners resemble early talkers: recoverability is observed to operate prior to mastery of syllable structure.

While early talkers seem to possess abilities (e.g., verbal memory capacity) superior to their age-mates, L2 learners often have literacy at their disposal to facilitate more rapid and complete storage of acoustic chunks. In both cases, it is not the maturation (or re-maturation) of recoverability, it is simply that the segmental information contained in underlying representations more closely approximates that in the adult/target underlying representations.

4 L2 Syllables: A Case of Interlanguage, but not Second Language Acquisition?

The data we have examined above do not yet allow us to conclude whether acquisition of syllable structure in adult L2 acquisition parallels that in L1 acquisition, except for the confounding factors of first language knowledge and cognitive maturity. The possibility exists that we are only witnessing the application of repair strategies in accordance with universal principles, which then do not result in rogue interlanguage phonologies. Is the adult second language learner's performance simply an example of accommodation of the L2 input to the L1, with no real change in the L1 system? While the studies discussed in section 3 point to adoption of syllable repair strategies which do not directly originate in the learner's L1 and which do not contravene the principles of prosodic organization, the evidence we have seen does not yet make a compelling case for full development of the syllable rhyme. This may, however, simply be due to the paucity of data which consider the status of the vowels in the nucleus and the interaction during development of syllable and metrical structure.

Longitudinal studies incorporating more than just production tasks might help to address these issues. A longitudinal study by Akita (1998) of three intermediate-level Japanese learners of English shows there is indeed scope for such studies. Akita's syllable structure perception data revealed that the least proficient learner accurately perceived the difference between CCV and CVCV structures (such as "street" vs. "sutoreet") only 66.3 percent of the time at the start of data collection, and after eight months in an English-speaking environment was able to do so 90 percent of the time. Parrondo-Rodriguez (1999) also incorporates the use of non-production tasks in her cross-sectional study of English-speakers' emerging Spanish syllable structure. A grammaticality judgement task involving nonsense words given to learners at varying levels of proficiency showed that, rather than starting with their English parameter setting, the beginners reverted to a default setting. With increased exposure to Spanish, learners' judgements as well as their production of syllables moved closer to that of the native speaking controls. Both Akita's study and Parrondo-Rodriguez's treat stress as well, thus also allowing investigation of the development of the syllable rhyme.

5   The Onset in L2 Phonology

In this and the following section, we return to a consideration of the syllable onset. In examining the rhyme, it was pointed out that a full treatment of the rhyme in L2 phonology must include stress, particularly where quantity-sensitive languages are involved (although as we saw, there is not yet sufficient research to permit such a treatment). In examining the L2 development of syllable onsets, we propose that it is necessary to make reference to segment structure.

5.1   Syllable structure as a projection of segment structure

Data from Broselow and Finer (1991), referred to above, as well as data from Eckman and Iverson (1993, 1994) demonstrate that speakers of L1s which lack onset clusters have difficulty with them in L2s which contain them. Archibald (1998) claims that the acquisition of new syllabic structure (at least in the onset) is not possible until the acquisition of new segmental structure takes place. This proposal involves an implicational hierarchy in which the presence of onset clusters involving an obstruent and liquid in a language implies the presence of an /l/ ~ /r/ contrast. However, the presence of an /l/ ~ /r/ contrast does not imply the presence of such onset clusters. Thus, the acquisition of a liquid contrast is directly related to the acquisition of branching onsets. We should therefore find learners with an /l/ ~ /r/ contrast who have not acquired onset clusters, but we should not find learners with onset clusters who have not acquired the /l/ ~ /r/ contrast.

5.2   Typological support

First let us consider typological evidence in support of the proposal that languages respect this condition. The statement "when there is only one liquid in a language, there are no onset clusters involving that liquid in the language" means that if branching onsets and liquid contrast were unrelated, such a pattern would not be expected. In other words, if a language were seeking to expand the number of possible syllables, without assuming an implicational hierarchy, there is no reason why a [pl] cluster should be blocked in a language that has /l/ but not /r/.

Maddieson (1984) lists the following languages as having a single liquid: Azerbaijani, Korean, Japanese, Dan, Dagbani, Senadi, Akan, Lelemi, Beembe, Teke, Vietnamese, Tagalog, Hawaian, Mandarin and Zoque. In investigating the syllable inventories of these (and other) languages, one finds no robust counterexamples to the claim that a language with a single liquid will not allow obstruent + liquid clusters.

Table 2.13 Branching onsets and liquid contrast

Language Family/Language	liquids	onset types
Amazonian		
Sanuma	/l/	C; isolated occurrences of [pl] and
(Borgman, 1990)		[kl] in onomatopoeic forms
Yagua	/r/	C
(Payne and Payne, 1990)		
African		
Kikiyu	/r/	C; homorganic N + C clusters
(Armstrong, 1940)		
Ganda	/l/	C; C + glide and N + C
(Cole, 1967)		
Akan	/r/	C; C + glide, N + C and [pr], [fr]
(Dolphyne, 1988)		derived from CVCV forms
Nkore-Kiga	one liquid	C; C + glide
(Taylor, 1985)		
Austronesian		
Japanese, Chinese, Korean, Vietnamese	one liquid	C; no obstruent + liquid clusters
Proto Austronesian	four liquids	CVCVC; CVCCVC (but
(Baldi, 1991)		syllabification of latter unclear)
North American		
Cayuga	/r/	C; [tr] and [kr], but they must be
(Dyck, personal communication, citing Chafe, 1977)		heterosyllabified to explain stress
Mesoamerican		
Proto-Aztecan	no liquids	C
Huichol	one liquid	C
Nahuatl	two liquids	CC
(Suárez, 1983)[11]		

Table 2.13 illustrates the correlation between lack of liquid contrast and lack of onset clusters. That it is the acquisition of the liquid contrast, not just the increase in inventory size that predicts emergence of onset clusters is suggested by the emergence in many languages in Mesoamerica of the phonemes /b, d, g, f, x, ñ, l, r and ʃ/ along with new consonant clusters with a stop or fricative plus a lateral or flap (Suárez, 1983).

5.4   Creoles

Data from creoles also seem to support the connection. Romaine (1988) notes that creoles typically have no initial or final consonant clusters and

Bender (1987) suggests the following prototypical consonant inventory for creoles: p, t, k, b, d, g, f, s, m, n, l/r, w, y. There are some interesting counterexamples to the no-cluster, single liquid character of creoles. A creole known as Pitcairnese, spoken on the island that was peopled by the mutineers from the *Bounty* and indigenous peoples, had clusters but this was most likely because of the nature of the Polynesian language. All of the English people died within ten years of settlement, and probably had no lasting effect on the creole (Romaine, 1988). Another interesting potential counterexample is the creole known as Russenorsk (used in northern Norway), which has clusters, but the creole also (exceptionally) has two liquids. Furthermore, we see this profile in Haitian Creole (Ritter, 1991), which has two liquids and allows onset clusters. It seems, then, that when creoles behave exceptionally in allowing clusters, they also have a liquid contrast in the segmental inventory.

In addition, we note in the case of Nigerian Pidgin English that the speakers modify the syllable structure of Yoruba (which is CV) to allow some CVC words when they are borrowed from English, but they never produce any consonant clusters.

5.5   First language acquisition

Vanderweide (1994) provided a reanalysis of Smith's (1973) acquisition of phonology study and noted that the subject, Amahl, first had no consonant clusters and then acquired heterosyllabic sequences of a sonorant plus an obstruent (e.g., *panda*). He then acquired heterosyllabic clusters of two obstruents (e.g., *doctor*). Finally, after acquiring the liquid contrast, he acquired tautosyllabic onset clusters (e.g., *black*).

6   Second Language Acquisition

At first it may seem to be coincidence that the acquisition of liquids is correlated with the acquisition of onset clusters. The researcher might be tempted to conclude that because consonant clusters are not allowed in the L1, lack thereof simply involves L1-influence. Why invoke such complex, abstract theoretical machinery to explain simple transfer? Yet the diverse array of evidence from sources such as language change, typology and first language acquisition suggests that there is a causal relationship which is also in evidence in second language acquisition. The theoretical framework of feature geometry and derived sonority provides the apparatus to explain what L2 learners are doing (and representing). In this respect, transfer is not always simple, in that complex structures transfer and interact with principles during L2 development. It is not merely canonical CV syllable structure which transfers; rather, it is a complex interaction of the properties of the segmental inventory determining the feature geometry of a segment that, in turn, influences the allowable sequences of segments.

6.1 Sonority distance

Let us apply this idea to a reanalysis of Broselow and Finer's (1991) study of the acquisition of initial clusters in English by Korean and Japanese speakers. Broselow and Finer got 24 Koreans and eight Japanese to produce words with the initial clusters [pr], [br], [fr], [py], and [fy]. Based on the Minimal Sonority Distance Parameter given in (4), they assume the markedness relationships (where C stands for any consonant) shown in (14). Korean and Japanese have a minimal sonority distance of 5 (which allows no clusters), compared with the minimal sonority distance of 3 for English.

(14)   Less marked......................More marked
         Cy............................Cr
         pC...........bC............fC

Although clusters do not exist in Japanese and Korean, in terms of markedness [py] should be the least problematic cluster and [fr] the most difficult. Table 2.14 presents the overall chart for the error rates of the Korean subjects, and by and large, supports Broselow and Finer's predictions with respect to markedness.

Broselow and Finer argue that differential error effects arise in those clusters that are not sanctioned in either L1. For example, neither Korean nor

Table 2.14   Korean onset cluster pattern errors

	py	pr	by	br	fy	fr
1 Total errors/n	3/384	2/383	5/384	16/384	15/384	21/382
%	5%[12]	3%	8%	26%	24%	34%
2 Errors → CV						
Epenthesis (CCV → CVCV)	0	1	1	12	0	0
Deletion (CCV → CV)	3	1	4	3	7	6
Total	3	2	5	15	7	6
3 Errors in manner						
Initial replacement	0	0	0	0	8(p)	13(p)
Medial replacement	0	0	0	1(y)	0	1(b) 1(y)
Total	0	0	0	1	8	15

	Cy	Cr	pC	bC	fC
4 Total errors/n	23/1152	39/1149	5/767	21/768	36/766
%	19%	31%	4%	17%	29%
5 Errors → CV	15/23	23/39	5/5	20/21	13/36
%	65%	59%	100%	95%	35%
6 Errors in manner	8/23	16/39	0	1/21	23/36
%	35%	41%	0	5%	64%

Japanese allow [pr] or [br] clusters and yet we see that [pr] clusters cause less difficulty. They claim that this is because of universal markedness effects, that can be described by the Minimal Sonority Distance Parameter (MSD), shown in (4), with the addition of voiceless and voiced stops, where voiceless stops are less sonorous than voiced ones. Under this version of the MSD, the sonority distance between [p] and [r] is greater than that between [b] and [r], therefore the [pr] cluster is less marked. Broselow and Finer's view is that second language learners have access to this parameter in UG, and that the starting point of their acquisition is their L1 setting (this is equivalent to the third position in (11), full transfer/full access).

Broselow and Finer note that if the L2 learners were simply transferring their L1 parameter settings to the L2, they would treat all clusters as if they were L1 sequences. However, we have seen that they treat clusters differently in a way which is consistent with the predictions of minimal sonority distance. In other words, they treat more marked clusters differently than less marked clusters.

On this basis, Broselow and Finer argue that their non-native speakers have adopted a parameter setting for the MSD that is somewhere between the native and target language settings.

6.2   A structural explanation: derived sonority

Archibald and Vanderweide (1996) argue that a phonologically defined notion of MSD will explain the performance of learners in a way that a phonetically based MSD will not. When we look at the differing repair strategies for Cy clusters versus other types, we notice an interesting pattern that is unexplained in Broselow and Finer's analysis. With one exception, when the second member of a cluster is a glide, it does not trigger epenthesis. In other words, subjects may well break up a [pr] or [br] cluster by inserting an epenthetic vowel between two consonants, but not do so for a [fy] or [by] cluster, even though the sonority distance is the same for these sets of clusters. As shown in Broselow (1987, 1988) and discussed in section 3 above, we find epenthesis in L2 acquisition used as a repair strategy, triggered by consonants in the input which are unsyllabifiable in the learner's interlanguage phonology. In the initial syllabification of the word "flaw" shown in (15a), the initial consonant [f] is left unsyllabified by L1 constraints which still operate in the learner's interlanguage and disallow consonant clusters. This unsyllabified consonant then triggers the insertion of an epenthetic vowel, resulting in the creation of a CV syllable (under the onset first principle given in (2)), and the well-formed structure shown in (15b).

(15)   a.   b.

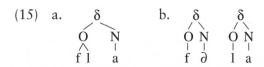

Now consider the possibility that glides are part of a complex nucleus and not of a complex onset – as has been argued for Korean by Kim-Renaud (1978) – then the glide would not trigger epenthesis as there is no unsyllabified onset consonant in the learner's interlanguage. This can be seen in the syllabification of the word "few" shown in (16).[13]

(16)

Archibald and Vanderweide propose that the behavior of the Korean subjects can be accounted for within a phonological framework which includes such structures as sub-syllabic constituents, feature geometry, and derived sonority. Here we will argue that such a model is able to account for the data observed by Broselow and Finer and is preferred for independent reasons. In addition, when we look at the behavior of the Finnish subject, we will see how this representation of segemental properties allows us to explain aspects of the syllabic structure. If the patterns were solely the result of the *phonetic* properties of the liquids, we would expect them to behave similarly cross-linguistically. What we will show is that the crucial information lies in the *phonological* properties of the liquids.

A model of hierarchical segment structure which treats sonority as a phonological construct derived from the complexity of the segmental representation reveals more about the mental representations of L2 learners and links their acquisition of segments to the acquisition of their L2 phonological inventory in the manner discussed in section 5 above.

In the following, we introduce feature geometry and phonological government and then go on to provide a reanalysis of Broselow and Finer's Korean data and, finally, present an analysis of data collected from a Finnish learner of English.

We adopt the model of segment structure shown in (17):

(17)

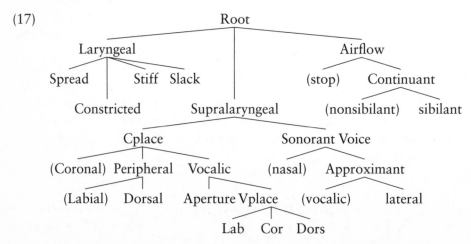

The Sonorant Voice (SV) node represents sonority. In general, the more SV structure a segment has, the more sonorous it is. This allows us to derive the sonority hierarchy shown in (18).

(18)

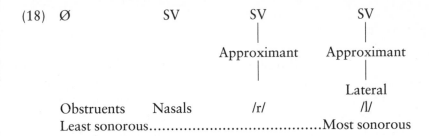

Obstruents have no SV structure and are, therefore, the least sonorant, while /l/ is the most sonorant, having the most SV structure. We note that glides are absent from the hierarchy in (18). We will assume that glides have the representation in (19), where SL refers to the Supralaryngeal node:

(19)

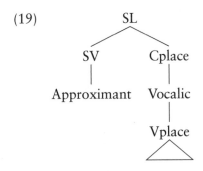

According to (19), glides have just as much sonority as liquids, but differ from other consonantal sounds in that they have both Cplace and Vplace nodes. As we shall see, this representation allows us to derive the tautosyllabicity of stop + glide clusters in English.

It is important to remember that the structure of a segment is based upon the contrasts it is involved in phonologically. Rice (1995) shows how the representation of a lateral is dependent on the contrasts found in the segmental inventory. The structures in (20) show how a Korean liquid could have quite a different representation from an English liquid:

(20)

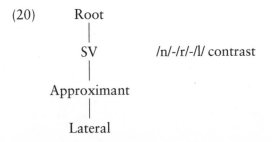

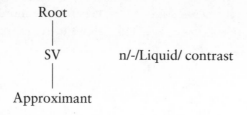

The acquisition of English [l], then, means the acquisition of the contrast between [l] and [r], which means the acquisition of the *representation* of [l]; not just the phonetic ability to produce a lateral. The acquisition of this representation is an essential step in acquiring English onset clusters. Vanderweide (1994) showed that children acquiring English as a first language did not start producing tautosyllabic onset clusters until they had acquired the appropriate representation for [l]. This is because English requires a Minimal Sonority Distance of two SV nodes within an onset cluster. Until the Koreans acquire the complex structure of [l] they will not have onset clusters.

The trees in (21) show the structures we are assuming for the English segments:

(21)

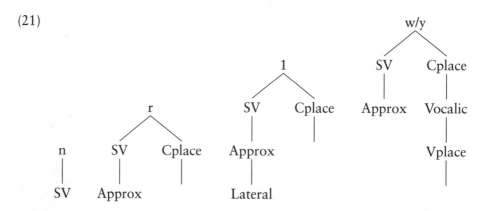

The trees in (22) show the structures we are assuming for the comparable Korean segments:

(22)

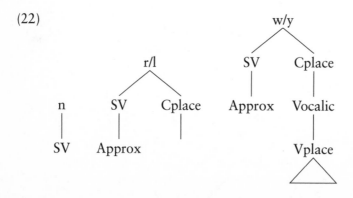

The structure of the liquids differs between the languages while the structure of the glide remains constant. What differs in the two languages is whether the onglide is found in the onset or the nucleus.

6.3   Phonological government

Following Rice (1992), we assume that phonotactic constraints result from universal principles of phonological government and syllabification determined by deriving sonority via the segmental structure discussed in the previous section. Following Vanderweide (1994), we adopt the definition of phonological government given in (23) and the syllabification algorithm given in (24).

(23)   *Government*
A segment governs an adjacent segment if it has more feature structure than the adjacent segment within a governing domain. Sonorant Voice, Supralaryngeal, and Root are governing domains.

(24)   *Syllabification Algorithm*
Process: A segment (A) governs a segment (B)?
Possibilities: Y (yes)/N (no)
Resulting Parse: Y → A and B are heterosyllabified
                          N → A and B are tautosyllabified

To account for the observed variation in allowable onset sequences cross-linguistically, we adopt the minimal sonority distance parameter given in (25).

(25)   *Minimal Sonority Parameter*
Parameter: SV government requires that the governor (B) must have at least X more nodes than the governee (A)
Settings: X = 1, 2, or 3
Default: X = 3

English and Korean have different settings of this minimal sonority distance parameter. English has a setting of X = 2 (allowing stop + liquid onsets) while Korean has a setting of X = 3 (prohibiting onset clusters).

Now, let's examine how these concepts, along with derived sonority and segmental representations, account for the differences in English and Korean syllabification. The trees in (26) show the allowable onset clusters in English:

(26)   English onset clusters (MSD = 2)

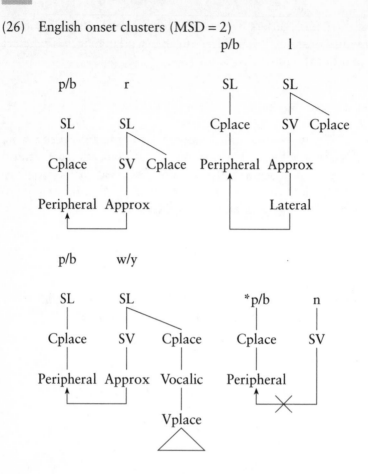

The first three clusters are well-formed tautosyllabically, since in each, the governor has at least two more SV nodes than the governee. The last cluster is not allowed in English, since the governor has only one more SV node than the governee.

The tree in (27) shows why Korean (with an MSD of 3) does not permit any consonant clusters.

(27)   Lack of Korean onset clusters

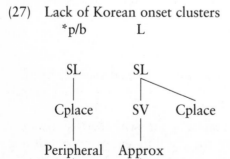

As shown in (27), an MSD of three prevents nasals, liquids and glides from entering into the onset in Korean, since in all cases, the governor never has at least three more nodes than the governee.

7   Finnish

To test this hypothesis further, we collected data from a single Finnish speaker and analyzed her consonant clusters.[14] Finnish has both [l] and [r] in the segmental inventory, and, historically, Finnish did not allow consonant clusters. Finnish words never begin with a cluster of consonants (Hakulinen, 1961).

In borrowing foreign words with an initial consonant cluster Finnish (like Proto-Finnic before it) has retained only the last consonant of the cluster. Consequently words which, in the Germanic languages from which Finnish has borrowed, began with skr-, str-, spr-, kr-, tr-, pr-, gr-, dr-, br-, fr- (and of course r-) all appear in Finnish with no more than r- as their initial consonant.

Examples of this can be seen in (28) (Kari Suomi, personal communication):

(28)   Swedish   Finnish

        Strand "waterfront"   Ranta
        Stol "chair"   Tuoli
        Klister "paste"   Liisteri

However, more recent borrowing shows a tendency to retain the clusters, as shown in (29):

(29)   English   Finnish

        Stress   Stressi
        Strategy   Strategia

Suomi (personal communication) states unequivocally, "it is no longer true to claim, as a sweeping generalization, that Finnish does not permit word-initial consonant clusters." These examples are from Standard Spoken Finnish, and there are reportedly dialects where cluster simplification continues to take place. However, Woiceshyn (personal communication) maintains that even earlier borrowings from Swedish retained their consonant clusters in slang. For example, the Swedish word *skol* "school" came into Finnish as *koulu*. Woiceshyn suggests that in slang the word could be pronounced with the initial s-cluster.

Traditionally, Finnish speakers have used consonant deletion to deal with initial clusters in L2 acquisition (Bannert, 1990; Hyltenstam and Lindberg,

1983). For example, it is common for Finnish speakers of Swedish to pronounce the three words *spruta* "syringe", *pruta* "(to) bargain", and *ruta* "square" all as [ruːta] (from N. Abrahamsson).

Our claim is that the existence of a liquid contrast in the Finnish consonantal inventory accounts for the ease of acquisition of consonant clusters historically in Finnish and in the interlanguage grammars of Finnish speakers of English.

Data were collected in spontaneous conversation with a native speaker of Finnish who has lived in Canada for 15 years. Table 2.15 illustrates the results for her onset clusters:

Table 2.15 English onset clusters of a Finnish speaker

Cluster	Accuracy	Cluster	Accuracy
pr	7/7	sp	5/5
tr	3/3	st	2/2
dr	1/1	sk	3/3
kr	1/1	sl	1/1
gr	3/3	sw	3/3
fr	2/2	str	1/1
θr	1/1	kl	1/1
tw	1/1	pl	1/1

Her overall accuracy on the onset clusters she produced was 37/37 (100 percent). Her accuracy in coda clusters can be seen in table 2.16:

Table 2.16 English coda clusters of a Finnish speaker

Cluster	Accuracy	Cluster	Accuracy
ts	3/3	ndz	1/1
ks	8/8	nst	2/2
st	8/8	nts	1/1
nd	3/5	rst	1/1
nz	7/7	rmz	1/1
rs	1/1	skt	1/1
rz	5/5	kst	2/2
dz	5/5	kts	1/1
rt	2/2	nt	4/4
rtʃ	2/2	ns	1/1
rdʒ	1/1	mz	2/2
ld	1/1	ntʃ	1/1
		ŋz	1/1

Her overall accuracy on the coda clusters was 65/67 (97 percent).

We would argue that this shows that the Finnish speaker was clearly able to produce English consonant clusters in both onset and coda position. If we viewed the relevant property of the first language as being "no consonant clusters" then we would have no way of distinguishing between the performance of the Korean and Finnish speakers. However, by viewing the relevant L1 property as the minimal sonority distance allowed by the feature geometry, we can see that the Korean speakers have to adjust their L1 feature geometry in a way that the Finnish speakers do not. The Finnish geometry is shown in (30).

(30)

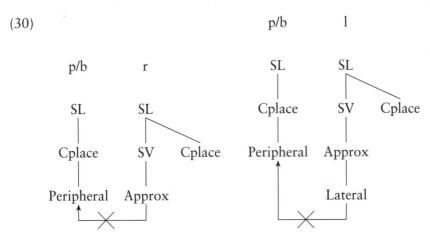

Finnish would have a minimal sonority distance of three (which would disallow clusters), but would have the necessary feature structure to support the English setting of two when confronted with positive evidence (in either borrowings or the L2) that consonant clusters were allowed. This is consistent with Brown's (1997) findings that Japanese speakers could not trigger the feature [coronal] in their L2 since it was not part of their L1 feature geometry.[15]

8 Conclusion

In this chapter, we have attempted to show that the acquisition of syllable structure in a second language is influenced both by universal principles of prosodic structure and by properties of the L1 syllabic structure. The question of whether new structure can be set up in the second language remains uncertain, though as in other linguistic domains, it looks as if the L1 representational structure is very difficult to overcome.[16]

Notes

1   Apart from the fact that, in general, most L2 research is carried out on English, reasons for the concentration of research on these languages can also be attributed to

the readily apparent difficulties posed by such languages for speakers of CV syllable languages. At first glance, there might seem to be little point in studying the acquisition of languages such as Spanish or Japanese by English speakers. However, as soon as one considers factors connected to syllable structure such as rhythmic timing in Spanish or pitch accent in Japanese, it is clear that such lines of investigation also merit attention.

2   The extent to which all principles are operable or whether the adult structure is present at the start of acquisition are issues as open to debate in phonology as they are in syntax (see note 3).

3   The violation of constraints both in children's emerging phonologies and in adult phonologies has led to the introduction of Optimality Theory, an approach involving the ranking of these constraints (Prince and Smolensky, 1993). Because OT constraints and their ranking are still under such intensive discussion, it is premature to include details of OT-based acquisition accounts here. However, some of the authors in this chapter have recently provided Optimality Theoretic accounts of their results (see also Hancin-Bhatt and Bhatt (1997) on L2 acquisition).

4   Where L2 perception data are more commonly collected is with respect to segmental phonology, see e.g., Flege (1995). Perception data also play an important role in investigating the acquisition both of intonation and of metrical stress (see e.g., Cruz-Ferreira, 1987; Archibald, 1993; and Pater, 1997, respectively). However, until recently investigation of L2 syllable structure through perception tasks has not been carried out (but see text to follow).

5   It should be noted that Demuth and Fee allow that not all children show evidence of a subminimal stage. See also Broselow and Park (1995) for a discussion of mora preservation in the English of Korean speakers.

6   Children learning English as a first language also show evidence of awareness of the exceptional status of some s-clusters insofar as they are (1) acquired later than other clusters: Smith's (1973) data shows that s-clusters violating the sonority sequencing generalization (e.g., [st]) are acquired later than non-violating clusters (e.g., [sn]); and they are (2) simplified differently (e.g., "blue" → [byu]; "spit" → [pIt]). This argues for the extrasyllabic status of /s/.

7   A parameter involving further attachment of consonants (e.g., /s/) will also be involved here.

8   A small sample of data collected from advanced Polish speakers of English suggests certain metrical parameters are resistent to resetting at their English values. The mis-stressings shown in (i) produced during conference presentations by university English teachers reveal that the pattern of errors Archibald found with respect to transfer of Polish penult stress and extrametricality persists:

(i)   Polish–English interlanguage stress errors

penult transfer	extrametricality
confeRENces	syLLAbuses
aREa	COMponents
purPOSEful	caTEgories
ATtack	peDAgogy
	PHYsician

These data point to the need for further investigation of the English rhymal structure adopted by Polish speakers to determine whether the quantity-sensitivity around which English stress revolves has been fully worked out in the rhyme.

9   We are, of course, making assumptions about the input, as in most cases the re-
      searchers do not state anything beyond what the learners were involved in at the time
      of testing. Nonetheless, we can assume that school children and German guest workers
      (Tropf's study) in their respective target language countries receive more aural than
      written input, and that secondary school and university students in foreign language
      settings (i.e., prior to arrival in the target language country) receive mostly written
      input.

10   It is controversial as to whether the omission of syllables is due to failure to perceive
      them, failure to store them (for some other reason) or constraints on their inclusion
      in production (see e.g., Jusczyk, 1997).

11   Huichol allowed the syllable types CV, CVC and CVVC.

12   For Broselow and Finer, this percent score reflects the percentage that a particular
      error made up of all the errors.

13   In fact, in native Japanese consonant glide sequences such as *ryoku* "inn" the glide
      must be analyzed as nucleic lest the false conclusion be drawn that Japanese has
      a minimal sonority distance of 1 (which would then permit impermissible onset
      clusters such as "sn-" and "fn-".)

14   We acknowledge the differences between the data collected by Broselow and Finer
      (many subjects in an elicitation task) and our Finnish data (one speaker in spontaneous
      conversation). The data, however, remain suggestive of real differences between the
      behavior of subjects from these languages.

15   Brown's work assumes a different representation for laterals (which we will not
      address here).

16   Given this stance, we are assuming that the change from non-branching onsets to
      branching onsets is not the acquisition of new structure. The structural node exists
      and its properties are reset based on the properties of the segmental inventory.

References

Abrahamson, N. (1997) Vowel epenthesis of initial /sC(C)/ clusters in Spanish speakers'
      L1 and L2 production. In J. Leather and A. James (eds.), *New Sounds 97*, pp. 8–16.
      University of Klagenfurt.

Akita, M. (1998) A longitudinal study of Japanese EFL learners' interlanguage phonology.
      Paper presented at EUROSLA 8. Paris, September, 10–12.

Anderson, J. (1987) The markedness differential hypothesis and syllable structure diffi-
      culty. In G. Ioup and S. Weinberger (eds.), *Interlanguage Phonology*. Rowley, MA:
      Newbury House.

Archibald, J. (1998) Second language phonology, phonetics and typology. *Studies in
      Second Language Acquisition* 20: 189–211.

—— (1993) *Language learnability and L2 phonology: The acquisition of metrical para-
      meters*. Dordrecht: Kluwer.

—— and Vanderweide, T. (1996, October) *Typological universals and phonological gov-
      ernment in L2 syllable structure*. Paper presented at the Second Language Research
      Forum, Tucson, AZ.

Armstrong, L. E. (1940) *The phonetic and tonal structure of Kikuyu*. London: Interna-
      tional African Institute.

Baldi, P. (ed.) (1991) *Patterns of change, change of patterns: Linguistic changes and
      reconstruction methodology*. Berlin: De Gruyter.

Bannert, R. (1990) *På väg mot svenskt utal*. Lund: Studentlitteratur.

Bender, L. M. (1987) Some possible African creoles: A pilot study. In G. Gilbert (ed.), *Pidgin and creole languages: Essays in memory of John Reinecke*. Honolulu: University of Hawaii Press.

Bongaerts, T., Planken, B. and Schils, E. (1995) Can late starters attain a native accent in a foreign language? A test of the critical period hypothesis. In Z. Lengyel and D. Singleton (eds.), *The Age Factor in Second Language Acquisition*. Clevedon: Multilingual Matters.

Borgman, D. (1990) Sanuma. In D. C. Derbyshire and G. K. Pullum (eds.), *Handbook of Amazonian languages*, pp. 15–248. Berlin: De Gruyter.

Broselow, E. (1988) Prosodic phonology and the acquisition of a second language. In S. Flynn and W. O'Neil (eds.), *Linguistic theory in second language acquisition*, pp. 295–308. Dordrecht: Kluwer.

—— (1987) Non-obvious transfer: On predicting epenthesis errors. In G. Ioup and S. Weinberger (eds.), *Interlanguage Phonology*. Rowley, MA: Newbury House.

—— and Finer, D. (1991) Parameter setting in second language phonology and syntax. *Second Language Research* 7: 35–59.

—— and Park, H.-B. (1995) Mora conservation in second language prosody. In J. Archibald (ed.), *Phonological acquisition and phonological theory*, pp. 151–68. Hillsdale, NJ: Erlbaum.

Brown, C. (1997) *Acquisition of segmental structure: consequences for speech perception and second language acquisition*. Ph.D. thesis, McGill University.

Chafe, W. (1977) Accent and related phenomena in the Five Nations Iroquois languages. In L. Hyman (ed.), *Studies in stress and accent*, pp. 169–81. Los Angeles: University of Southern California Press.

Clements, G. N. and Keyser, J. (1983) *CV Phonology: A Generative Theory of the Syllable*. Cambridge, MA: MIT Press.

Cole, D. T. (1967) *Some features of Ganda linguistic structure*. Johannesburg, South Africa: Witwatersrand Press.

Cruz-Ferreira, M. (1987) Non-native interpretative strategies for intonational meaning: An experimental study. In A. James and J. Leather (eds.), *Sound Patterns in Second Language Phonology*. Dordrecht: Foris.

Demuth, K. and Fee, E. J. (1995) Minimal prosodic words in early phonological development. MS., Brown University.

Dolphyne, F. A. (1988) *The Akan (Twi-Fante) language*. Accra, Ghana: Ghana Universities Press.

Eckman, F. (1981) On the naturalness of interlanguage phonological rules. *Language Learning* 31–195–216.

—— and Iverson, G. (1994) Pronunciation difficulties in ESL: Coda consonants in English interlanguage. In M. Yavas (ed.), *First and second language phonology*, pp. 251–65. San Diego, CA: Singular Press.

—— and —— (1993) Sonority and markedness among onset clusters in the interlanguage of ESL learners. *Second Language Research* 9: 234–52.

Fikkert, P. (1994) *On the Acquisition of Prosodic Structure*. Amsterdam: Holland Institute of Generative Linguistics.

Flege, J. E. (1995) Second language speech learning. Theory, findings and problems. In W. Strange (ed.), *Speech Perception and Linguistic Experience*, pp. 233–77. Timonium, MD: York Press.

Hakulinen, Lauri (1961) *The Structure and Development of the Finnish Language*. Translated by John Atkinson. Uralic and Altaic Series, vol. 3. Bloomington: Indiana University Press.

Hancin-Bhatt, and Bhatt, R. (1997) Optimal L2 syllables: interactions of transfer and developmental effects. *Studies in Second Language Acquisition* 19: 331–78.

Hayes, B. (1989) Compensatory lengthening in moraic phonology. *Linguistic Inquiry* 20: 253–306.

Hyams, N. (1992) The genesis of clausal structure. In Meisel, J. (ed.), *The acquisition of verb placement: Functional categories and V2 phenomena in language acquisition.* Dordrecht: Kluwer, 371–400.

Hyltenstam, K. and Lindberg, I. (1983) Invanrares svenska. En kritisk genomgång av materialet I projectet Svenska för invandrare (Josefson 1979). Särskilt med avseende på det insamlade materialets användningsmöjligheter. *SSM Report 9, Studium av ett invandrarsvenskt språkmaterial*: 5–51. Stockholms universitet, Insitutionen för Lingvistik.

Ingram, D. (1989) *First Language Acquisition*. Cambridge: Cambridge University Press.

Ioup, G., Boustagui, E., El Tigi, M. and Moselle, M. (1994) A case study of successful adult second language acquisition in a naturalistic environment. *Studies in Second Language Acquisition* 16: 73–98.

Jusczyk, P. W. (1997) *The Discovery of Spoken Language*. Cambridge: MIT Press.

Kahn, D. (1980) *Syllable-based Generalizations in English Phonology*. New York: Garland.

Kehoe, M. and Stoel-Gammon, C. (1997) Review article: The acquisition of prosodic structure: An investigation of current accounts of children's prosodic development. *Language* 73: 113–44.

Kim-Renaud, Y.-K. (1978) The syllable in Korean phonology. In C.-W. Kim (ed.), *Papers in Korean Linguistics*, pp. 85–98. Hornbeam Press.

Lleó, C. and Prinz, M. (1997) Syllable structure parameters and the acquisition of affricates. In S. J. Hannahs and M. Young-Scholten (eds.), *Focus on Phonological Acquisition*. Amsterdam: Benjamins.

Maddieson, I. (1984) *Patterns of sounds*. Cambridge, MA: Blackwell.

Major, R. (1987) Foreign accent: Recent research and theory. *IRAL* 25: 185–202.

Neufeld, G. (1980) On the adult's ability to acquire phonology. *TESOL Quarterly* 14: 285–98.

Newport, E. (1990) Maturational constraints on language learning. *Cognitive Science* 14: 11–28.

Oller, D. K. (1974) Towards a general theory of phonological processes in first and second language learning. Paper presented at the Western Conference on Linguistics, Seattle.

Parrondo-Rodriguez, A. (1999) *L2 Acquisition of Syllable Structure and Stress in Spanish*. Unpublished Ph.D. thesis, University of Durham (UK).

Pater, J. (1997) Metrical parameter missetting in second language acquisition. In S. J. Hannahs and M. Young-Scholten, *Focus on Phonological Acquisition*. Amsterdam: Benjamins.

Patkowski, M. (1990) Age and accent in a second language. A reply to James Emil Flege. *Applied Linguistics* 11: 73–89.

Payne, D. and Payne, T. (1990) Yagua. In D. C. Derbyshire and G. K. Pullum (eds.), *Handbook of Amazonian languages*, pp. 249–474. Berlin: De Gruyter.

Prince, A. S. and Smolensky, P. (1993) *Optimality Theory: Constraint Interaction in Generative Grammar*. RuCC Technical Report #2. Rutgers University Center for Cognitive Science.

Radford, A. (1995) Children – Architects or brickies? In D. MacLaughlin and S. McEwen (eds.), *Proceedings of the 19th Annual Boston University Conference on Language Development*, pp. 1–19. Sommerville, MA: Cascadilla Press.

Rice, K. (1995) *What is a lateral?* Paper presented at the Canadian Linguistics Association annual meeting, Montreal, Quebec.

—— (1992) On deriving sonority: A structural account of sonority relationships. *Phonology* 9: 61–99.

Riney, T. (1990) Age and open syllable production in interlanguage phonology. In H. Burmeister and P. Rounds (eds.), *Variability in Second Language Acquisition. Proceedings of the 10th Meeting of the Second Language Research Forum*, vol. 2. Eugene: Department of Linguistics, University of Oregon.

Ritter, E. (1991) Déplacement de NP en haïtien: oui ou non? [Does Haitian creole have NP movement?] In A. Kihm (ed.), *Recherches linguistiques de Vincennes: La créolisation, théorie et applications*, pp. 65–85. Paris: Université Paris VIII.

Romaine, S. (1988) *Pidgin and Creole Languages*. New York: Longman.

Sato, C. (1984) Phonological processes in second language acquisition: Another look at interlanguage syllable structure. *Language Learning* 34: 43–57.

Scupin, E. and Scupin, G. (1907) *Bubis erste Kindheit*. Leipzig: Griebens.

Selkirk, E. (1982) The syllable. In H. van der Hulst and N. Smith (eds.), *The Structure of Phonological Representations*. Foris.

Smith, N. V. (1973) *The Acquisition of Phonology: A Case Study*. Cambridge: Cambridge University Press.

Stern, C. and Stern, W. (1907) *Die Kindersprache*. Leipzig: Barth.

Stoel-Gammon, C. and Dale, P. (1988) Aspects of phonological development of linguistically precocious children. Paper presented at the Midwest Child Phonology Conference, Champaign, Illinois.

Suárez, J. (1983) *The Mesoamerican Indian Languages*. New York: Cambridge University Press.

Tarone, E. (1980) Some influences on the syllable structure of interlanguage phonology. *IRAL* 18: 139–52.

Taylor, C. (1985) *Nkore-Kiga*. London: Croom Helm.

Tropf, H. (1987) Sonority as a variability factor. In A. James and J. Leather (eds.), *Sound Patterns in Second Language Acquisition*. Dordrecht: Foris.

Vainikka, A. (1993/1994) Case in the development of English syntax. *Language Acquisition* 3: 257–325.

Vanderweide, T. (1994) *Government Phonology and principles of L1 syllabification*. MA thesis, University of Calgary.

Verma, M., Firth, S. and Corrigan, K. (1992) The developing system of Punjabi/Urdu speaking children learning English as a second language in Britain. *New Sounds 92*. Amsterdam: University of Amsterdam.

Weinberger, S. (1988) *Theoretical Foundations of Second Language Phonology*. Ph.D. dissertation, University of Washington.

Wexler, K. (1994) Finiteness and head movement in early child grammars. In D. Lightfoot and N. Hornstein (eds.), *Verb Movement*, pp. 305–50. Cambridge: Cambridge University Press.

White, L. (1989) *Universal Grammar and Second Language Acquisition*. Amsterdam: Benjamins.

Young-Scholten, M. (1997) Second language syllable simplification: Deviant development or deviant input? In J. Leather and A. James (eds.), *New Sounds 97*. Klagenfurt, Austria.

—— (1995) The negative effects of positive evidence on L2 phonology. In L. Eubank, L. Selinker and M. Sharwood Smith (eds.), *The Current State of Interlanguage*. Amsterdam: Benjamins.

—— (1994) On positive evidence and ultimate attainment in L2 phonology. *Second Language Research* 10: 193–214.

—— (1993) *The Acquisition of Prosodic Structure in a Second Language*. Tübingen, Niemeyer.

——, Akita, M. and Cross, N. (1999) Focus on form in phonology: Orthographic Exposure as a Promoter of Epenthesis. In P. Robinson and J. O. Jungheim, *Pragmatics and Pedagogy*. Proceedings of the Third PacSLRF, vol. 2. Tokyo: Aoyama Gakuin University.

3

Mapping Features to Forms in Second Language Acquisition*

Donna Lardiere

1 Introduction

In this chapter I examine the relation of morphological form to syntactic competence in second language acquisition. By *morphological form* I mean overtly realized inflectional affixation (or other phonological modification to lexemes, such as ablaut, suppletion, etc.). The type of *syntactic competence* of concern to us here is the mental representation of syntactic phrase structure, what Chomsky (1995:3), citing Jespersen, refers to as a "notion of structure," and in particular the representation of nonsubstantive functional categories and features which occupy such a central position in recent linguistic theory and language acquisition research (see also White, this volume, chapter 4).

Within current generative grammar models, such as the Minimalist Program (Chomsky, 1995), the featural properties associated with functional categories are presumed to drive syntactic movement via *feature-checking* computations. For example, the functional head T[ense] includes the feature [± finite] and, if T is [+ finite], a nominative case feature is assigned to subject DPs and checked within the T[ense] P[hrase] (Chomsky, 1995:240, 308). Presumably, the specification of syntactic features such as "finite" or "nonfinite" implicates the acquisition (or prior existence) of some functional category in the phrase structure, such as T, with which that particular feature is associated.

What I am calling *syntactic features* are also often referred to in the syntactic literature as "morphological", necessitating a conceptual distinction

---

* I would like to thank Bonnie Schwartz and two anonymous reviewers for their thoughtful comments.

between abstract (morpho)syntactic features, such as "[+ finite]", and their (morpho)phonological reflexes, such as -[s] as in *He walk-s to school* or Ø as in *I walk to school*. This conceptual distinction between feature and form, which is sometimes referred to in morphological theory as the *Separation Hypothesis*, lies at the heart of the problem of characterizing grammatical development in both native and non-native language acquisition.[1] It is the nature of this distinction (assuming there is one) in SLA that is the main topic of this chapter.

In a theory of Universal Grammar based on fixed general principles and language-specific setting of parameters, functional categories and features have been identified as a locus of variation (i.e., parameterization) among grammars. This variation, as Chomsky (1995:169) points out, must be somehow detectable to the language acquirer in the primary linguistic data, either via particular lexical properties, word order, or (most importantly for our purposes), morphological form.

A central question for both native and non-native language acquisition, then, is how a learner manages to associate the particular featural specifications of the target language – that is, a syntactic representation – with their overt realization in the input. With respect to morphology in particular, we may ask about its association with syntax: Do language learners derive syntactic representations of functional categories solely from exposure to the relevant morphological forms of their particular target language, such that acquiring the morphology is a prerequisite condition for projecting an associated category? Or rather do they already have some featural knowledge which gives them some idea of what they're looking for – that is, of what they're trying to match up with the forms they hear in the input? Both positions have been defended in the acquisition literature; in this chapter I shall try to sift through some of this literature, and to highlight some of the methodological difficulties surrounding the kind of syntactic competence we can ascribe to second language learners whose L2 morphological form diverges considerably from that of the target language input. In addition, the question of prior knowledge of features is highly interesting, particularly in L2 acquisition, where we can ask if it is possible to ascribe such knowledge to influence from the L1.

The rest of the chapter is organized as follows: Section 2 provides some of the relevant theoretical background regarding the interaction of overt morphological form with syntactic parameterization and especially notions of feature "strength". Section 3 broadly reviews current thinking on the relation of morphological to syntactic development in L1 acquisition, as these views, together with the theoretical proposals outlined in section 2, constitute the basis (or at least a departure point) for much current generative L2 acquisition research. Section 4 then directly examines this L2 research, specifically from the viewpoint of answering the questions posed above; in this section I also highlight some of the results of my own studies which bear on these questions. The final section attempts to sketch a more explicit model of the morphological component in second language grammars. Throughout all the sections of this chapter, I focus as specifically as possible on the relation of overt morphological form to syntactic competence, occasionally at the expense of overlooking other interesting findings of the relevant literature (for which I apologize).

2   Some Theoretical Background

Within the last several years, there have been numerous attempts to link the complexity of the verbal morphological paradigm, particularly for subject–verb agreement, to specific parametric variations in syntax, such as those associated with the licensing of null subjects and/or overt verb-raising. Because recent theoretical suggestions for the specific relation of morphological paradigms to syntactic verb-raising have been quite explicit and especially pertinent to recent proposals for language acquisition, I will outline three of them in some detail here, assessing them throughout within a larger context of acquisition research.

2.1   Morphological form and verb-raising

A close relation between morphological subject–verb agreement paradigms and overt verb-raising in the syntax has been hypothesized in much recent work. Following Pollock's (1989) Split-Infl Hypothesis – further differentiating IP into T[ense]P and Agr[eement]P in syntactic phrase structure – the robustness of inflectional agreement paradigms has come to be associated with a "strong" Agr feature which triggers overt verb-raising in the syntax. In pre-Minimalist approaches, the verb raised in order to join with agreement inflection (located in Agr); in more recent theory, an already-inflected verb raises to Agr to have its inflectional phi features checked there. Current generative approaches seem to endorse Halle and Marantz's (1993) Distributed Morphology model in assuming some version of the Separation Hypothesis, in that verbal inflection may be abstractly featural, rather than phonetically spelled-out (Chomsky, 1995:381).[2] However, there have been several recent attempts focused on finding a formula relating overt morphological form to those abstract features, particularly to the feature "strength" of Agr.

   An important issue for our purposes here concerns the problem of independently determining for any particular language whether Agr is "strong" or "weak", a distinction presumed to be parameterized. The problem is how to define "strength" in a way which avoids circularity: "strong" features trigger overt raising for feature-checking, but the only way to set the parameter value for "strong" Agr is by seeing whether or not there is overt raising. In other words, without independent criteria for what constitutes "strength", it is really not clear what stands to be gained beyond simply stating that verbs raise in some languages but not others.[3]

Some researchers have attempted to address this problem by trying to formulate independent criteria for defining feature strength; these efforts have concentrated on tying syntactic feature "strength" to the complexity of morphological form, primarily agreement affixation in verbal morphological paradigms. Three recent attempts along these lines are notable for their implications for language acquisition – these are proposals by Rohrbacher (1994), Vikner (1995, 1996) and Pollock (1997). Because so much current work in acquisition rests on the nature of the relation between verbal affixation and syntactic operations such as verb-raising, let us take a somewhat more detailed look at each of them in turn.

Rohrbacher (1994) tied syntactic verb-raising to rich agreement, defining feature "strength" as first and second person distinctively marked from each other, from the third person and from the infinitive, in at least one number (singular or plural) of one tense of regular verbs. Under this analysis, a parameter which determines verb-raising is roughly formulated as: "Inflectional paradigm does (not) distinctively mark [1st], [2nd] and [singular]" (p. 6).

Rohrbacher moreover argues for two qualitatively different kinds of morphological Infl-affixes – those belonging to paradigms which do mark [first, second, singular] distinctively and those affixes (if there are any) belonging to paradigms which do not. In the former ("distinctive") case, the entire paradigmatic set of Infl-affixes is considered "referential" and "substantive elements with non-grammatical meanings" (p. 115), and therefore listed in the lexicon along with other substantive lexical-category items such as nouns and verbs. In contrast, the latter ("nondistinctive") types of Infl-affixes (such as English third person, singular -s or the entire affixal paradigm for Faroese) are considered "nonreferential"; these are not listed in the lexicon but rather are merely PF reflexes of abstract feature bundles on syntactic nodes postsyntactically affixed to the verb by PF spell-out rules (p. 115ff).[4]

Some advantages of this explanation, according to Rohrbacher, are: (a) that a single parameter involving *overtly detectable* morphological properties of a functional category has far-reaching syntactic consequences; (b) that it correctly predicts that older variants of English and mainland Scandinavian which had strong agreement also had V to I raising, and that raising was eventually lost in these languages as a consequence of their loss of distinctive feature-marking; and (c) that it renders the morphological-formal notion of "paradigm" linguistically relevant to syntax, since one must have access to entire paradigms in order to determine that a language has distinctive feature marking and thus V to I raising. The latter point in particular has important implications for language acquisition, to which we return shortly.

Vikner (1995, 1996), while endorsing Rohrbacher's general approach, objects to the requirement that first and second person forms be distinct from third person and infinitive forms, calling it "conceptually unmotivated"

(1996:10). Revising Rohrbacher's formulation, Vikner proposes that verb-raising is entailed if and only if synthetic, affixal person morphology is found on regular verbs in all "core" (non-periphrastic) tenses. Vikner argues that his reformulation better accounts for the diachronic facts of Middle English; he admits, however, that his primary objection to Rohrbacher's analysis – namely, that children must "keep track of such a large amount of elements and verb forms during acquisition" – is also a problem for his own account (p. 11).

Examining this problem a little more closely for a moment, let us consider the knowledge required by a language learner trying to ascertain whether or not Agr is "strong" and thus whether or not verbs raise in the language being acquired.

Under Rohrbacher's analysis, the (first or second) language learner would need to have acquired (a) the distinction between singular and plural forms of the verbal agreement paradigm, (b) the forms for first, second and third person of the relevant singular or plural side of the relevant tense paradigm, and (c) the verbal infinitive form (as opposed to, say, a participial or imperative form, both of which are probably very frequent in the input).

Under Vikner's account, the learner would need to know (a) what constitutes a "core" tense (e.g., not compound tense or subjunctive or imperative forms), even though for some languages such as French or German such core tense paradigms such as those for simple or historical past are relatively infrequent in the input, and (b) at least two different person affixes in each of the relevant core tense paradigms. Moreover, as Vikner points out, other cross-linguistic differences concerning verb-movement, such as the positions of participles in Romance and infinitives in Germanic and Romance, do not seem to be linked to inflectional "strength" (1996:4, n. 5), thus adding to the complexity of the acquisition problem.

However, developmental data from much child language acquisition research suggest that children know extremely early whether verbs raise or not in the language they are acquiring, almost certainly long before they've acquired the myriad relevant morphological distinctions required under either Rohrbacher's or Vikner's analysis (e.g., Déprez and Pierce, 1993; Meisel, 1994; Pierce, 1992; Poeppel and Wexler, 1993; Verrips and Weissenborn, 1992). We return to this point below in section 3.

Finally, a somewhat different approach to defining inflectional strength is taken by Pollock (1997), who argues that person/number agreement *per se* is not directly related to verb movement, and that individual inflectional heads are "strong" only if they are "morphologically identified." *Morphological identification* is defined by Pollock as the unambiguous alternation of distinct morphemes within the same inflectional category across a morphological paradigm P in a particular language L (p. 265).

To give an example from French, Pollock proposes the following morphological description for the present indicative 1pl. form *parlons* "we speak" in which the Mood and Tense heads presumed to reflect the underlying syntactic structure contain null morphemes (p. 265, (91)):

(1)   [[[[$_{Root}$ parl] -∅ $_{Mood}$] -∅ $_T$] -ons $_{Agr}$]

In "regular, productive paradigms" in French, according to Pollock, the null Mood morpheme -∅ unambiguously alternates with -er in the future tense, as in *parlerons* "we will speak" (p. 274, n. 21, (i)):

(2)   [[[[$_{Root}$ parl] -er $_{Mood}$] -∅ $_T$] -ons $_{Agr}$]

Likewise, the null Tense morpheme -∅ as in (1) and (2) above alternates with -i as in the conditional and imperfect forms *parlerions* "we would speak" and *parlions* "we were speaking" shown below (p. 274, n. 21, (ii–iii)):[5]

(3)   [[[[$_{Root}$ parl] -er $_{Mood}$] -i $_T$] -ons $_{Agr}$]

(4)   [[[[$_{Root}$ parl] -∅ $_{Mood}$] -i $_T$] -ons $_{Agr}$]

Thus these three inflectional heads – Mood, Tense and Agr – are strong in French because they are morphologically identified, i.e., at least one morpheme within each category can alternate with another.

Under this analysis, English is somewhat problematic because Tense morphemes alternate between {-ed, -∅} (for past and nonpast respectively) and Agr morphemes alternate between {-s, -∅} (for 3sg. and elsewhere, respectively), incorrectly predicting that both these categories are morphologically identified and thus strong. However, Pollock proposes a solution arguing that, whereas Tense *is* strong in English, Agr is in fact actually weak or nonexistent: the -s affix marks a [singular] number feature rather than person agreement, and the "bare" forms of (non-3sg.) agreement are quite literally bare, i.e., not associated with any -∅ agreement affix; therefore -s has no alternant and fails to be morphologically identified.

Once again, it appears that this analysis places a considerable burden on the language learner, who must compare affixes across the present indicative, future, conditional, imperfect, etc. paradigms. And again, developmental data indicate that children know the verb-raising facts about their language long before they've acquired these extensive morphological distinctions. Moreover, one additional complication is that the knowledge imputed to the learner must be capable of distinguishing *null* morphemes from *no* morphemes (say, in the case of English verbs); in a system such as Pollock's where morphological form so iconically reflects syntactic clausal structure, it is not clear how the learner could ever figure this difference out.

2.2 Summary

To summarize so far, the purpose of this section has been to illustrate some recent theoretical attempts to independently define the notion of inflectional "strength" presumed to be responsible for various syntactic phenomena such as verb movement. All of the proposals examined above share a common assumption that overt morphological form plays a prominent role in this definition, and to varying extents, assume identity between overt morphemes and the abstract features that undergo checking operations in the syntax.

However, the learnability requirements associated with various proposals do not appear to square with what we do already know about early developmental syntax – namely, that children acquire knowledge of verb-raising long before they acquire the relevant morphological distinctions required by these models to inform them of the status of inflectional strength in the language they are acquiring. In this respect, the proposals we have seen to date have a typological rather than truly explanatory flavor; Chomsky, for example, has characterized the correlation between rich morphological form and overt syntactic movement as a "tendency" for which "a principled explanation is lacking" (1995:277).

In the sections to follow, particularly section 4, I will highlight the results of acquisition studies which suggest that the link between verbal affixal paradigms and Agr feature strength is less direct than claimed in the preceding analyses. Obviously, however, the inquiry into the nature of this relationship is ongoing and much more research is needed to resolve the matter.

3 L1 Acquisition

3.1 On the relevance of L1 to L2 acquisition research

Since L1 acquisition is widely presumed to be constrained by UG, some L2 researchers have sought to interpret apparent developmental commonalities between L1 and L2 acquisition as providing support for the view that UG similarly constrains L2 acquisition (e.g., Epstein, Flynn and Martohardjono, 1996; Flynn, Foley, Lust and Martohardjono, 1998; Vainikka and Young-Scholten, 1996). By the same token, divergent L2 developmental data have sometimes been used to argue that UG does not constrain L2 grammars (e.g., Clahsen and Muysken, 1986; Bley-Vroman, 1989). However, neither conclusion is logically necessary, particularly if we assume a significant role for prior L1 knowledge in influencing the course and outcome of L2 development (see Schwartz, 1995, 1996; Schwartz and Sprouse, 1994, 1996 for some detailed elaboration of this point).

Rather, the data available from child L1 studies serve to establish one kind of baseline against which a comparison of the similarities and differences in L2 development can be isolated and fruitfully examined within a generative analytical framework – quite aside from debates on access to UG *per se* but rather with an eye toward investigating interesting questions concerning grammatical representation, maturation, modularity, and the scope of UG.

There is little doubt that both native and non-native language acquisition exhibit early stages during which the forms associated with functional categories are often omitted or only variably produced; these are functional elements such as tense and agreement morphology on verbs, appropriate case marking on nouns, pronouns and their modifiers, and other elements such as auxiliaries, modals, complementizers, determiners, etc. Given the enhanced role of morphological features *and* forms in recent syntactic theory as discussed above, the omission of such functional elements assumes correspondingly greater significance in our characterization of early grammatical knowledge. In particular, we may ask: does this apparent commonality between L1 and L2 acquisition share a similar epistemological basis? If so, what are we to make of the fact that L1 acquisition uniformly converges on the morphologically complete target grammar, whereas L2 acquisition may not?

I have already alluded in section 2 to the existence of developmental data from L1 acquisition studies indicating that young children exhibit knowledge of the status of verb-raising in their language well before they exhibit the kind of extensive paradigmatic knowledge of morphological form presupposed by the specific proposals of Rohrbacher, Vikner or Pollock. However, in line with general theoretical attempts to define the relation between overt morphological form and syntactic feature-checking, much L1 acquisition research has also suggested that the variable (non-)production of morphological forms is not random, but rather systematically correlated with certain syntactic developments, such as the incidence of null subjects in non-null subject languages, the position of negation elements, and the occurrence of verb-raising in those languages which have it.

In fact, it appears that only one major featural distinction might be needed for learners to ascertain whether or not verbs raise or (null) subjects can be licensed – the distinction between finite vs. non-finite. The overwhelming bulk of evidence indicates that children do seem to be aware of this distinction from the earliest stages of acquisition. (It is the emergence and grammatical significance of the more finely individuated components of finiteness, such as tense distinctions and the various phi features associated with person and number agreement, that generate more heated debate. I return to this issue below.)

3.2 A case in point: root infinitives

One much-studied area of L1 acquisition concerns children's variable production of non-finite verb forms in contexts where the adult target language (and thus the bulk of the input available to the child) requires finite verbs – a phenomenon referred to as "*optional*" or "*root*" *infinitives* (henceforth RIs) (Wexler, 1994; Rizzi, 1993/1994). This particular research area provides perhaps the richest vein of inquiry into the nature of the interaction between morphological form and syntactic feature-checking available, although there is not yet a clear consensus on the proper analysis of RIs in child language. Specifically, there are two closely related contentious issues which concern us here, namely, (a) whether morphologically non-finite forms are also syntactically non-finite, and (b) whether the acquisition (however this is defined) of finite morphology is a necessary precondition for the syntactic representation of functional categories associated with finiteness, such as Tense and Agr. (As a part of (b), we also need to consider the extent of morphological acquisition – how much of which morphological paradigms are needed to trigger knowledge of the relevant syntactic features, and, as a methodological issue, how we can assess this.)

Although there are different ways of dividing up the various schools of thought here, I will settle on an approach which simply distinguishes between whether or not the omission of some morphological form from production data is presumed to stem from some absence or underspecification of one or more functional features or categories in the child's syntax.

Several studies have suggested a robust statistical correlation between the production of RIs and null subjects in non-null subject languages (such as French, German, Dutch, and Flemish) and a corresponding significant drop in RIs co-occurring with finite-marked verbs (e.g., Haegeman, 1995; Krämer, 1993; Phillips, 1995, 1996; Poeppel and Wexler, 1993). One language which does not seem to conform to this correlation, however, is English. Phillips (1996) notes that the exceptionality of English is contrary to the cross-linguistic uniformity we would expect to find if the correlation between RIs and null subjects were due to RI clauses being *syntactically* non-finite. He argues, therefore, that RI clauses are in fact syntactically finite, and that the "non-finite" verb is actually a default form of the verb which fails to undergo raising to combine with its finite inflection.[6]

Phillips suggests that languages in which finite verbs do raise (unlike English) may require verb-raising in order to license nominative case on subjects (since there is no verb-raising in the adult target grammar of English in any event, subjects must get their case-licensing some other way). This analysis is moreover compatible with two additional widely recognized phenomena throughout the data: first, the observation that finite-marked verbs in raising languages mostly appear in their raised positions whereas non-finite or "default" verbs do not; and second, that when finite inflections are used, they tend to be used correctly (i.e., there are very few "mismatches" between form and feature).

Note the extent to which Phillips' analysis does, in fact, depend on the acquisition of finite inflectional forms – in other words, the appropriate "spell-out" forms must be available – in order for the verb to undergo raising in the syntax. In this respect, Phillips' approach does seem to assume that the acquisition of morphological form is a prerequisite for syntactic *derivation*. On the other hand, we find under this analysis a separation of syntactic finiteness features from their morphological spell-out, in that verb-raising and correct finite inflection need not occur; hence, Phillips claims, there is no syntactic *representational* deficit – all functional categories are available at early stages of acquisition quite apart from their morphological spell-outs.

A similar conclusion is drawn by Borer and Rohrbacher (1997), who propose that the absence of functional elements in early stages of acquisition actually provides evidence for, rather than against, the existence of functional categories in the syntax. This is because the child who has not yet acquired the morphological paradigm avoids using inappropriate or mismatched inflectional forms which, when checked against the required inflectional features, would cause the syntactic derivation to crash. (Again, note that under this approach, the morphology must nonetheless be acquired in order for feature-checking derivation to proceed.) If no such feature-checking mechanism were already in place, they argue, we would expect to find random or mismatched agreement marking; however, as noted earlier, this is generally not a characteristic of early child speech. Interestingly, Borer and Rohrbacher show that inappropriate inflectional marking apparently does characterize the speech of agrammatic aphasic patients, who may have indeed suffered some loss of functional structure.

Borer and Rohrbacher thus also conclude that all functional categories are in place and available for syntactic feature-checking from the earliest stages of L1 acquisition. They moreover argue that children must have a priori knowledge of which universal semantic features and categories are (morpho)syntactically grammaticizable,[7] and therefore already have some idea of what to look for when determining the function of affixal material, "rather than the other way around" (p. 27).

The analyses of Phillips (1995) and Borer and Rohrbacher (1997) contrast with other L1 studies which claim that children do start out with a syntactic representational deficit of some sort, for which RIs (and other missing functional material) constitute some evidence. I will briefly touch on a few representative examples of approaches which crucially depend on the acquisition of particular morphological distinctions to trigger the development of syntactic competence.

In line with the theoretical view that functional categories and features are the only sites for parameterized variation among language-specific grammars, some researchers have argued that the syntactic representation of functional projections must be input-driven; i.e., children only gradually construct functional phrase structure by the prior acquisition of actual affixes associated with the heads of functional categories instantiated in their particular language. To give an explicit example of this type of approach, Clahsen (1990/1991) and Clahsen and Penke (1992) have claimed that the (comparatively late) acquisition of a specific morpheme in German – the 2sg. verbal agreement suffix -*st* – constitutes the trigger for projecting an AgrP in German L1 acquisition (although this specific claim has been refuted by others, e.g., Meisel, 1994; Poeppel and Wexler, 1993; Verrips and Weissenborn, 1992).[8]

Alternative accounts have proposed that all functional projections are available but may fail to be projected (e.g., Grimshaw, 1994; Haegeman, 1995; Rizzi, 1993/1994), or that certain specific features associated with functional categories are missing or underspecified. Examples of the latter type of analysis include Wexler (1994), who proposes that early child grammars lack a fully-specified Tense head, and Hoekstra, Hyams and Becker (1997), who argue that it is the underspecification of Number which gives rise to RIs.

These analyses, contra Phillips (1995, 1996) and Borer and Rohrbacher (1997), assume that RI clauses are both morphologically *and syntactically* non-finite. Since non-finite root clauses are disallowed in the adult grammars of the languages under consideration, RIs are thus presumed to stem from some type of non-targetlike representational deficit, such as the failure to project functional categories or to grammatically encode a specific feature on a specific head. However, much recent work (with a few notable exceptions such as Radford, 1990, 1996; Vainikka, 1993/1994) indicates that there is *at least* one functional category projection in the earliest stages of acquisition which is featurally specified for at least a [+/−] finiteness distinction; such a projection is needed, according to Poeppel and Wexler, "to account for even the simplest facts of very early grammar" (1993:21).

3.3 Summary

As we have seen, analyses differ on the extent to which morphological deficits of early L1 production data reflect true syntactic deficits as well. However, several points emerge from the literature which seem to enjoy surprisingly wide consensus, summarized below:

1   Children's variable omission of morphological material is apparently not random, but rather is somehow correlated in a systematic way with certain syntactic properties, such as the licensing of null subjects (in non-null subject languages) and failure to raise verbs (in raising languages).
2   In verb-raising languages, there is a statistically significant tendency for finite-inflected verbs to raise, and for non-finite or "default"-inflected (RI) verbs to remain in situ.
3   Finite inflections, when produced, are overwhelmingly produced correctly – the errors children do make with morphological form are largely those of omission.
4   Children acquiring very highly inflected languages with "rich" agreement are less likely to produce RIs as frequently or for as long as children acquiring less highly inflected languages.

Taken together, the above points seem to indicate, as Phillips puts it, that "children clearly seem to know the syntactic consequences of their morphological simplifications" (1996:595), which in turn suggests that a rudimentary mapping between morphological form and syntactic features (specified for strength and finiteness) is already in place. This knowledge does not appear to be contingent on the prior acquisition of the various and more extensive paradigmatic criteria set forth in the theoretical analyses we have seen.

4 L2 Acquisition

Returning to the initial questions posed in this chapter, we may ask whether the development – and, in particular, the deficits and variability – of morphological form observed in second language acquisition are tied to syntactic knowledge in the same way as has been suggested for L1 acquisition. (Of course, it should be kept in mind that even in L1 acquisition, the question of the precise nature of the relation between morphology and syntax is far from settled!) In other words, is the acquisition of some set of actual morphemes or morphologically realized forms a *prerequisite* for acquiring knowledge of the syntactic features involved in syntactic feature-checking operations?

In the following sections, I would like to consider this issue from various angles, e.g., to what extent affixes are identified with features by L2 acquirers, whether we find systematic variability in L2 acquisition of the sort proposed for L1 acquisition, the role of native L1 influence in the L2 acquisition of both features and forms, and how to begin to account for morphological non-convergence (or "fossilization") with respect to the target language as opposed to virtually inevitable convergence in L1 acquisition.

4.1   Features vs. forms in L2 acquisition

Recall from section 1 that under the theoretical assumptions of the Separation Hypothesis, grammatical (or conceptual) features such as tense/time distinctions, person, number and/or gender phi features, etc. are claimed to be distinct from their phonetic spell-outs; thus we need not assume a priori that the omission or variable production of particular affixes necessarily indicates lack of knowledge of those features. However, because the particular features which any specific language chooses to morphologically encode may obviously vary from one language to another, it has been common in L2 acquisition research (as in L1 research and recent syntactic theory) to assume that it is indeed the "detectable" properties of morphological form which inform the learner as to which particular functional categories should be projected in the interlanguage phrase structure.[9] In other words, an approach compatible with some form of theoretical model along the lines of Rohrbacher (1994) or Vikner (1995) would maintain that syntactic knowledge of functional categories or feature "strength" may essentially only be derived for a particular language from the productive acquisition of (some set of) actual affixes of that language's morphological paradigm.

In a well-known series of papers, for example, Vainikka and Young-Scholten (1994, 1996) have claimed that early-stage L2ers lack knowledge of the inflectional (IP) categories and features of the L2 (German, in this case), that such knowledge is not available via L1 transfer and that it may only be acquired as a *consequence* of learning the affixes of the verbal agreement paradigm.[10] They argue, moreover, that at early stages of L2 acquisition where verb agreement paradigms still appear incomplete, this may be attributed to the fact that "there is no Infl or Agr position for base-generating *suffixes*" (1994:281, my emphasis).[11]

Eubank (1993/1994) and Eubank et al. (1997) also appear to equate overt morphological forms with the syntactic features they encode, assuming that the specification of the value for feature strength is contingent on the presence "in the lexicon" of the relevant paradigmatic affixes. Since, as Eubank observes, bound affixes are generally assumed not to transfer from the L1 to the L2, neither, he argues, do the feature values associated with those affixes. If affixes did transfer, he writes, "then one would expect to find associated values; if not, then related values may likewise be absent" (1993/1994:206).[12]

These approaches illustrate a non-separationist treatment of bound affixes as lexical items which are isomorphic with their abstract features, and the *absence* of these items in learner production data is interpreted as a kind of evidence for absence of some associated syntactic knowledge. So let us consider two ways of going about investigating the nature of L2 learner omissions (or misspelling) of morphological form: the first is to ask if such omissions exhibit the same systematicity in L2 as in L1 acquisition, which would suggest a close link between syntactic and morphological development; the second is to see whether we can find other kinds of evidence for syntactic knowledge even in the absence of correct overt morphology.

4.2   Are morphological omissions or errors random in L2 acquisition?

Recall that findings from L1 studies appear to suggest that the omission of morphological affixes in early stages of L1 acquisition seems to be systematically correlated with particular syntactic properties such as licensing of null subjects and the underspecification of feature strength for verb-raising. One study which has specifically asked the question of whether this kind of correlation also holds for L2 acquisition is that of Prévost and White (to appear), who hypothesize (following Rizzi, 1993/1994 for L1 acquisition) that RIs in early L2 acquisition are a consequence of grammatical truncation.

Under the Truncation Hypothesis, the language learner's representation of clausal structure may (optionally) be truncated at any category below CP, generating some specific predictions for morphological marking; for example, root projections below IP should exhibit non-finite morphology (RIs), including on modals or auxiliaries, whereas clauses which are clearly CPs should require finite verbal affixation and should not exhibit null subjects. It is a theoretical model which does take the presence or absence of morphological form as an indication of underlying syntactic representational competence, and posits a contingent relation between their development.

The data for Prévost and White's study come from four children and four adults learning French or German in a naturalistic setting. Their findings suggest an age effect for the childen vs. adults in the occurrence of non-finite morphology on verbs. Prévost and White report that for the children in their study, the incidence of RIs correlates with the predicted syntactic effects, whereas non-finite morphological marking is more variable and random among the adults. These results seem to indicate that grammatical truncation is indeed an option for young L2 learners, whose inflectional affixation for finiteness vs. non-finiteness seems to more closely mirror the actual syntactic properties associated with featural finiteness (although cf. Phillips, 1996, who argues otherwise for L1 acquisition).

In contrast to these data, however, Haznedar and Schwartz (1997) argue that in their longitudinal study of a four-year-old Turkish child acquiring English, the English L2 data show no developmental relation between finite affixation and the disappearance of null subjects, contrary to what the Truncation Hypothesis would predict. Gavruseva and Lardiere (1996) also report the frequent occurrence (23–75 percent) of non-finite verb forms in obligatory finite CP contexts for an eight-year old Russian child acquiring English, a finding again at odds with Truncation predictions.

Another question of interest in considering variability of morphological form is whether not just omissions but also errors, e.g., agreement mismatches, occur. Recall that L1 data robustly indicate that, although young children omit agreement morphology, they rarely use the wrong person-agreement affix. Both Grondin and White (1996) and Haznedar and Schwartz (1997) report similar results for the child L2 data they examined (for the acquisition of French and English respectively); i.e., children omit affixes but generally get them right when they do use them.

The results for adults seem decidedly more mixed. Vainikka and Young-Scholten (1994) indicate that there are agreement mismatches for adult acquirers of German; they note that early-stage learners use either the (infinitive) -n suffix or no suffix most of the time, but that "[w]hen other suffixes are used, they are usually used incorrectly" (p. 289). Prévost and White however, report that preliminary analyses of the adult data from their study indicate that inaccurate morphological form "most commonly" consists of missing, rather than faulty, inflection (p. 26). Preliminary analysis of adult L2 English data from the Patty corpus (see Lardiere, 1998b and section 4.3 below) also show that agreement mismatches are rare – virtually restricted to a few occurrences of 3sg. forms of *be* overextended to plural contexts with quantifiers (e.g., *so two of us was living in Chinatown; all of us is able to do it*). In these cases, the presence of the quantifier seems to be complicating the phi-feature computation for agreement.

Other more clearcut cases of erroneous morphological affixation in adult L2 acquisition do exist and are in themselves quite interesting, since even the production of a "wrong" affix does not always appear to be random. For example, Lardiere and Schwartz (1997) argue that L2 English acquirers' choice of *-ing* rather than *-er* in the productive coining of agentive deverbal compounds (e.g., **cookie-eating* or **eating-cookie* vs. the target form *cookie-eater*) may be a principled one: both *-ing* and *-er* can be affixed to verbs to derive 3sg. nominalizations; the "agentive" role that additionally gets morphologically encoded in *-er* but not in *-ing* may instead be transferred from the L1 (Spanish) as *pro*, which has been independently argued to bear the same role in such compounds in the L1 (di Sciullo, 1992; Lardiere, 1994). The use of *-ing* in agentive deverbal compounds, therefore, may represent an overgeneralization which nonetheless is compatible with respect to the required feature-marking.

Another interesting case of "incorrect" affixation comes from a study by Orr (1987), who investigated the L2 acquisition of noun-class and agreement morphology in Chichewa, a Bantu language, by native speakers of Chingoni (another Bantu language with a very similar noun-class and agreement marking system) and Gujarati, an Indo-Aryan language spoken by Indian immigrants in Malawi, where the research was conducted. Orr found that the successful acquisition of the extensive noun-class morphology system of Chichewa was strongly dependent on the subjects' L1, with the Chingoni speakers outperforming the Gujarati speakers on inflectional accuracy by far, especially at lower levels of comparable proficiency in communicative competence (determined by Foreign Service Institute (FSI) ratings). The data showed that the native Chingoni speakers all exhibited a "sophisticated ability to supply class prefixes for nouns covering a broad spectrum of types" (p. 118) even at the lowest levels of proficiency examined. Native Gujarati speakers, on the other hand, relied to a much greater extent and for far longer (i.e., through higher levels of FSI proficiency ratings) on a single overgeneralized noun class and agreement prefix.

The use of an overgeneralized default affix (as opposed to no affix or random affixation) suggests that the Gujarati speakers do indeed have a functional representation of Agr in Chichewa. Though the initial source of this knowledge is unclear, Gujarati does have (less extensive) noun class distinctions and agreement, so that the transfer of a functional category for agreement from the L1 is certainly possible. Although it appears that neither L1 group has a categorial (representational) deficit for Agr in L2 Chichewa, native Chingoni speakers will clearly have an immense advantage over the Gujarati speakers in figuring out where to begin to look for the corresponding spell-outs (e.g., as prefixes rather than suffixes) and how finely Chichewa lexical noun classes need to be individuated within morphological form.

The data from the native Gujarati speakers learning Chichewa at first glance seem amenable to the type of analysis proposed for L1 acquisition by Phillips (1996) and Borer and Rohrbacher (1997) (outlined earlier in section 3.2), whereby we find the use of a default Agr form to prevent a feature-checking derivation from crashing.[13] Orr, however, provides at least anecdotal evidence that even native speakers of other Bantu languages acquiring L2 Chichewa do exhibit "fossilized" noun-class agreement errors in their Interlanguage, or what Orr in fact more accurately refers to as "idiosyncratic approaches to Chichewa noun class morphology" (p. 2), and presumably their derivations do not crash. In sum, it seems hardly controversial to maintain that a variety of factors (e.g., differing conditions of exposure to input, L1 background, etc.) play a role in whether inflectional "errors" (as opposed to simple omissions) persist in adult L2 acquisition, quite unlike most findings for L1 acquisition.

4.3   Other kinds of evidence for L2 syntactic competence

In L2 as in L1 acquisition, morphological deficiency in production data has often been assumed to reflect a corresponding deficit in the underlying syntactic representation of functional features and phrase structure. As suggested earlier, several studies have proposed, on the basis of sub-criterial rates of verbal affixation, that full clausal phrase structure (i.e., including IP and/or CP) is either altogether absent (e.g., Vainikka and Young-Scholten, 1994, 1996; Eubank and Grace, 1996; Eubank et al., 1997; Beck, in press), optionally truncated (Prévost and White, in press), featurally underspecified (Eubank, 1993/1994, 1996) or otherwise "impaired" (Beck, in press). This view is certainly not surprising given the theoretical assumptions outlined in section 2 and the hypothesized relation between RIs and various syntactic effects observed in L1 acquisition. Nevertheless, I will argue against it here for L2 acquisition, summarizing some results of my own research (Lardiere, 1998a, 1998b).[14] These results suggest that the contingent relation which has been argued to hold (for both L1 and L2 acquisition) between the acquisition of verbal morphological paradigms and syntactic knowledge of functional categories is in fact untenable for L2 acquisition.

The relevant data come from three recordings of naturalistic speech covering a span of about eight-and-a-half years, from Patty, a native Chinese speaker who acquired English as an adult. The first recording was made after Patty had lived in the US for about ten years; from that point until the last recording nearly nine years later, she'd been totally and virtually exclusively immersed in L2 English. (See Lardiere, 1998a for additional subject background details.) Patty's suppliance of morphological marking on English verbs has apparently "fossilized" at a production rate far below any of the criterial levels for acquisition generally assumed throughout the literature; nevertheless, we can still find surprisingly robust evidence for grammatical knowledge that crucially implicates the presence of the functional categories usually associated with verbal inflection, suggesting that the development of syntactic competence (i.e., a "notion of structure") and of morphological form in L2 acquisition are largely independent.

Let us consider the data for three alternative types of evidence which seem to indicate syntactic knowledge that is sharply dissociated from verbal morphological marking: pronominal case on subjects, word order with respect to negation and adverb placement, and the extensive presence throughout the data of clauses (subordinate, relative, free relative, wh-questions) both with and without overt complementizers that could presumably only be analyzed as CPs.

4.3.1 Tense and pronominal case

Recall from section 1 that under Minimalist assumptions (and in fact under pre-Minimalist approaches as well), there is a close relation between a [±finite] feature specification in IP/TP and the assignment of nominative case to subjects (e.g., Chomsky, 1995:308). The theory predicts that if I^0 or T^0 is available and fully specified in the learner's syntactic representation, it will check the case of a subject DP which has raised into its checking domain (because T^0 is strong in English), and if it is specified for [+finite], we should expect to find nominative case marking on the subject. Since case is expressed morphologically only on pronouns in English and since certain pronouns (in the first and third persons) are suppletively unrealizable without marking case distinctions, unlike regular tense affixation on verbs, pronominal case-marking constitutes a good test for investigating whether T^0 is available and specified for strength and finiteness.

The data from Patty yield interesting and strong results: First, suppliance of past tense in obligatory past finite contexts remains stable and very low at approximately 34 percent over the entire eight-and-a-half year time span. This rate is far lower than most researchers posit for acquisition of the associated functional category (see, for example, n. 10). However, the second result is that the distribution of case on pronouns in Patty's data is absolutely perfect and clearly a function of finiteness, such that we find nominative pronouns as subjects of finite clauses, but non-nominative (object) forms wherever required, including for subjects in non-finite contexts such as infinitive, Exceptional Case Marking (ECM) and small clauses.[15] These findings indicate that Patty's grammatical representation includes T^0, with features specified for strength and finiteness.

4.3.2   Agreement and optional verb-raising

A recent set of L2 acquisition studies has appeared which takes as its theoretical basis the hypothesized link between the verbal morphological paradigm and Agr feature strength as proposed, for example, in the theoretical literature outlined in section 2. A strong feature, recall, is held to be responsible for main verb-raising (past Neg and/or adverbs) in the computational derivation. Two related but somewhat different strands of thought have emerged from these studies. The first hypothesizes that until learners acquire the relevant verbal agreement affixes of the L2 paradigm, the feature value for Agr "strength" remains unspecified or "inert". This in turn predicts that until the paradigm is mastered and the Agr feature value set to either "strong" or "weak", learners should exhibit "optional" verb-raising, even if neither the L1 nor the L2 has overt verb-raising (Eubank, 1993/1994, 1996; Eubank and Grace, 1996; Eubank et al., 1997). The second, even stronger, claim that has been made is that while there is indeed a theoretical link between Agr feature-strength and verbal morphological form (which constrains L1 acquisition as part of UG), this feature is permanently "impaired" among adult L2 acquirers, presumably due to critical period effects. This impairment results in optional verb-raising regardless of whether the agreement paradigm is ever acquired or not (because this piece of UG linking the morphology to the syntax is inaccessible to adults) (Beck, in press).

Investigating the optionality of verb-raising in Patty's data, Lardiere (1998b) found that Patty's comparable rate of agreement affixation on lexical main verbs (i.e., for the same type of contexts for the same L1–L2 combination as that examined by Eubank and Grace and Eubank et al.) remains stable but extremely low – nearly absent, in fact – at around only 4 percent suppliance over the eight-and-a-half-year time period. However, an examination of possible Neg and adverb contexts for verb-raising shows that verb-raising does not occur, and does not appear to be an option – the correct result for English.[16]

Again, the results seem to indicate that lack of overt agreement affixation on main verbs is a fossilized characteristic of Patty's Interlanguage English, but that there is no featural deficit in her syntactic representation. The data suggest that even when such affixation is *never* acquired, it is still possible for an adult learner to determine the status of verb-raising in the target L2.

4.3.3   Evidence for a CP projection

At the same time that we find extremely low suppliance rates for finite tense and agreement marking on verbs, we also find clear evidence in Patty's data for the representation of fully extended clausal phrase structure, i.e., a CP projection. Lardiere (1998a) reports that the first recording alone includes at least 65 CP clauses; among these we find multiple embeddings, relative and free relative clauses, wh- and yes–no questions and various overt complementizers. A few examples from the data follow:

(5)   *can I have onion?*
      why do you want me to go?
      something that have to show the unbeliever that you are in spirit
      he have the inspiration to say what he want to say
      maybe we are the one who chosen
      everyone who believe it can get it

Under most proposals for both L1 and L2 acquisition, the presence of a CP implicates the presence of all lower functional projections as well, an assumption stated explicitly for "structure-building" and "minimal-projection" accounts (e.g., Grimshaw, 1994; Radford, 1990, 1996; Vainikka, 1993/1994 for L1 acquisition; Vainikka and Young-Scholten, 1994, 1996 for L2 acquisition) and optional truncation (Rizzi, 1993/1994 for L1; Prévost and White (in press) for L2) as well as most "full competence" models (see White, this volume, chapter 4, for an overview). Indeed, it appears that Patty's representation of functional projections is complete, despite impoverished morphological affixation. This suggests that the development of syntactic phrase structure in second language acquisition is not contingent on the acquisition of morphological paradigms.

4.3.4   Summary

I have used the data from Patty to highlight other potential sources of evidence that can indicate whether the features thought to be responsible for UG-constrained operations such as subject raising, nominative case licensing, verb raising, etc. are present and fully specified in the L2 grammar. In Patty's case, these features do seem to be operational despite deficient morphological affixation. Unlike the proposals we have seen for L1 acquisition, accurate affixal spell-out does not appear to be a prerequisite for either representational *or derivational* syntactic competence. Rather, the data suggest that syntactic and morphological development are autonomous in L2 acquisition, related via a mapping from one system to the other that is itself indirect and, at least for adult L2 acquisition, subject to greater, perhaps permanent, variability or breakdown. I return to the nature of this mapping in section 5.

The fact that syntactic derivation is available despite possibly incomplete morphological development further suggests that there may not be any necessary contingency at all between morphological paradigms and inflectional feature strength such as that posited by Rohrbacher (1994), Vikner (1995) or Pollock (1997). It may be that morphological and syntactic knowledge co-develop side by side in child language acquisition, being mapped one to the other from early stages of acquisition but not necessarily contingently or implicationally linked. In children, this may be difficult to tease apart since both systems may be developing simultaneously. Thus one advantage of look-ing at adult L2 steady-state data is that we might get a clearer picture of the modularity of grammatical domains by seeing where the two developmental paths diverge; what we consider post-"critical period" deficits might result from a decreasing ability to construct the mapping from feature to form as easily as child language acquirers do. In any case, the L2 data indicate that acquiring this mapping does not appear to be a prerequisite condition for carrying out syntactic computations based on feature strength and finiteness, nor for building a syntactic representation of the target grammar.

However, there is one large caveat here: As I have indicated so far in a string of notes throughout, suppletive forms are acquired earlier and more robustly than affixal forms, certainly at least for adult language acquisition. If morphologically detectable properties should indeed turn out to be required in order to specify features and trigger the projection of functional categories, then I see no reason why suppletive forms cannot fulfill this function. Of course, in this case the theoretical models which explicitly require affixal paradigmatic knowledge would need to be reworked, and acquisitional models which have posited particular developmental stages based on production data that excluded suppletive forms from consideration (e.g., Clahsen and Penke, 1992 for L1 and Vainikka and Young-Scholten, 1994 for L2 acquisition) would similarly need to be revised.

Otherwise (that is, if we insist on a contingent role for morphology in L1 acquisition of functional categories, as the L1 data suggest), the most coherent explanation for the L2 data is that, at least for second language acquisition, learners already have knowledge of functional categories and features via prior language knowledge (as proposed by Schwartz and Sprouse, 1994, 1996); apparently they do not need to rely on L2 morphological form to trigger syntactic representation and/or derivation. For L2 acquirers, the problem lies in figuring out how (and whether) to spell out morphologically the categories they already represent syntactically, i.e., the "mapping problem". Clearly, further research will be needed to distinguish between the alternative possibilities.

5   Mapping to Morphological Form: Conclusion

In this final section I would like to elaborate in somewhat more detail on what I take to be the basis for much of the divergence between adult and child language acquisition outcomes. As I have argued elsewhere (Lardiere, 1998a:20), the available data suggest that the abstract features which motiv-ate syntactic computations are modularly "insulated" from the specific details of morphophonological spell-outs. Rather, the morphological component "reads" the output of this computation, identifying the features which condition morphological operations resulting in phonological modifications to lexemes (see Beard, 1995, for a very explicit processing model of the morphological component). It is in this post-syntactic area where Patty (and many adult L2 acquirers) appear to falter with respect to the target language.

Consider first a very simple example of an acquisition problem which will nonetheless illustrate this basic point about modularity (and turn out not to be so simple) – the acquisition of gender distinctions in English third-person pronouns. Unlike languages with more complex gender (i.e., noun class) distinctions, the assignment of morphological gender to third-person pronouns in English is virtually co-extensive with the semantic or conceptual notion of "natural gender" associated with sex distinctions of "male," "female" and "neuter" (i.e., something like "neither saliently male nor female"). The mapping between semantic "sex" and pronominal "gender" in English is therefore a seemingly quite simple and direct one-to-one correspondence, in which the sex of the discourse referent of a third-person pronoun (along with case) determines which morphological form of the pronoun to select.

It is puzzling, therefore, that many L2 learners of English, including Patty, often confuse the "masculine" and "feminine" forms, since presumably all L2 learners (probably from early childhood) have a clear conceptual distinction between "male" and "female". The difficulty in getting to the correct PF obviously resides elsewhere – in the syntactic computation, perhaps, which must assign case, or especially in the mapping to morphology which must identify the semantic feature "sex of discourse referent" rather than some other feature (such as "agreement with head noun in an NP", as in Romance languages) as the conditioning factor for the choice of spell-out. If the latter mapping fails, then we do expect to find variability with respect to gender-marking. In this case, L1 transfer may initially play an important role – say, for a native French speaker acquiring English whose morphology picks out the "wrong" (i.e., the L1 "agreement") feature to encode, resulting in something like *her wife* where a native speaker would say *his wife*.

In Patty's case, one could conceivably "blame" L1 transfer only to the extent that (spoken) Chinese does not morphologically distinguish any pronominal gender at all, leaving her with no knowledge of the category and perhaps making it harder to acquire. However, this explanation is quite unsatisfactory, since neither does her L1 morphologically distinguish pronominal case, and as demonstrated earlier, her case-marking is perfect.

My own (admittedly sketchy) view of the matter is that the Infl features that motivate case assignment are far more fundamental to the derivational computation than gender, such that Patty may have already had some a priori knowledge of what to "look for" in the L2 input. Grammatical gender, on the other hand, is a more purely morphological category, requiring an additional "layer" of mapping.

To illustrate what this means, let us digress briefly by way of comparison to Russian, for an example *par excellence* of intricate mapping from feature to form for case, based on an example from Beard (1995:256–7). Similar to English, subjects of finite clauses in Russian are assigned nominative case; subjects of infinitives are assigned dative case (of course, English selects "object" pronouns for these). Subjects of NPs, as in "Ivan's appearance" are, also similar to English, assigned genitive case. Once computational feature-checking has occurred, the syntax-to-morphology mapping proceeds via an algorithm that Beard roughly characterizes as follows (p. 256, (11.2)):

(6)   Iff Subject and within domain NP, then Genitive;
      Iff Subject and within domain [– Infl], then Dative;
      Iff Subject and within domain [+ Infl], then Nominative.

Focusing on genitive case assignment, Beard points out that mapping from the syntax to the morphological entity "Genitive" still does not directly predict the correct spell-out; rather, another complex algorithm is required to map the morphological category "Genitive" to Phonetic Form (PF) based on noun class, number and/or stem phonology. For Russian, this looks something like the following (p. 257, (11.4)):

(7)   If Genitive, and:
      a.   Class 1, suffix /a/;
      b.   Class 2/3, suffix /i/;
      c.   Class 4 (plural), then
           (i)   if stem ends on /j/ or a "nonsharp" consonant, suffix /ov/;
           (ii)   if stem ends on a "sharp" consonant, suffix /ej/;
           (iii) otherwise, null.

Of course, the Russian case system is much more complex than that of English, interacting with a more complicated noun class system and marking case on all NPs rather than just pronouns. The point of going through this example, however, is to analogously illustrate the complexity of English for a learner whose L1 marks neither case nor gender – in very broad terms, note the overall similarity to the mapping procedure for spelling out English possessive pronouns. Once the syntax licenses case assignment (or derivational feature-checking takes place, in minimalist terms) and maps the output to "Genitive" in the morphological component, yet another mapping is required which for third-person pronouns will be further conditioned (as in Russian) by gender (i.e., noun class) and number, along the (oversimplified) lines of the following:

(8)   If Genitive, third-person, and:
      a.   "Class 1" (masc.), select "his";
      b.   "Class 2" (fem.), select "her";
      c.   "Class 3" (neuter), select "its";

In other words, although the English case system is "simple" compared with that of Russian, there are still multiple layers of complexity involved in mapping to PF. Patty's English Interlanguage flawlessly executes the first mapping – to Case – but occasionally falters with the next added layer – the additional mapping to gender required for third-person pronouns. This also happens to be a layer farther removed from the syntactic computation (see n. 13).

Patty's verbal affixation shows similar evidence of difficulties with feature-to-form mapping in that her morphology misses or mis-identifies the features conditioning "affix-hopping" which in English interacts with modality, perfective aspect and negation in a somewhat complicated way. Patty occasionally produces utterances which exemplify this difficulty (from Lardiere, 1998a):

(9)   *I was still wrote to my friend*
      I'm start to have a lot of friends
      my heart would bounding
      I can never got that right

And finally, there is the obvious discrepancy between the rates for suppletive vs. affixal marking – apparently robust throughout the (adult) L2 literature, which similarly points to a post-computational mapping problem.

To conclude, I suspect that it is among the increasingly complex "outer"-layer mappings from morphology to PF that we are likely to find the greatest vulnerability to "fossilization" and "critical period" effects. Ultimately, the issue of whether (adult) second language acquisition is constrained by UG or not will thus only be resolvable if we are able to clarify for ourselves whether by "UG" we mean only the syntactic computational component (as is often traditionally assumed), or also the mapping procedures that get us from the syntax to PF, and which seem to be the source of much of the divergence between adult and child language acquisition outcomes. Since, as Aronoff (1994:166) points out, even the most complex morphological systems of natural languages must be learnable and hence, conform to "universal principles of grammar," the study of these systems in second language grammars will play an important role in contributing to this clarification.

Notes

1   The term "Separation Hypothesis" is particularly associated with Beard, especially his (1995), but see other morphological literature as well which relies on this distinction or "separation" between feature and form, e.g., Anderson (1992), Aronoff (1994) and Halle and Marantz (1993).

2   Under DM, however, this is true only to the extent that *all* lexical items receive their phonological matrices post-syntactically; in other words, unlike other current

lexeme-based models (e.g., Anderson, 1992; Aronoff, 1994; Beard, 1995), DM does not treat grammatical morphemes differently from lexemes (both are referred to as "vocabulary").

3 Chomsky's (1995:233) own description of "strength" is as follows:

> A strong feature has two properties. First, it triggers an overt operation, before Spell-Out. Second, it induces cyclicity: a strong feature cannot be "passed" by α that would satisfy it, and later checked by β . . . Apart from its problems and limitations, formulation of strength in terms of PF convergence is a restatement of the basic property, not a true explanation. In fact, there seems to be no way to improve upon the bare statement of the properties of strength. Suppose, then, that we put an end to evasion and simply define a strong feature as one that a derivation "cannot tolerate": . . . a strong feature triggers an *overt* operation to eliminate it by checking. [Emphasis in original.]

4 As Rohrbacher points out, one problem with assuming referential, substantive status for agreement affixes is that it (incorrectly) predicts that in verb-raising languages such as French there should be no "non-natural" person/number agreement such as that found in the colloquial use of the 3sg. form for impersonal *on* to express 1pl. meaning. To this we might add the potential learnability difficulties for children in figuring out what it is exactly that makes agreement affixes in one language "referential" but in others not. For extensive discussion on the (non-) lexemic status of affixes, see Beard (1995).

5 Pollock analyzes -*er* as a [–realis] Mood marker, and -*i* as a past Tense marker.

6 Phillips notes that although this default form is often the infinitive, it need not be; other forms, such as participles, may be selected as the default.

7 See Beard (1995), Bybee (1985) and Pinker (1984) for related discussion on this point.

8 One interesting characteristic of early L1 production data found not only by Clahsen but by other researchers as well is the correct use of suppletive agreement (e.g., the differentiated forms of *be* in English or *sein* and modal forms in German) at a (comparatively) early stage, i.e., well before the regular lexical verb paradigm is acquired. Clahsen and Penke (1992) note, for instance, that from a very early stage of Simone's development "there are practically no errors in the use of modals and *sein*" (p. 199). Clahsen and Penke do not count suppletives as instances of productive agreement because such forms are "listed in the lexicon" and "not subject to regular affixation" (p. 199). However, with respect to syntactic feature-matching, it is not at all clear that suppletive forms are irrelevant, since the appropriate feature-matching suppletive must still be selected and the feature must be checked. Especially recast within the Minimalist Program, under which all items drawn from the lexicon are already (featurally) inflected, the early correct use of suppletive agreement forms suggests that a feature-checking mechanism must already be in place by that point; otherwise we might expect to find random or mismatched suppletive forms (along the lines suggested earlier by Borer and Rohrbacher). I return to this point below.

9 Of course, this assumption itself rests on the somewhat circular theoretical notion that all inflectional morphology must have a functional categorial correlate, or "mirror" à la Baker (1988), in the syntactic representation, raising the possibility that we are in some sense conflating notational description with the (substantive) object of that description.

10 Vainikka and Young-Scholten (1994) operationalized "acquisition" as the production of a correct agreement affix in at least 60 percent of raised lexical verbs (i.e., excluding the copula, modals and auxiliaries) and a minimum of two correct instances

of at least four different suffixes of the verbal agreement paradigm. Similar to Clahsen and Penke (1992) (see n. 8), Vainikka and Young-Scholten excluded auxiliary/copular/modal forms from consideration, contending that these "do not reflect the productive paradigm in German" (1994:279). Interestingly, however, they note that the distinct suppletive forms of *sein* "to be" do appear to be acquired considerably earlier than the regular affixal paradigm (compatible with the L1 findings of Clahsen and Penke, 1992) and may function as a more salient "trigger" for projecting AgrP among adults (p. 296).

Again, given the theoretical assumptions of the Minimalist Program, the early differentiated use of suppletive forms suggests that some feature-checking mechanism is indeed in place, implicating the presence in the syntactic representation of a functional Agr category.

11 Although this assumption would presumably be different under the Minimalist Program, where lexical items are inserted fully inflected. The question still arises, however, of whether by "inflected" we are referring to feature assignment or morphological spell-out.

12 Given that Eubank assumes that affixes are "lexical items" and also given standard assumptions of Saussurian arbitrariness between the features of lexical items and their phonological form, it is not clear (except for cognate items) why learners would ever transfer· actual affixes – i.e., their PF spell-out – any more than they would transfer the PF spell-out for any other lexical item (e.g., *book*), and, by the same token, why knowledge of the features associated with L1 affixes would be any more or less available than knowledge of the features for other L1 lexical items. (And cf. Selinker and Lakshmanan, 1993 and especially Odlin, 1998 for a discussion of bound morphology transfer.)

13 It is not clear to what extent the kind of feature-specification required for the extensive noun-class agreement system in Bantu languages is similar to the specification of (conceptual) phi-features for person/number commonly assumed for the Indo-European languages that have formed the basis for most acquisition (and theoretical) analyses. Though the arrangement of Chichewa nouns into 18 or so noun classes seems clearly lexically determined, it also seems unlikely that these grammaticalized class-denoting *affixes* are themselves in any way "referential" or "lexemic" in Rohrbacher's (1994) sense; rather they seem closer to Aronoff's (1994) depiction of purely morphological categories or "morphology by itself."

14 For additional arguments, see also Epstein, Flynn and Martohardjono, 1996; Grondin and White, 1996; Schwartz and Sprouse, 1994, 1996; White, 1996.

15 Genitive casemarking on pronouns is also virtually perfect (we find one instance of *mine* instead of target *my*). However, *affixal* genitive casemarking on full DPs (e.g., *John's book*) is sometimes missing, suggesting once again that suppletive forms are more likely to be acquired than affixal ones in adult L2 acquisition, as suggested by Vainikka and Young-Scholten (1996) (and see n. 10). The perfect distribution of pronominal case (which is suppletive in English) along with the better results for suppletive vs. affixal agreement presented in the next section strongly suggest a spell-out, rather than a syntactic computational problem as an explanation for variability in morphological form and fossilization. I will return again to this issue in section 5.

16 An additional interesting and important aspect of the data is that suppletive agreement for all finite nonpast contexts of auxiliary and copular *be* is highly accurate (78–95 percent), again raising a question about whether these contexts should really be eliminated from consideration when assessing agreement, as is routinely the case in most studies.

References

Anderson, S. (1992) *A-morphous Morphology*. Cambridge: Cambridge University Press.

Aronoff, M. (1994) *Morphology by Itself: Stems and Inflectional Classes*. Cambridge, MA: MIT Press.

Baker, M. (1988) *Incorporation: A Theory of Grammatical Function-changing*. Chicago: University of Chicago Press.

Beard, R. (1995) *Lexeme-morpheme Base Morphology*. Albany, NY: SUNY Press.

Beck, M.-L. (in press) L2 acquisition and obligatory head movement: English-speaking learners of German and the Local Impairment Hypothesis. To appear in *Studies in Second Language Acquisition*.

Bley-Vroman, R. (1989) What is the logical problem of foreign language learning? In S. Gass and J. Schachter (eds.), *Linguistic Perspectives on Second Language Acquisition*. NY: Cambridge University Press.

Borer, H. and Rohrbacher, B. (1997) Features and projections: arguments for the Full Competence Hypothesis. In E. Hughes, M. Hughes and A. Greenhill (eds.), *Proceedings of the 21st Annual Boston University Conference on Language Development*, vol. 1, pp. 24–35. Somerville, MA: Cascadilla Press.

Bybee, J. (1985) *Morphology: A Study of the Relation Between Meaning and Form*. Amsterdam: John Benjamins.

Chomsky, N. (1995) *The Minimalist Program*. Cambridge, MA: MIT Press.

Clahsen, H. (1990/1991) Constraints on parameter setting: a grammatical analysis of some acquisition stages in German child language. *Language Acquisition* 1: 361–91.

—— and Muysken, P. (1986) The availability of Universal Grammar to adult and child learners. *Second Language Research* 2: 93–119.

—— and Penke, M. (1992) The acquisition of agreement morphology and its syntactic consequences. In J. Meisel (ed.), *The Acquisition of Verb Placement: Functional Categories and V2 Phenomena in Language Acquisition*, pp. 181–223. Dordrecht: Kluwer.

Déprez, V. and Pierce, A. (1993) Negation and functional projections in early grammar. *Linguistic Inquiry* 24: 25–67.

di Sciullo, A. M. (1992) Deverbal compounds and the external argument. In I. M. Roca (ed.), *Thematic structure: Its Role in Grammar*, pp. 65–78. Dordrecht: Foris.

Epstein, S., Flynn, S. and Martohardjono, G. (1996) Second language acquisition: theoretical and experimental issues in contemporary research. *Behavioral and Brain Sciences* 19: 677–714.

Eubank, L. (1996) Negation in early German–English interlanguage: more valueless features in the L2 initial state. *Second Language Research* 12: 73–106.

—— (1993/1994) On the transfer of parametric values in L2 development. *Language Acquisition* 3: 183–208.

—— and Grace, S. (1996) Where's the mature language? Where's the native language? In A. Stringfellow, D. Cahana-Amitay, E. Hughes and A. Zukowski (eds.), *Proceedings of the 20th Annual Boston University Conference on Language Development*, pp. 189–200. Somerville, MA: Cascadilla Press.

——, Bischof, J., Huffstutler, A., Leek, P. and West, C. (1997) "Tom eats slowly cooked eggs": thematic verb-raising in L2 knowledge. *Language Acquisition* 6: 171–99.

Flynn, S., Foley, C., Lust, B. and Martohardjono, G. (1998) Mapping from the initial to the final state: UG at the interface in L1 and L2 acquisition. Paper presented at the Annual Meeting of the Linguistic Society of America, New York.

Gavruseva, L. and Lardiere, D. (1996) The emergence of extended phrase structure in child L2 acquisition. In A. Stringfellow, D. Cahana-Amitay, E. Hughes and A. Zukowski (eds.), *Proceedings of the 20th Annual Boston University Conference on Language Development*, pp. 225–36. Somerville, MA: Cascadilla Press.

Grimshaw, J. (1994) Minimal projection and clause structure. In Lust, B., Suñer, M. and Whitman, J. (eds.), *Syntactic Theory and First Language Acquisition: Cross-linguistic Perspectives*, vol. 1. Hillsdale, NJ: Lawrence Erlbaum.

Grondin, N. and White, L. (1996) Functional categories in child L2 acquisition of French. *Language Acquisition 5*: 1–34.

Haegeman, L. (1995) Root infinitives, tense and truncated structures. *Language Acquisition 4*: 205–55.

Halle, M. and Marantz, A. (1993) Distributed morphology and the pieces of inflection. In Hale, K. and Keyser, S. J. (eds.), *The View from Building 20: Essays in Linguistics in Honor of Sylvain Bromberger*, pp. 111–67. Cambridge, MA: MT Press.

Haznedar, B. and Schwartz, B. D. (1997) Are there optional infinitives in child L2 acquisition? In E. Hughes, M. Hughes and A. Greenhill (eds.), *Proceedings of the 21st Annual Boston University Conference on Language Development*, vol. 1, pp. 257–68. Somerville, MA: Cascadilla Press.

Hoekstra, T., Hyams, N. and Becker, M. (1997) The underspecification of Number and the licensing of root infinitives. In E. Hughes, M. Hughes and A. Greenhill (eds.), *Proceedings of the 21st Annual Boston University Conference on Language Development*, vol. 1, pp. 293–306. Somerville, MA: Cascadilla Press.

Krämer, I. (1993) The licensing of subjects in early child language. In Phillips, C. (ed.), *Papers on Case and Agreement II. MITWPL 19*: 197–212.

Lardiere, D. (1998a) Case and tense in the "fossilized" steady-state. *Second Language Research 14* (1): 1–26.

—— (1998b) Dissociating syntax from morphology in a divergent L2 end-state grammar. *Second Language Research 14* (4): 359–75.

—— (1994) The Acquisition of Word-formation Rules for English Synthetic Compounding. Ph.D. dissertation, Boston University.

—— and Schwartz, B. D. (1997) Feature-marking in the L2 development of deverbal compounds. *Journal of Linguistics 33*: 325–53.

Meisel, J. M. (1994) Getting FAT: finiteness, agreement and tense in early grammars. In Meisel, J. (ed.), *Bilingual First Language Acquisition: French and German Grammatical Development*, pp. 89–129. Amsterdam: John Benjamins.

Odlin, T. (1998) Some evidence for the transferability of bound morphology. Paper presented at the Meeting of the American Association of Applied Linguistics, Seattle, March 1998.

Orr, G. J. (1987) *Aspects of the Second Language Acquisition of Chichewa Noun Class Morphology*. Doctoral dissertation, UCLA.

Phillips, C. (1996) Root infinitives are finite. In A. Stringfellow, D. Cahana-Amitay, E. Hughes and A. Zukowski (eds.), *Proceedings of the 20th Annual Boston University Conference on Language Development*, pp. 588–99. Somerville, MA: Cascadilla Press.

—— (1995) Syntax at age two: crosslinguistic differences. *MITWPL 26*.

Pierce, A. (1992) *Language Acquisition and Syntactic Theory: A Comparative Analysis of French and English Child Grammars*. Dordrecht: Kluwer.

Pinker, S. (1984) *Language Learnability and Language Development*. Cambridge, MA: Harvard University Press.

Poeppel, D. and Wexler, K. (1993) The full competence hypothesis of clause structure in early German. *Language 69*: 1–33.

Pollock, J.-Y. (1997) Notes on clause structure. In L. Haegeman (ed.), *Elements of Grammar*, pp. 237–79. Dordrecht: Kluwer.

—— (1989) Verb movement, Universal Grammar, and the structure of **IP**. *Linguistic Inquiry* 20: 365–424.

Prévost, P. and White, L. (in press) Truncation and missing inflection in second language acquisition. To appear in M. A. Friedmann and L. Rizzi (eds.), *The Acquisition of Syntax*. Longman.

Radford, A. (1996) Phrase structure and functional categories. In P. Fletcher and B. MacWhinney (eds.), *The Handbook of Child Language*, pp. 483–507. Oxford: Blackwell.

—— (1990) *Syntactic Theory and the Acquisition of English Syntax*. Oxford: Blackwell.

Rizzi, L. (1993/1994) Some notes on linguistic theory and language development: the case of root infinitives. *Language Acquisition* 3: 371–93.

Rohrbacher, B. (1994) The Germanic VO Languages and the Full Paradigm. Ph.D. dissertation, University of Massachusetts, Amherst.

Schwartz, B. D. (1996) Now for some facts, with a focus on development and an explicit role for the L1. [Comment on Epstein, Flynn and Martohardjono]. *Behavioral and Brain Sciences* 19: 739–40.

—— (1995) "Transfer" and L2 acquisition of syntax: where are we now? Plenary address at the Second Language Research Forum, Cornell University, Ithaca, NY, Oct. 1. MS., University of Durham.

—— and Sprouse, R. A. (1996) L2 cognitive states and the Full Transfer/Full Access model. *Second Language Research* 12: 40–72.

—— and —— (1994) Word order and nominative case in nonnative language acquisition: a longitudinal study of (L1 Turkish) German interlanguage. In T. Hoekstra and B. D. Schwartz (eds.), *Language Acquisition Studies in Generative Grammar*, pp. 317–68. Amsterdam: John Benjamins.

Selinker, L. and Lakshmanan, U. (1993) Language transfer and fossilization: the Multiple Effects Principle. In S. Gass and L. Selinker (eds.), *Language Transfer in Language Learning*, pp. 197–216. Amsterdam: John Benjamins.

Vainikka, A. (1993/1994) Case in the development of English syntax. *Language Acquisition* 3: 257–325.

—— and Young-Scholten, M. (1996) Gradual development of L2 phrase structure. *Second Language Research* 12: 7–39.

—— and —— (1994) Direct access to X'-theory: evidence from Turkish and Korean adults learning German. In T. Hoekstra and B. D. Schwartz (eds.), *Language Acquisition Studies in Generative Grammar*, pp. 265–316. Amsterdam: John Benjamins.

Verrips, M. and Weissenborn, J. (1992) Routes to verb placement in early German and French: the independence of finiteness and agreement. In J. Meisel (ed.), *The Acquisition of Verb Placement: Functional Categories and V2 Phenomena in Language Development*, pp. 283–331. Dordrecht: Kluwer.

Vikner, S. (1996) V^0–to-I^0 movement and inflection for person. Unpublished MS., Rutgers University, forthcoming in L. Haegeman (ed.), *The New Comparative Syntax*. Longman.

—— (1995) V^0–to-I^0 movement and inflection for person in all tenses. *Working papers in Scandinavian syntax* 55: 1–27.

Wexler, K. (1994) Optional infinitives, head movement and the economy of derivations. In D. Lightfoot and N. Hornstein (eds.), *Verb Movement*, pp. 305–50. Cambridge, Cambridge University Press.

White, L. (1996) Clitics in L2 French. In H. Clahsen (ed.), *Generative Perspectives on Language Acquisition: Empirical Findings, Theoretical Considerations, Crosslinguistic Comparisons*, pp. 335–68. Amsterdam: John Benjamins.

4

Second Language Acquisition: From Initial to Final State*

Lydia White

Introduction

Over the last two decades, researchers interested in investigating the linguistic competence of second language (L2) learners have drawn heavily on current generative grammar in order to understand the nature of the mental representation, or interlanguage grammar, attained by L2 learners. The enriched relationship between linguistic theory and L2 acquisition theory can largely be attributed to the introduction of the Principles and Parameters framework (Chomsky, 1981). This framework accommodated variation between languages by introducing the concept of parameters; in addition, proposals for universal principles became much more highly developed than they had been in earlier versions of generative grammar. The emphasis on parameters allowed L2 researchers to look at variation between languages and the role of language transfer, investigating whether or not parameters of Universal Grammar (UG) can be (re)set in L2 acquisition (e.g., Flynn, 1987; White, 1985b). As far as universal principles are concerned, much research focused on the general question of whether UG remains available in non-primary acquisition, and whether interlanguages are natural languages, constrained by principles of UG (e.g., Bley-Vroman, 1990; Schachter, 1989; White, 1988).

* An earlier version of this chapter was presented at the 1995 Boston University Conference on Language Development and appears in the Proceedings (White, 1996b). This research was conducted with the support of research grants from the Social Sciences and Humanities Research Council of Canada and the Fonds pour la Formation de Chercheurs et l'Aide à la Recherche. I would like to thank Kevin Gregg and Gita Martohardjono for comments and suggestions.

More recently, L2 research has explored the nature of developing inter-language grammars, as well as looking at the initial and final states of inter-language knowledge. In this chapter, I identify and discuss three main themes in L2 acquisition research conducted within the UG framework:

1 Theories about the L2 initial state and the kind of grammatical know-ledge that the L2 learner starts out with.
2 Theories about stages of development, the nature of the stages, and the kind of grammar development that takes place.
3 Theories about the final state or ultimate attainment possible in L2 acquisition.

Research on these three areas has not taken a chronological path. In the first decade of UG-based L2 acquisition research (starting in the early 1980s), the main thrust of research was on whether or not UG is available to L2 learners during the course of acquisition. Assumptions about the initial state and final outcome were often implicit; research concentrated primarily on various points in development, looking for evidence as to whether learners' hypotheses are constrained by principles of UG and whether they can set or reset parameters. Detailed investigation of the L2 initial state is very much a current concern, while ultimate attainment has received increasing attention in recent years, often in the context of the critical periods hypothesis.

L1 Acquisition

In first language (L1) acquisition, the learner's task is to acquire a grammar on the basis of input, a grammar which constitutes a mental representation of the language being acquired, and which is involved in the comprehension and production of language. L1 acquisition is assumed to be constrained by UG, since the input is "deficient" in various respects, underdetermining the final grammar (the so-called "poverty of the stimulus" argument or the "logical problem of language acquisition"). UG provides a system of constraints (in the form of principles and parameters) which limit the hypothesis space that the child has to search through, restricting the range of possible grammars to be considered. Acquisition proceeds on the basis of input interacting with principles and parameters of UG, leading to the construction of a grammar or series of grammars; eventually, the child arrives at a steady state grammar, as schematized in figure 4.1.

In a sense one can think of L2 acquisition research as starting from where L1 acquisition research ends. In the L2 acquisition field, implicit or explicit assumptions are made about the end result of L1 acquisition (that is, about the steady state grammar achieved by native speakers). Linguistic theory provides some idea of what is attained in L1 acquisition; unfortunately, linguistic

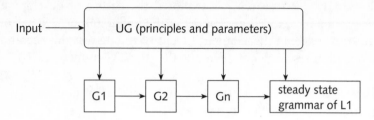

Figure 4.1 L1 acquisition

theory and L1 acquisition theory do not tell us what happens to aspects of UG that are not required in any particular L1. However, there are major implications for L2 acquisition, depending on whether properties of grammar which have not been activated in a particular L1 wither away or become otherwise inaccessible.

Functional categories, such as determiner (Det), inflection (Infl) and complementizer (Comp) and their associated projections, DP, IP and CP, provide an example. Theories about L1 acquisition of functional categories can be divided into two main positions:

1 All functional categories are available from the beginning; this is referred to as the "full competence" or "strong continuity" approach (e.g., Hyams, 1992; Poeppel and Wexler, 1993). On some versions of the full competence hypothesis, however, certain functional categories may initially lack fully specified features (Hoekstra and Hyams, 1995; Wexler, 1994).
2 Functional categories are initially absent and emerge gradually in response to triggering input according to the "lexical learning" or "weak continuity" hypothesis (Clahsen, Eisenbeiss and Vainikka, 1994) or as a result of maturation (Radford, 1990) or as a combination of both maturation and input ("structure building", Guilfoyle and Noonan, 1992).

The full competence approach assumes that all functional categories are present in the child's initial state. The question of relevance to L2 acquisition is what happens to functional categories that any particular L1 happens not to realize. One possibility is that grammars retain all possible functional categories, even those they do not make use of. Another possibility is that functional categories that are not required in a particular grammar wither away in some sense.

On the weak continuity approach, functional categories are assumed not to be present from the beginning; some or all are unavailable initially. Functional categories emerge as triggered by input. Thus, languages (and language acquirers) draw from an inventory of possible functional categories and associated features; a particular grammar instantiates only a subset of the available possibilities. Again, the question of interest to L2 researchers is what happens to the functional categories that are not triggered in the course of L1 acquisition. They do not form part of the L1 grammar – does the full inventory remain available via UG so that acquisition of new L2 functional categories can successfully take place?[1]

These theories differ in their assumptions about the L1 initial state, as well as the course of grammar development. Possibly, they also differ over the end state (namely whether or not all functional categories are represented in all grammars) but because this has no particular consequences for native speaker grammars, this issue is not pursued. However, there are consequences for L2 acquisition. Do functional categories, principles or parameter settings unused in the L1 "wither" and become inaccessible in L2 acquisition or is the full inventory present and accessible?

As we shall see, certain L2 researchers effectively assume withering – the L2 learner is left with nothing more than those categories, features and settings instantiated in the L1 grammar, any other options effectively disappearing. In contrast, other researchers assume that the full range of options remains available after L1 acquisition is over, including options that have not been exercised in the L1.

The L2 Initial State

The L2 acquisition task is similar to the L1 task: the learner must acquire a mental representation on the basis of deficient input (White, 1985a, 1989b). But the means, the process and the end result may well be different; indeed these are matters that have been the subject of extensive debate. What does the L2 learner start from? What mechanisms does the L2 learner use? What does the L2 learner achieve? At issue within the framework we are adopting is whether or not interlanguage grammars are subject to the constraints of UG.

Current research focuses particularly on the nature of the linguistic knowledge available at the commencement of L2 acquisition, including consideration of the extent to which the L2 learner is influenced by the L1 grammar (if at all), whether the L1 grammar is adopted as the L2 learner's initial theory of the L2 and, if so, whether all or only parts of the L1 grammar are adopted. Much of this debate centers on the nature, availability and role of functional categories and associated functional features, drawing on recent developments in linguistic theory and L1 acquisition theory.

Five different perspectives on the L2 initial state can be identified. They can be distinguished from each other on the basis of two issues: the extent of presumed involvement of the L1 grammar (full transfer, partial transfer or no transfer) and the extent to which UG constrains interlanguage representations. The debate over UG is often phrased in terms of "access" (full access versus partial or no access), although there are problems with this terminology, as we shall see.

Full Transfer/Partial Access

Extending Schwartz and Sprouse's (1996) terminology, I shall refer to the first approach to the initial state as Full Transfer/Partial Access. This is the position that the L1 grammar constitutes the learner's representation of the L2 and is used to analyze the L2 input; in other words, the L2 initial state consists of the L1 final state. Properties of UG not instantiated in the L1 grammar are not available; for this reason, this position is sometimes referred to as the "no access" position (e.g., by Epstein, Flynn and Martohardjono, 1996). However, the term "no access" is misleading; most proponents assume that certain UG effects will, in fact, be manifested in interlanguage grammars, albeit weakly via the L1, as is the case, for example, for Bley-Vroman's (1990) Fundamental Difference Hypothesis.[2] Indeed, this position is also sometimes known as the "no-parameter resetting" hypothesis, which is perhaps a more accurate reflection of what it stands for.

This view also has implications for the course of development: interlanguage grammars (ILGs) will not show new parameter settings (Clahsen and Hong, 1995; Clahsen and Muysken, 1989) or new feature specifications (Hawkins and Chan, 1997; Liceras and Díaz, in press), as well as for ultimate attainment, which will necessarily be different from the grammar of a native speaker. This position is illustrated in figure 4.2.

Although Full Transfer/Partial Access takes the L1 grammar as the starting point, this does not mean that proponents are committed to the impossibility of grammar development, though they differ radically over what kind of change is assumed to take place and the extent to which L1 principles and parameters can accommodate L2 input. Earlier versions of this approach assumed no parameter resetting and relative inflexibility of UG principles, such that a principle existing in the L1 could not accommodate a totally new situation in the L2 (e.g., Schachter, 1989). More recently there have been suggestions that UG principles remain active, even if these principles are available only via the L1, such that L2 learners can arrive at UG-consistent grammars which differ from the L1 (Tsimpli and Roussou, 1991).

An example of an L1-based UG principle being active enough to constrain the acquisition of novel properties of the L2 is provided by Kanno (1996).[3]

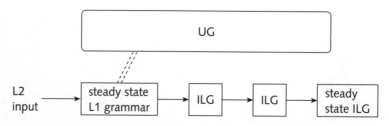

Figure 4.2 Full Transfer/Partial Access

She shows that beginning learners of Japanese are highly sensitive to a subject/object asymmetry in case particle deletion: they recognize that accusative case particles can be freely dropped, whereas nominative particles cannot, even though the L1 (English) has no such phenomenon. Kanno attributes knowledge of this distinction to the operation of the Empty Category Principle (available via the L1 grammar) in a new domain (found in the L2 but not the L1).

No Transfer/Full Access

The next approach, which I will call No Transfer/Full Access, assumes that the L2 grammar is acquired on the basis of UG principles and parameters interacting directly with L2 input, as shown in figure 4.3.[4] On this view, the L1 final state does not constitute the L2 learner's grammar or mental representation at any stage. (Figure 4.3 illustrates this by dissociating the L1 grammar from the L2 acquisition system. This is not meant to imply that UG was not involved in the acquisition of the L1, nor that it is no longer implicated in adult L1 knowledge.) Instead, UG is assumed to constitute the initial state for L2 acquisition. Thus the L2 learner's initial state parallels that of the L1 acquirer, and L1 and L2 developing grammars are also expected to be similar. All properties of UG are available for L2 acquisition, including new parameter settings, functional categories, and feature values. In other words, any options or choices not exemplified in the L1 still remain available; the content of UG itself (a) does not change as a result of L1 acquisition (that is, nothing withers away) and (b) is accessible in non-primary acquisition at any age.

This position is advanced by Epstein, Flynn and Martohardjono (1996, 1998), Flynn and Martohardjono (1994) and Flynn (1996). Somewhat confusingly, although these researchers explicitly exclude properties of the L1 grammar from the interlanguage representation, they nevertheless assume some role for the L1, without specifying or clarifying its precise status. Indeed, their position is inconsistent. In spite of their claim that the L1 grammar does not constitute the initial state for the L2 learner, Flynn (1987, 1996) and Flynn and Martohardjono (1994) argue that L2 acquisition involves the assignment of "additional" parametric values where L1 and L2 do not match

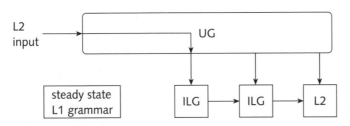

Figure 4.3   No Transfer/Full Access

in parameter settings. It is surely only if the L2 learner starts from the possibilities exemplified in the L1 that the issues of match and mismatch arise.

Another recent proponent of the No Transfer/Full Access view is Platzack (1996) who argues that both L1 and L2 learners resort to unmarked grammars, defined by him in terms of the Minimalist assumption that movement is costly (Chomsky, 1995). Platzack claims that all features in initial grammars are weak (thus not motivating movement in the syntax). For L2 acquisition, this means that the learner will initially assume weak feature values even if the L1 grammar has strong features and even if the L2 input motivate strong features. (White's (1991a, 1991b, 1992a) results indicate that French learners of English transfer a strong Agr feature from the L1, hence inappropriately allowing verb movement over adverbs in the L2, which has weak Agr, suggesting that Platzack's proposal is incorrect.)

As far as development is concerned, No Transfer/Full Access predicts that the grammars of L1 and L2 acquirers should be essentially alike; furthermore, there will be no differences in developing interlanguage grammars attributable to the mother tongue of the learner. This view further predicts that the L2 learner should in principle converge on the L2 grammar; in other words, ultimate attainment should be similar to that of native speakers.

Full Transfer/Full Access

Figure 4.4 illustrates the third position, Full Transfer/Full Access (Schwartz, 1998; Schwartz and Sprouse, 1994, 1996, this volume, chapter 5). According to this approach, L1 and L2 acquisition differ with respect to their starting point but are similar with respect to involvement of UG. The kind of transfer that is assumed is not transfer of surface properties but transfer of the L1 grammar with associated "deep" consequences (clustering of parametric properties, syntactic consequences of certain functional categories and feature values, etc.). Full Transfer/Full Access shares characteristics of the two previously discussed approaches. As in Full Transfer/Partial Access, the L1 grammar is assumed to constitute the L2 initial state. As in No Transfer/Full Access, properties of UG not exemplified in the L1 are assumed still to be available to constrain interlanguage grammars. The learner, faced with L2 input that must be accounted for, initially uses a representation based entirely on the L1

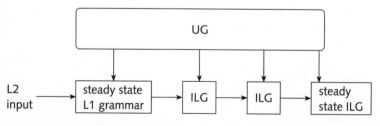

Figure 4.4   Full Transfer/Full Access

grammar. However, where properties of the L2 input suggest that the L1 grammar is inadequate, there is restructuring. When the L1 grammar is unable to accommodate the L2 input, the learner has recourse to UG options, including new parameter settings, functional categories and feature values, in order to arrive at an analysis more appropriate to the L2 input.

An earlier version of this position was exemplified by my own work on parameters (e.g., White, 1985b, 1989a), which maintained that L2 learners initially apply the L1 value of a parameter to the L2 data, with subsequent resetting in response to L2 input. Schwartz (1998) and Schwartz and Sprouse (1994, 1996, this volume, chapter 5) extend this view, arguing that it is not just L1 parameter settings that are applied to the L2 but the L1 grammar in its entirety.

According to Full Transfer/Full Access, the L1 is seen as the initial state; nevertheless, there is no commitment as to how long this state lasts. L2 data might motivate change more or less immediately. There will also be circumstances depending on the L1s and L2s in question, where the positive L2 input will not motivate restructuring (Schwartz and Gubala-Ryzak, 1992; Schwartz and Sprouse, 1994; White, 1989a, 1989b). In effect, the grammar that the learner has hypothesized acts as a filter, preventing certain aspects of the L2 input from being noticed; hence, reanalysis does not take place. (See Brown, this volume, chapter 1, for related proposals for phonology.)

Full Transfer/Full Access predicts that grammars of L1 and L2 learners will differ, prior to any parameter resetting, as will the grammars of learners of different L1s. It is also not expected that learners will necessarily converge on the L2 grammar, since properties of the L1 grammar may prevent the learner from noticing relevant properties of the L2, in effect leading to fossilization at a point short of native-like competence.

Partial Transfer/Full Access

There are a number of researchers who hold that the L2 initial state draws on properties of both the L1 and UG concurrently (varying in what aspects of the L1 grammar they assume to be present in the initial state, as well as what aspects of UG). This situation, which we will term Partial Transfer/Full Access, is diagrammed in figure 4.5.

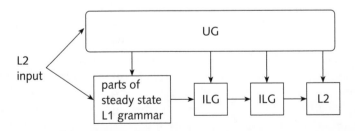

Figure 4.5   Partial Transfer/Full Access

Proponents are Vainikka and Young-Scholten (1994, 1996a, 1996b), who propose that only L1 lexical categories are found in the initial L2 grammar. Functional categories are not transferred. In the initial state, then, L2 learners are assumed to project NP and VP (with L1 headedness) but not DP, IP, or CP. In this respect, L2 learners are like L1 acquirers, who are also assumed, on the weak continuity hypothesis, to lack functional categories initially (Clahsen, Eisenbeiss and Vainikka, 1994). In response to L2 input, learners gradually project functional categories (drawing on the full inventory in UG), just as L1 acquirers are assumed to do. In principle, L2 learners should converge on the L2 grammar.

Eubank (1994a, 1994b) takes a somewhat different view, maintaining that both L1 lexical categories and L1 functional categories are found in the L2 initial state. Features, however, do not take on L1 values (strong/weak) but are initially unspecified, or inert. In consequence, apparent optionality of certain word orders in early L2 grammars is accounted for. In this work, Eubank assumed that functional categories will eventually become specified for L2 feature values.

In the above views, only part of the L1 grammar is represented in the L2 initial state (either lexical categories alone or lexical and functional categories, the latter lacking their feature strength). White (1996a) makes a somewhat different claim, arguing that L1 lexical and functional categories as well as feature values are adopted in the L2 initial state where possible. However, she maintains that there will be cases where the L1 grammar simply could not constitute an initial theory of the L2, appropriate or inappropriate. The L2 acquisition of functional projections which are not realized in the L1 constitutes such a case, e.g., the acquisition of French clitics by English speakers. In such cases, the L2 learner resorts immediately to options made available by UG, successfully acquiring L2 clitic projections.[5] (See Schwartz, in press, for an opposing view.)

Partial Transfer/Partial Access

In recent work, Beck (1997, in press), Eubank, Beck and Aboutaj (1997) and Eubank, Bischof, Huffstutler, Leek and West (1997) have proposed what amounts to Partial Transfer/Partial Access. In particular, they depart from Eubank (1994a, 1994b), claiming instead that certain functional features never become specified for strong/weak values in the course of L2 development. In other words, L2 grammars are permanently impaired in a local domain (the local impairment hypothesis (Beck, in press)), with a range of consequences not found in native speaker grammars. Since inflectional features are never specified, there is permanent variability in word order, with verbs sometimes raising and sometimes not. On this view, ultimate attainment is necessarily non-native-like. This position is schematized in figure 4.6.

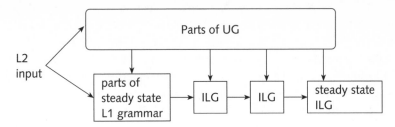

Figure 4.6   Partial Transfer/Partial Access

Evidence for the Initial State: What Counts as Data?

It is not always clear what constitutes appropriate evidence to distinguish between the approaches outlined above, what the relevant data would be or what the existing data show. In part, this is because the positions share a considerable amount of common ground; they make overlapping predictions and certain data simply do not provide the means of distinguishing between them. Indeed, relevant evidence is not confined to data drawn from initial systems.

In investigating the L2 initial state, a number of problems arise relating to data, problems which also have arisen in investigating L1 acquisition. The first problem concerns the use of "absence of evidence as evidence of absence". Radford (1990) and Guilfoyle and Noonan (1992) have used spontaneous production data which show a lack of material associated with functional categories (such as absence of determiners, tensed verbs, agreement, complementizers, etc.) to argue for the absence of functional categories in the initial L1 grammar; Vainikka and Young-Scholten (1994) do the same for L2. However, as a number of researchers have pointed out (Epstein et al., 1996; Grondin and White, 1996), relying only on production data can often lead to an underestimation of an L2 learner's linguistic competence. One cannot automatically assume that late use of a form indicates late acquisition. An abstract category may be acquired even though its morphological realization is lacking; indeed, various syntactic consequences of functional categories may be present in the L2 grammar even in the absence of the relevant morphology (Lardiere, 1998a, 1998b, this volume, chapter 3; Prévost and White, in press).

A related question involves accuracy. Does a learner's use of agreement or tense, for example, have to be accurate in order for one to be able to conclude that Agr or T is present in the grammar? Poeppel and Wexler (1993) argue, for L1 acquisition, that where there is accuracy in agreement, this is compelling evidence for the existence of the associated functional category. However, the converse does not follow; morphological inaccuracy or lack of morphology does not necessarily mean lack of corresponding functional categories. The presence of incorrect agreement markers can be indicative of agreement; such errors would suggest that the learner has certain functional categories in the grammar but has not yet worked out the details of how the categories are realized in the L2 (Epstein et al., 1996; Grondin and White, 1996; Lardiere and Schwartz, 1997). (In fact, Grondin and White (1996) and Prévost and White (in press) report that agreement marking, when present, is accurate in the interlanguage grammars of children and adults.)

Determining how many occurrences of a form are sufficient to count as evidence for the presence of some grammatical property is another area where there has been considerable disagreement. Traditionally, if a form was produced in 90 percent of obligatory contexts, it was counted as having been acquired (Brown, 1973). Vainikka and Young-Scholten (1994) take 60 percent of correct usage as an indication of acquisition of L2 functional categories. Again, usage does not necessarily reflect knowledge or acquisition; some property may be instantiated in the grammar even though it is not used consistently (Epstein et al., 1996; Grondin and White, 1996; Valian, 1991). Emergence may be a more appropriate measure of acquisition than a high incidence of correct use (Meisel, Clahsen and Pienemann, 1981).

Finally, there is the problem that one can never be sure that the first data obtained from any particular learner are in fact relevant to the initial state, even if data elicitation started as soon as the learner first began to speak. After all, there may well be grammar acquisition in the "silent period" that often precedes first productions. Thus, if a theory predicts the non-occurrence of certain phenomena but these are found, it can always be argued that they would have been absent from earlier data. For example, Vainikka and Young-Scholten (1994), on finding evidence suggesting the presence of functional categories in early German L2, suggest that such evidence would have been lacking at an earlier stage. Conversely, if a theory predicts the presence of certain phenomena (such as transfer effects) but these are not found, it could always be argued that they would have been evident at an earlier stage.

Interlanguages and Stages of L2 Development

As a set of constraints on representation, UG places limitations on the form of the grammar, rather than on the acquisition process itself (Borer, 1996; Carroll, 1996; Gregg, 1996). Thus, claims for UG access during the course of acquisition are simply claims that interlanguage grammars will fall within a limited range, specified by UG. Dekydtspotter, Sprouse and Anderson (1998) comment that instead of talking about "full access", we should consider a term like "full restriction", which better represents the role of UG.

With this caveat in mind, let us consider what the various approaches to the initial state have to say about later grammars. Claims about transfer (whether full or partial) relate particularly to the initial state, in that L1-based representation is assumed in the early stages of L2 acquisition but not necessarily beyond (though this is certainly not precluded). Development, then, is in some sense progress away from the L1 grammar, with restructuring in response to the L2 input. Claims about UG access, on the other hand, are crucially relevant beyond the initial state. Whether L2 learners start from UG or the L1 representation (in whole or in part), if UG constrains developing grammars, this will affect the nature of interlanguage grammars at different stages, as well as the final outcome – grammars will fall within the hypothesis space permitted by UG. If there is only partial access to UG, certain kinds of changes to the grammar will not be possible, for example, parameter resetting, and interlanguage grammars may reveal properties not otherwise found in natural language.

Development: Transfer versus No Transfer

Even though full or partial transfer are claims about the initial state, the effects of transfer may be observed in later stages of acquisition, depending on whether or not restructuring of the initial state grammar takes place. All positions except No Transfer/Full Access predict differences between L1 and L2 acquisition and differences between learners of different L1s; that is, they predict evidence of properties of the L1 grammar, although they differ as to what these properties will be and how long they will last. In so far as L1 properties are found in initial grammars or subsequently, the No Transfer/Full Access model is disconfirmed. Research on developmental stages suggests that L2 learners with different mother tongues behave differently with respect to certain properties; for example, White (1985b) found that the interlanguage grammars of French-speaking and Spanish-speaking learners of English differ, with the Spanish speakers at different stages in the acquisition process treating English as if it were a null subject language, while the French speakers did not do so. Vainikka and Young-Scholten (1996b) show that L2 learners of German initially assume word order that reflects the L1: OV if they are native speakers of Korean or Turkish, VO if they are native speakers of Romance. Hawkins and Chan (1997) demonstrate that French-speaking and Chinese-speaking learners of English differ in how they treat English restrictive relative clauses. They argue that the Chinese speakers arrive at an analysis, based on the L1, which does not involve wh-movement, in contrast to the French speakers.

In contrast, other work on developing interlanguage grammars has claimed similarities between learners of different L1s and between L1 and L2 acquisition. If the L2 initial state does not involve the L1 at all, similarities are expected in the grammars adopted at various stages by learners of different L1s. Epstein et al. (1996, 1998) and Flynn (1996) appear to believe that successful acquisition of an L2 property which is not exemplified in the L1 is sufficient to demonstrate lack of L1 involvement in the interlanguage representation; they argue that child and adult Japanese speakers who are intermediate level learners of English successfully acquire English functional categories, hence that they have access to UG independent of the L1.

However, successful attainment of L2 properties in intermediate learners who have been in the L2 environment for a number of years is hardly compelling evidence against transfer. Later similarity in the performance of different groups of learners is consistent both with early differences and with early similarities. If intermediate level learners of different L1s are found to behave similarly, or if learners successfully acquire properties in the L2 which are not found in the L1, such results are equally consistent with Full Transfer, Partial Transfer or No Transfer. Once parameters have been set to L2 values, all Full Access theories predict largely the same kind of grammar development for learners of different L1s, as well as certain similarities between L1 and L2 acquisition and successful attainment of L2 properties. The onus, then, is on those who predict similarity across different learners from the beginning stages to provide data that do indeed address this issue; data from later stages that suggest mastery of L2 properties such as the functional categories investigated by Epstein et al. (1996, 1998), while in principle relevant to the access issue,[6] are in fact irrelevant to the transfer issue.

Development: Full versus Partial Access

As far as UG availability is concerned, the approaches described above cannot be fully assessed without considering interlanguage grammars beyond the initial state. In order to determine whether UG fully or partially constrains interlanguage representations, it is necessary to look at later stages. As we have already seen, No Transfer/Full Access and Full Transfer/Full Access are distinguishable only by their claims about the role of the L1, since both approaches assume UG is actively implicated, with parameter resetting possible in principle, new functional categories and feature values acquirable, etc. As far as partial versus full access claims are concerned, both Full Transfer/Partial Access and Full Transfer/Full Access assume the same initial state (namely the L1 grammar). Thus, the only evidence that can be used to decide between them is evidence about what happens later, namely, presence or absence of parameter resetting, emergence of new functional categories, changes in feature values, or lack thereof, and the presence or absence of UG-inconsistent grammars.

Much former work on the operation of principles and parameters in L2 development tested predictions of the full versus partial access positions. Proponents of Full Transfer/Partial Access focused on apparent failure to observe principles of UG. For example, Schachter's (1989) results showed that L2 learners whose L1s lack syntactic wh-movement fail to recognize Subjacency violations in L2s with wh-movement, thus supporting her claim that they lack the Subjacency Principle. In contrast, research by Thomas (1991, 1993) on L2 reflexive binding suggests that adult L2 learners' grammars are UG-consistent, observing principles such as c-command, and that the L1 is not the source of knowledge of L2 reflexives, since L2 learners acquire properties of reflexives which are very different from those of the L1. More recently, researchers have demonstrated that L2 learners observe the Overt Pronoun Constraint (OPC), whereby in null subject languages an overt pronoun cannot take a quantified antecedent (Montalbetti, 1984). Kanno (1997) has shown that English-speaking learners of Japanese at the intermediate level observe the OPC, as have Perez-Leroux and Glass (1997) for English-speaking learners of Spanish at an advanced level. Since English is not a null subject language and overt pronouns in English can take quantified antecedents, there appears to be nothing in the L1 from which knowledge of this principle could originate, suggesting availability of UG principles independently of the L1.

As far as parameters are concerned, there has been considerable research on parameter resetting, investigating whether parametric properties cluster in the interlanguage grammar, including studies on adjacency (White, 1989a), null subjects (e.g., Lakshmanan, 1994; Liceras, 1989; White, 1985b), verb movement (e.g., White, 1991a, 1991b, 1992a), word order (e.g., Clahsen and Muysken, 1986; Flynn, 1987; Schwartz and Sprouse, 1994) and binding (e.g., Finer and Broselow, 1986; Hirakawa, 1990; Thomas, 1991, 1993). If the L2 initial state consists of the L1 final state (in whole or in part) and UG continues to operate, the L2 learner should restructure the grammar in response to L2 input and the resulting grammar should be UG-constrained, exhibiting properties associated with particular parameter settings. Thus, evidence in favour of parameter resetting is evidence for full access, whereas evidence against it supports partial access. Evidence has, in fact, proved quite conflicting and the debate on parameter resetting continues, currently centering largely on the availability of L2 functional categories and feature values (e.g., Beck, in press; Eubank et al., 1997; Hawkins and Chan, 1997; Liceras and Díaz, in press; Meisel, 1997; Schwartz and Sprouse, 1994; White, 1992a).

In considering the UG access question in L2, there are other outcomes besides successful resetting that can help to determine the extent of UG involvement. If L2 learners arrive at settings which are sanctioned by UG but are those of neither the L1 nor the L2, such outcomes are consistent with full access but are precluded on partial access positions, since, if the L2 learner's only access to UG is via the L1, no other parameter settings are predicted to be acquirable. A number of cases of this kind have been reported, for example by Finer and Broselow (1986) who suggest that L2 learners acquire a parameter value for the Governing Category Parameter which is that neither of the L1 nor L2; as a result, Korean-speaking learners of English treat English reflexives like Russian. In a related vein, duPlessis, Solin, Travis and White (1987) show that learners of German may arrive at a combination of parameter settings which are those of neither L1 nor L2; a similar proposal is made by Schwartz and Sprouse (1994). Clahsen and Hong's (1995) results can also be interpreted in this way; they argue that Korean-speaking learners of German are unable to reset the null subject parameter from the + null subject setting of the L1 to the − null subject of the L2. Specifically, two properties, namely acquisition of agreement and loss of null subjects, do not covary in the interlanguage grammars in the way they do in L1 acquisition of German. However, some of the subjects who failed to arrive at the L2 German value of the parameter in fact seem to have hit upon the Italian value (i.e., allowing rich agreement and null subjects), again suggesting that parameters can be reset to values other than those found in the L1.[7]

Finally, there is another kind of grammar which should not be found in the course of L2 development if there is full access to UG. All Full Access positions predict that interlanguage grammars are necessarily UG-consistent; hence, "wild" grammars (that is, grammars that fail to observe UG constraints) should not be found. Clahsen and Muysken (1986) claimed that the interlanguages of L2 learners of German were unnatural, allowing rightward movement possibilities not found in natural language; duPlessis et al. (1987) and Schwartz and Tomaselli (1990) argued against this position, reanalyzing the German L2 data to show that, on the assumption that these learners had reset the head direction parameter to the L2 value, their grammars fell within the bounds of UG. Similarly, White (1992b), Martohardjono and Gair (1993) and Hawkins and Chan (1997) have argued that L2 grammars showing apparent non-operation of Subjacency (Schachter, 1989) are in fact not "wild" at all; rather, L2 learners of certain L1s adopt a non-movement analysis of English wh-movement, involving the postulation of *pro* (which does not move, hence is not subject to Subjacency). More problematically, Klein (1993, 1995) has found that L2 learners of a variety of ages, levels and L1s assume that null prepositions are possible in wh-questions, while they are never found in this context in natural languages, according to Klein. However, Dekydtspotter et al. (1998) argue, contra Klein, that grammars allowing null prep do in fact fall within the constraints of UG.

Where results suggest problems with parameter resetting, or the setting of only some of a cluster of properties associated with a parameter value, the question arises as to how long one can be expected to wait for evidence of successful parameter resetting. If one investigates the interlanguage grammars of L2 learners at any particular point of development and finds no evidence for parameter resetting, the possibility of grammar change in a subsequent stage cannot be ruled out. (This is reminiscent of the problem of always being able to appeal back to an earlier unobserved stage; here we are appealing forward to a stage not yet passed through.) For this reason, the final state (ultimate attainment) of the L2 learner must be investigated (Borer, 1996; Smith and Tsimpli, 1995; White and Genesee, 1996). We turn now to evidence about the ultimate attainment of L2 learners.

The L2 Final State

In L1 acquisition, the working assumption is that all acquirers of the same language or dialect achieve essentially the same end-state. But this is not the case in L2 acquisition, where we have relatively little idea of what the steady state grammar looks like. Anecdotally, it seems obvious that L2 learners differ from each other in their ultimate attainment, even when one considers learners of the same mother tongue learning the same L2. It appears that people "stop" acquiring their L2 at different points ("fossilization"), thus ending up with different grammars. In recent years there has been a move to investigate the nature of the ultimate achievement of L2 learners. Researchers have deliberately sought out subjects who can be deemed to have completed the L2 acquisition process – they have got as far as they are going to get. Two related issues have been investigated in the context of ultimate attainment: critical periods and near nativeness. More recently, researchers have looked specifically at the issue of non-convergence on the L2 grammar in the final state.

The theories described above make different predictions regarding the final outcome of L2 acquisition. No Transfer/Full Access predicts that convergence on the L2 system will necessarily occur. Indeed, Flynn (1996:150) claims that full access to UG implies exceptionless attainment of L2 competence and that any other view is incoherent. Partial Transfer/Full Access as exemplified by Vainikka and Young-Scholten also predicts convergence. Full Transfer/Partial Access and Partial Transfer/Partial Access, on the other hand, predict that the L2 final state will necessarily be different from native speakers (unless the L1 and L2 happen to coincide with respect to all UG properties). Full Transfer/Full Access and certain versions of Partial Transfer/Full Access do not assume that convergence is guaranteed. Whether or not convergence is possible will depend specifically on the L1s and L2s in question, and relates to whether positive L2 input is available to disconfirm inappropriate L1-based analyses. Second language learners starting with different L1 grammars as the initial state will not in fact be taking the same developmental path. The initial representation, as well as UG, will constrain subsequent hypotheses. In some cases the current grammar may in fact appear to accommodate the L2 input adequately and thus change will not be motivated, not because of lack of availability of UG but rather because the current grammar effectively acts as a filter. Divergent outcomes, then, would not be surprising.

Critical periods

One way of addressing the ultimate attainment issue has been to look at whether there are maturational effects in L2 acquisition, particularly whether there is a sudden decrease in UG availability at puberty or a gradual decline, or no decline at all. In other words, the idea is that UG might wither away but only at the end of some critical period for language acquisition.

Johnson and Newport (1991) showed that proficient L2 speakers who learned English as adults and who were native speakers of Chinese performed significantly below native controls on Subjacency violations, incorrectly accepting many of them. When these subjects were compared with adult Chinese speakers who learned English at various ages (4–7 years, 8–13 years and 14–16 years), results showed a continuous decline in performance and a correlation between performance and age of arrival in the USA, suggesting that access to UG is subject to maturation and that the ultimate attainment of adult learners is likely to be different in essence from that of child learners.

Others, however, have not found evidence of lack of UG principles in adult learners. For example, White and Juffs (1998) found that native speakers of Chinese who were proficient English L2 speakers and learned English as adults were not significantly different from native speakers of English in their performance on Subjacency violations. White and Genesee (1996) found native-like performance on Subjacency and no evidence of age effects for learners of English who were assessed, by independent measures, as being of near-native proficiency.

Near-native speaker competence

As we have seen, the Full Transfer/Partial Access position assumes that parameters cannot be reset (Clahsen and Hong, 1995; Clahsen and Muysken, 1989; Hawkins and Chan, 1997; Smith and Tsimpli, 1995; Tsimpli and Roussou, 1991), the implication being that the grammar ultimately attained by L2 learners will necessarily fail to be native-like. Recently, there has been interest in the linguistic competence of near-native speakers (people who can pass as native speakers of a language which is not in fact their mother tongue or who can pass as such except for their L2 phonology). If their competence (not just their performance) proves to be native-like, this suggests the active involvement of UG beyond what is given by the L1 grammar, with parameter resetting possible in principle.

Experimental results on the ultimate attainment of near-native speakers are conflicting: some report that fluent L2 speakers do not achieve native-like competence in certain domains, even if they pass as near-native speakers (Coppieters, 1987; Sorace, 1993) while others report few or no differences between near-natives and natives (Birdsong, 1992; Ioup, Boustagui, El Tigi and Moselle, 1994; White and Genesee, 1996). Indeed, results from various studies on near-native competence suggest that there may be certain areas where divergence between native and near-native grammars is found and others where ultimate attainment is fully native-like. This is unexpected on the No Transfer/Full Access position but can be explained on the views that assume full access together with full or partial transfer. If properties of the initial representation (drawn from the L1 grammar) act as a filter, there will be cases where L2 input will never motivate grammar change. If so, we expect differences in degree of near-nativeness achieved for the same property by learners of different L1s; learners of certain L1s may be more likely to notice properties of the L2 input because of features of the L1. This is what is reported by Sorace (1993) who shows that English-speaking and French-speaking near-native speakers of Italian differ as to how they represent unaccusatives (verbs whose sole argument is a theme) in the L2. Sorace suggests that the French-speaking learners of Italian were more sensitive to auxiliary choice (i.e., when to use *essere* "to be" or *avere* "to have") in certain syntactic contexts with unaccusative verbs than English-speaking learners, because French overlaps (though by no means coincides) with Italian with respect to auxiliary selection with unaccusatives.

Non-convergent final outcomes

Near-native competence represents one extreme as far as the L2 final state is concerned. But most L2 learners do not achieve even near native performance. In such cases, it is of considerable interest as to whether the interlanguage grammar is in fact different from the grammar of native speakers, that is, whether non-native performance reflects non-native competence and, if so, in what respects. This issue is investigated by Lardiere (1998a, 1998b, this volume, chapter 3) who examines the end-state competence of an L2 speaker who has fossilized at a point short of the L2, English. The subject is a native speaker of Chinese who has lived in an English-speaking environment for many years. Spontaneous production data gathered after ten years and after 18 years in the USA show that incidence of overt tense and agreement morphology is very low, suggesting that the functional categories Tense and Agr might be lacking or deficient in features. Lardiere argues, however, that this would be a mistaken interpretation of the data, since there are other reflexes of the categories Tense and Agr in this subject's grammar. In particular, use of nominative versus accusative case on pronouns, depending on a +/− finite tense distinction, is totally accurate, as is verb placement, the verb never being inappropriately raised, which follows if Agr is weak. These results suggest that, even in the absence of inflectional morphology, functional categories and their feature specifications are present in the grammar and function in ways appropriate for the L2. In this case, then, the underlying grammar does in fact converge on the native grammar, even though the surface morphology is very divergent.

Conclusion

The various approaches to the operation of UG and the role of the L1 that have been discussed in this chapter are summarized in table 4.1, which

Table 4.1 Summary of claims on UG availability and transfer

	FT/PA	NT/FA	FT/FA	PT/FA	PT/PA
Initial state	L1	UG	L1	UG and parts of L1	Parts of UG and L1
Grammar development	UG principles (via L1)	UG principles	UG principles	UG principles	(Some) UG principles
	L1 parameter settings + local adjustments	L2 parameter settings	Parameter resetting from L1 → L2/Ln	Parameter resetting from L1 → L2	Parameters associated with functional features remain unspecified
	Possibility of "wild" grammars	No wild grammars	No wild grammars	No wild grammars	Locally wild grammars
Final state	L1 (+ local adjustments) L2 not attainable	L2	Ln (L2 possible but not inevitable)	L2 (Ln)	L2 not attainable

compares the claims that each position makes for the L2 initial state, subsequent grammars during development, as well as the final state. What is presented in table 4.1 necessarily represents an oversimplification, since, as we have seen, there are in fact different versions of all of the positions that have been discussed. But what table 4.1 makes clear is that these positions have a great deal in common in terms of their underlying assumptions and there is considerable overlap in the predictions that they make. Perhaps, then, it is time to adopt a less global approach.

Looking at the UG debate in terms of full versus partial transfer and full versus partial access has yielded fruitful research questions and interesting empirical results over the years, such that our understanding of the nature of interlanguage grammars has advanced considerably. However, there are some problems with continuing to insist on these distinctions, or at least on these distinctions in their current form. One problem relates to the difficulty of disentangling properties of the L1 grammar from properties of UG. As Hale (1996) notes in his commentary on Epstein et al. (1996), it may be impossible to distinguish empirically between the possibility that UG-like knowledge comes only from the L1 (partial access) and the possibility that it comes directly from UG (full access). This suggests that we should avoid thinking in terms of a dichotomy: Does interlanguage knowledge come from UG or from the L1? Many of the studies reviewed here have shown that L2 learners can acquire subtle and abstract properties of the L2 which are not obviously present in the L1 and which are underdetermined by the L2 input. In other words, these studies suggest that interlanguage grammars can be pushed in new directions, whether the more abstract underlying principles come from UG, the L1 or both.

Another problem is that the concept of partial access has, in the past, been treated globally, whereas in fact this is by no means an all-or-nothing issue. Currently, a number of researchers are actively pursuing the possibility that there may be quite specific or local impairments to interlanguage grammatical systems; for example, L2 learners may be "stuck" with L1 feature values (Hawkins and Chan, 1997; Liceras and Díaz, in press) or with no feature values at all (Beck, in press; Eubank et al. 1997). Regardless of the ultimate correctness of such proposals, it seems promising to investigate detailed properties of the interlanguage grammar without assuming that problems in one domain necessarily imply problems everywhere, or that success in one domain necessarily implies success in another.

Indeed, we might be better off if we considered the UG question in terms of unimpaired versus impaired operation. If UG operation is impaired, in what respects? What are the consequences for interlanguage grammars? If it is unimpaired, what precisely is the domain of operation of UG? What explains discrepancies between "defective" surface properties of interlanguage grammars (often morphological) and more abstract underlying knowledge? (See Haznedar and Schwartz, 1997; Lardiere, 1998a, 1998b, this volume, chapter 3; Prévost and White, in press.) In order to further explore these questions, we need detailed investigation of the precise nature of interlanguage grammars at various points in acquisition, considered as systems in their own right.

Notes

1   See relevant discussion by Brown and Matthews (1997) and Brown (this volume) on L1 acquisition of feature geometry and the implications for L2 acquisition of phonological features.
2   Clahsen and Muysken (1986) present a genuinely no access claim, since they assume that interlanguage grammars are constrained by neither UG nor the L1. A similar position is adopted by Meisel (1997).
3   It is not clear whether Kanno is in fact a proponent of Full Transfer/Partial Access or of Full Transfer/Full Access, since she does not discuss this issue. Her data are consistent with either position.
4   Somewhat misleadingly, Epstein et al. (1996) equate full access with the strong continuity hypothesis. However, this is misconceived, since the weak continuity hypothesis also assumes full access to UG (Vainikka and Young-Scholten, 1996c). Flynn (1996) uses the term "full access" but restricts this to the position that argues for no involvement of the L1 grammar in the mental representation of the L2. Again, this constitutes a serious misunderstanding of the various positions in the field: Full Transfer/Full Access assumes that transfer is compatible with full access to UG.
5   It is possible that what White (1996a) describes is in fact Full Transfer/Full Access but where the L1–based initial state lasts for such a short time that it is unobservable.
6   Although relevant in principle, there are considerable methodological problems such that it is not clear that the data show anything other than reasonable imitation abilities on the part of L2 learners. See commentaries on Epstein et al. (1996).
7   This is my interpretation of their results. They do not entertain this possibility.

References

Beck, M. (In press) L2 acquisition and obligatory head movement: English-speaking learners of German and the local impairment hypothesis. *Studies in Second Language Acquisition.*
—— (1997) Viruses, parasites, and optionality in L2 performance. Paper presented at the Second Language Research Forum, Michigan State University, October 1997.
Birdsong, D. (1992) Ultimate attainment in second language acquisition. *Language* 68: 706–55.
Bley-Vroman, R. (1990) The logical problem of foreign language learning. *Linguistic Analysis* 20: 3–49.
Borer, H. (1996) Access to Universal Grammar: the real issues. *Behavioral and Brain Sciences* 19: 718–20.
Brown, C. (This volume) The interrelation between speech perception and phonological acquisition from infant to adult. In J. Archibald (ed.), *Second Language Acquisition and Linguistic Theory.* Oxford: Blackwell.

—— and Matthews, J. (1997) The role of feature geometry in the development of phon-emic contrasts. In S. J. Hannahs and M. Young-Scholten (eds.), *Focus on Phonological Acquisition*, pp. 67–112. Amsterdam: John Benjamins.

Brown, R. (1973) *A First Language: The Early Stages*. Cambridge, MA: Harvard Univer-sity Press.

Carroll, S. (1996) Parameter-setting in second language acquisition: explanans and explanandum. *Behavioral and Brain Sciences* 19: 720–1.

Chomsky, N. (1995) *The Minimalist Program*. Cambridge, MA: MIT Press.

—— (1981) *Lectures on Government and Binding*. Dordrecht: Foris.

Clahsen, H. and Hong, U. (1995) Agreement and null subjects in German L2 develop-ment: new evidence from reaction-time experiments. *Second Language Research* 11: 57–87.

—— and Muysken, P. (1989) The UG paradox in L2 acquisition. *Second Language Research* 5: 1–29.

—— and Muysken, P. (1986) The availability of Universal Grammar to adult and child learners: a study of the acquisition of German word order. *Second Language Research* 2: 93–119.

——, Eisenbeiss, S. and Vainikka, A. (1994) The seeds of structure: a syntactic analysis of the acquisition of Case marking. In T. Hoekstra and B. Schwartz (eds.), *Language Acquisition Studies in Generative Grammar*, pp. 85–118. Amsterdam: John Benjamins.

Coppieters, R. (1987) Competence differences between native and near-native speakers. *Language* 63: 544–73.

Dekydtspotter, L., Sprouse, R. and Anderson, B. (1998) Interlanguage A-bar dependencies: binding construals, null prepositions and Universal Grammar. *Second Language Re-search* 14.

duPlessis, J., Solin, D., Travis, L. and White, L. (1987) UG or not UG, that is the question: a reply to Clahsen and Muysken. *Second Language Research* 3: 56–75.

Epstein, S., Flynn, S. and Martohardjono, G. (1998) The strong continuity hypothesis in adult L2 acquisition of functional categories. In S. Flynn, G. Martohardjono and W. O'Neil (eds.), *The Generative Study of Second Language Acquisition*, pp. 61–77. Hillsdale, NJ: Erlbaum.

——, —— and —— (1996) Second language acquisition: theoretical and experimental issues in contemporary research. *Brain and Behavioral Sciences* 19: 677–714.

Eubank, L. (1994a) Optionality and the initial state in L2 development. In T. Hoekstra and B. Schwartz (eds.), *Language Acquisition Studies in Generative Grammar*, pp. 369–88. Amsterdam: John Benjamins.

—— (1994b) Towards an explanation for the late acquisition of agreement in L2 English. *Second Language Research* 10: 84–93.

——, Beck, M-L. and Aboutaj, H. (1997) OI effects and optionality in the interlanguage of a Moroccan-Arabic speaking learner of French. Paper presented at the American Association of Applied Linguistics, Orlando.

——, Bischof, J., Huffstutler, A., Leek, P. and West, C. (1997) "Tom eats slowly cooked eggs": thematic-verb raising in L2 knowledge. *Language Acquisition* 6: 171–99.

Finer, D. and Broselow, E. (1986) Second language acquisition of reflexive-binding. In S. Berman, J.-W. Choe, and J. McDonough (eds.), *Proceedings of NELS 16*, pp. 154–68. University of Massachusetts at Amherst: Graduate Linguistics Students Association.

Flynn, S. (1996) A parameter-setting approach to second language acquisition. In W. Ritchie and T. Bhatia (eds.), *Handbook of Second Language Acquisition*, pp. 121–58. San Diego: Academic Press.

—— (1987) *A Parameter-Setting Model of L2 Acquisition*. Dordrecht: Reidel.

—— and Martohardjono, G. (1994) Mapping from the initial state to the final state: the separation of universal principles and language-specific principles. In B. Lust, M. Suner, and J. Whitman (eds.), *Syntactic Theory and First Language Acquisition: Cross-Linguistic Perspectives. Volume 1: Heads, Projections and Learnability*, pp. 319–35. Hillsdale, NJ: Lawrence Erlbaum.

Gregg, K. (1996) The logical and developmental problems of second language acquisition. In Ritchie, W. and Bhatia, T. (eds.), *Handbook of Second Language Acquisition*, pp. 49–81. San Diego: Academic Press.

Grondin, N. and White, L. (1996) Functional categories in child L2 acquisition of French. *Language Acquisition* 5: 1–34.

Guilfoyle, E. and Noonan, M. (1992) Functional categories and language acquisition. *Canadian Journal of Linguistics* 37: 241–72.

Hale, K. (1996) Can UG and the L1 be distinguished in L2 acquisition? *Behavioral and Brain Sciences* 19: 728–30.

Hawkins, R. and Chan, Y. C. (1997) The partial availability of Universal Grammar in second language acquisition: the "failed features" hypothesis. *Second Language Research* 13: 187–226.

Haznedar, B. and Schwartz, B. (1997) Are there optional infinitives in child L2 acquisition? In E. Hughes, M. Hughes and A. Greenhill (eds.), *Proceedings of the 21st Annual Boston University Conference on Language Development*, pp. 257–68. Somerville, MA: Cascadilla Press.

Hirakawa, M. (1990) A study of the L2 acquisition of English reflexives. *Second Language Research* 6: 60–85.

Hoekstra, T. and Hyams, N. (1995) The syntax and interpretation of dropped categories in child language: a unified account. *Proceedings of WCCFL XIV*. CSIL, Stanford University.

Hyams, N. (1992) The genesis of clausal structure. In J. Meisel (ed.), *The Acquisition of Verb Placement*. Dordrecht: Kluwer.

Ioup, G., Boustagui, E., El Tigi, M. and Moselle, M. (1994) Reexamining the critical period hypothesis: a case study of successful adult SLA in a naturalistic environment. *Studies in Second Language Acquisition* 16: 73–98.

Johnson, J. and Newport, E. (1991) Critical period effects on universal properties of language: the status of Subjacency in the acquisition of a second language. *Cognition* 39: 215–58.

Kanno, K. (1997) The acquisition of null and overt pronominals in Japanese by English speakers. *Second Language Research* 13: 265–87.

—— (1996) The status of a non-parameterized principle in the L2 initial state. *Language Acquisition* 5: 317–34.

Klein, E. (1995) Evidence for a "wild" L2 grammar: when PPs rear their empty heads. *Applied Linguistics* 16: 87–117.

—— (1993) *Toward Second Language Acquisition: a Study of Null-Prep Phenomenon*. Dordrecht: Kluwer.

Lakshmanan, U. (1994) *Universal Grammar in Child Second Language Acquisition*. Amsterdam: John Benjamins.

Lardiere, D. (This volume) Mapping features to forms in second language acquisition. In J. Archibald (ed.), *Second Language Acquisition and Linguistic Theory*. Oxford: Blackwell.

—— (1998a) Case and tense in the "fossilized" steady state. *Second Language Research* 14: 1–26.

—— (1998b) Dissociating syntax from morphology in a divergent end-state grammar. *Second Language Research* 14.

—— and Schwartz, B. (1997) Feature-marking in the L2 development of deverbal compounds. *Journal of Linguistics* 33: 327–53.

Liceras, J. (1989) On some properties of the "pro-drop" parameter: looking for missing subjects in non-native Spanish. In S. Gass and J. Schachter (eds.), *Linguistic Perspectives on Second Language Acquisition*, pp. 109–33. Cambridge: Cambridge University Press.

—— and Díaz, L. (in press)The interface with the perceptual and the conceptual systems: verb morphology and null versus overt subjects in Spanish non-native grammars. In M. Beck (ed.), *Morphology and the Interfaces in Second Language Knowledge*. Amsterdam: John Benjamins.

Martohardjono, G. and Gair, J. (1993) Apparent UG inaccessibility in second language acquisition: misapplied principles or principled misapplications? In F. Eckman (ed.), *Confluence: Linguistics, L2 Acquisition and Speech Pathology*, pp. 79–103. Amsterdam: John Benjamins.

Meisel, J. (1997) The acquisition of the syntax of negation in French and German: contrasting first and second language acquisition. *Second Language Research* 13: 227–63.

——, Clahsen, H. and Pienemann, M. (1981) On determining developmental stages in natural language acquisition. *Studies in Second Language Acquisition* 3: 109–35.

Montalbetti, M. (1984) After binding: on the interpretation of pronouns. Unpublished Ph.D. dissertation, MIT.

Perez-Leroux, A. T. and Glass, W. (1997) OPC effects in the L2 acquisition of Spanish. In A. T. Perez-Leroux and W. Glass (eds.), *Contemporary Perspectives on the Acquisition of Spanish. Volume 1: Developing Grammars*, pp. 149–65. Somerville, MA: Cascadilla Press.

Platzack, C. (1996) The initial hypothesis of syntax: a minimalist perspective on language acquisition and attrition. In H. Clahsen (ed.), *Generative Perspectives on Language Acquisition: Empirical Findings, Theoretical Considerations, Crosslinguistic Comparisons*, pp. 369–414. Amsterdam: John Benjamins.

Poeppel, D. and Wexler, K. (1993) The full competence hypothesis of clause structure in early German. *Language* 69: 1–33.

Prévost, P. and White, L. (In press) Accounting for morphological variation in L2 acquisition: Truncation or missing inflection? In M. A. Friedemann and L. Rizzi (eds.), *The Acquisition of Syntax: Issues in Comparative Developmental Linguistics*. London: Longman.

Radford, A. (1990) *Syntactic Theory and the Acquisition of English Syntax*. Oxford: Blackwell.

Schachter, J. (1989) Testing a proposed universal. In S. Gass and J. Schachter (eds.), *Linguistic Perspectives on Second Language Acquisition*, pp. 73–88. Cambridge: Cambridge University Press.

Schwartz, B. (In press) Some specs on Specs in L2 acquisition. In D. Adger, S. Pintzuk, B. Plunkett and G. Tsoulas (eds.), *Specifiers: Minimalist Approaches*. Oxford: Oxford University Press.

—— (1998) On two hypotheses of "Transfer" in L2A: Minimal trees and absolute influence. In S. Flynn, G. Martohardjono and W. O'Neil (eds.), *The Generative Study of Second Language Acquisition*, pp. 35–59. Hillsdale, NJ: Erlbaum.

—— and Gubala-Ryzak, M. (1992) Learnability and grammar reorganization in L2A: against negative evidence causing the unlearning of verb movement. *Second Language Research* 8: 1–38.

—— and Sprouse, R. (This volume) When syntactic theories evolve: consequences for L2 acquisition research. In J. Archibald (ed.), *Second Language Acquisition and Linguistic Theory*. Oxford: Blackwell.

—— and —— (1996) L2 cognitive states and the Full Transfer/Full Access model. *Second Language Research* 12: 40–72.

—— and —— (1994) Word order and nominative case in nonnative language acquisition: a longitudinal study of (L1 Turkish) German interlanguage. In T. Hoekstra and B. Schwartz (eds.), *Language Acquisition Studies in Generative Grammar*, pp. 317–68. Amsterdam: John Benjamins.

—— and Tomaselli, A. (1990) Some implications from an analysis of German word order. In W. Abraham, W. Kosmeijer and E. Reuland (eds.), *Issues in Germanic Syntax*, pp. 251–74. Berlin: Walter de Gruyter.

Smith, N. and Tsimpli, I.-M. (1995) *The Mind of a Savant*. Oxford: Blackwell.

Sorace, A. (1993) Incomplete and divergent representations of unaccusativity in nonnative grammars of Italian. *Second Language Research* 9: 22–48.

Thomas, M. (1993) *Knowledge of Reflexives in a Second Language*, Amsterdam, John Benjamins.

—— (1991) Universal Grammar and the interpretation of reflexives in a second language. *Language* 67: 211–39.

Tsimpli, I. and Roussou, A. (1991) Parameter resetting in L2? *UCL Working Papers in Linguistics* 3: 149–69.

Vainikka, A. and Young-Scholten, M. (1996a) The early stages of adult L2 syntax: additional evidence from Romance speakers. *Second Language Research* 12: 140–76.

—— and —— (1996b) Gradual development of L2 phrase structure. *Second Language Research* 12: 7–39.

—— and —— (1996c) Partial transfer, not partial access. *Behavioral and Brain Sciences* 19: 744–5.

—— and —— (1994) Direct access to X'-theory: evidence from Korean and Turkish adults learning German. In T. Hoekstra and B. Schwartz (eds.), *Language Acquisition Studies in Generative Grammar*, pp. 265–316. Amsterdam: John Benjamins.

Valian, V. (1991) Syntactic subjects in the early speech of American and Italian children. *Cognition* 40: 21–81.

Wexler, K. (1994) Optional infinitives, head movement and the economy of derivations. In D. Lightfoot and N. Hornstein (eds.), *Verb Movement*, pp. 305–50. Cambridge: Cambridge University Press.

White, L. (1996a) Clitics in L2 French. In H. Clahsen (ed.), *Generative Perspectives on Language Acquisition: Empirical Findings, Theoretical Considerations, Crosslinguistic Comparisons*, pp. 335–68. Amsterdam: John Benjamins.

—— (1996b) The tale of the ugly duckling (or the coming of age of second language acquisition research). In A. Stringfellow, D. Cahana-Amitay, E. Hughes and A. Zukowski (eds.), *Proceedings of the 20th Annual Boston University Conference on Language Development*, pp. 1–17. Somerville, MA: Cascadilla Press.

—— (1996c) Universal grammar and second language acquisition: current trends and new directions. In W. Ritchie and T. Bhatia (eds.), *Handbook of Language Acquisition*, pp. 85–120. New York: Academic Press.

—— (1992a) Long and short verb movement in second language acquisition. *Canadian Journal of Linguistics* 37: 273–86.

—— (1992b) Subjacency violations and empty categories in L2 acquisition. In H. Goodluck and M. Rochemont (eds.), *Island Constraints*, pp. 445–64. Dordrecht: Kluwer.

—— (1991a) Adverb placement in second language acquisition: some effects of positive and negative evidence in the classroom. *Second Language Research* 7: 133–61.

—— (1991b) The verb-movement parameter in second language acquisition. *Language Acquisition* 1: 337–60.

—— (1989a) The principle of adjacency in second language acquisition: do L2 learners observe the subset principle? In S. Gass and J. Schachter (eds.), *Linguistic Perspectives on Second Language Acquisition*, pp. 134–58. Cambridge: Cambridge University Press.

—— (1989b) *Universal Grammar and Second Language Acquisition*. Amsterdam: John Benjamins.

—— (1988) Island effects in second language acquisition. In S. Flynn and W. O'Neill (eds.), *Linguistic Theory in Second Language Acquisition*, pp. 144–72. Dordrecht: Reidel.

—— (1985a) Is there a logical problem of second language acquisition? *TESL Canada* 2.2: 29–41.

—— (1985b) The pro-drop parameter in adult second language acquisition. *Language Learning* 35: 47–62.

—— and Genesee, F. (1996) How native is near-native? The issue of ultimate attainment in adult second language acquisition. *Second Language Research* 12: 238–65.

—— and Juffs, A. (1998) Constraints on wh-movement in two different contexts of non-native language acquisition: competence and processing. In S. Flynn, G. Martohardjono and W. O'Neil (eds.), *The Generative Study of Second Language Acquisition*, pp. 111–29. Hillsdale, NJ: Erlbaum.

5

When Syntactic Theories Evolve: Consequences for L2 Acquisition Research

Bonnie D. Schwartz and Rex A. Sprouse

Introduction

One of the central tenets of generative grammar since its inception has been that Universal Grammar (UG) places severe restrictions on the class of grammars that human beings can acquire. This assertion accounts, in principle, for the rapidity and apparent effortlessness with which children normally acquire their native language (L1): since in acquiring the grammar of their L1, children are selecting from only a small subset of the logically possible formal systems (the relatively small set given by UG), exposure to random, contextualized utterances suffices as their only direct (external) evidence.

The leading question animating generative research on non-native language (L2) acquisition is, presumably, whether Interlanguage "grammars" fall within the bounds set by UG, and if they do not, then just what their formal properties are. The Strong UG hypothesis states that L2 acquisition, even by adults, is always constrained by the principles of UG. If it can be shown, however, that adult L2 acquirers create systems which lie outside the small class of grammars permitted by UG, then the basic question of L2 acquisition research within the generative paradigm is answered: UG does not constrain (adult) L2 acquisition.

It was the ground-breaking work of Lydia White that set in motion this research strategy for testing L2 data against the formal constraints of UG. White has frequently emphasized the importance of the poverty of the stimulus in generative L2 acquisition research. For example, in her 1989 book, she observes:

that the three problems with the input . . . identified for L1 acquisition [under-determination, degenerate input, lack of negative evidence] remain problematic for L2 . . . The most important of these problems is underdetermination. When one considers the L2 acquisition task and the assumed complexity of the gram-mar attained by successful L2 learners, this grammar appears to go far beyond the input, suggesting that there must be something like UG guiding L2 acquisi-tion. (White, 1989:45)

Indeed, armed with the sophisticated tools of modern linguistic theory and a well-articulated logical problem in need of explanation, generative L2 research has gleaned a wealth of information over the last 15 years.

Still, generative L2 research faces the hazard of losing its grounding, when-ever it considers only the analysis of L2 data sets and ignores the logical problem of language acquisition. Whether trying to defend or refute the Strong UG hypothesis, the issue of underdetermination needs to be addressed. Let us first consider trying to muster support for the Strong UG hypothesis. Here it is crucial to demonstrate that the Interlanguage phenomena under investigation pose a poverty-of-the-stimulus problem and not merely that the phenomena are "UG-compatible". This is because particular subsets of sen-tences or sentence-meaning pairs generated by many non-UG-constrained formal systems will be UG-compatible. For example, our electronic mail systems are able to generate the sentence "I'm going home in ten minutes". It is easy enough to provide a UG-compatible analysis of this data set, but certainly no one would as a result conclude that our electronic mail systems are constrained by UG. Simply stated, a UG-compatible analysis of an L2 data set does not, on its own, constitute an argument for the Strong UG hypothesis; what is required, to repeat, is the demonstration of UG-derived poverty-of-the-stimulus effects.

Similar reasoning extends to undermining the Strong UG hypothesis, i.e., attempts at establishing the existence of "rogue" or "wild" L2 grammars. Here it is crucial to demonstrate that an Interlanguage system violates well-established universals of human language. This cannot be done merely by constructing an analysis of an Interlanguage data set in such a way that the analysis is "UG-incompatible" on the adoption of some particular theory of UG. One can always concoct a UG-incompatible analysis of data – that is, even data sets of known natural languages are amenable to infinitely many UG-incompatible treatments (Tomaselli and Schwartz, 1990:26–7). To not locate a UG-compatible analysis of a set of L2 data may simply show lack of imagination, since there may well be a UG-compatible analysis of the data after all. Given that the lynchpin of the argument for UG is the logical prob-lem of language acquisition, then UG-incompatible analyses must be supple-mented by demonstrating that L2 acquisition is not underdetermined by the input in the same way that L1 acquisition is. In short, a UG-incompatible analysis of an L2 data set does not, on its own, constitute an argument against the Strong UG position.

The reason, then, for the looming potential hazard to generative L2 acquisition research is quite clear: it is by no means a priori given which class of grammars, precisely, UG permits. Methodologically, linguists begin by assuming the narrowest empirically motivated class of grammars and then design theories of UG that will permit just this class. However, it is always the case that subsequent comparative research, say, in the realm of syntax, may reveal that the class of actually attested human languages is a bit broader than that class assumed at the outset. Thus, syntactic theory will have to be weakened correspondingly to accommodate this slightly larger class of languages, and hence the theory of UG will have to be changed. There is, then, a natural tension between the desire to formulate the maximally restrictive syntactic theory and the need to accommodate the observed cross-linguistic syntactic variation. This natural tension obviously has consequences for various types of L2 acquisition research which are dependent on theories of UG.

In generative L2 acquisition research, the issue of UG often goes hand-in-hand with the issue of L1 influence. In order to determine whether UG continues to constrain (adult) L2 acquisition, an attempt must be made to exclude the possibility that so-called UG effects are the result, in actuality, of the L1 grammar. Recently the issue of L1 transfer, long central to the field, has been approached with a new degree of rigor and precision: specific, principled hypotheses have been put forward about the nature and form of morphosyntactic influence from the L1. This welcome innovation might be seen as a double-edged sword, however. This is because the positions are generally tied to particular linguistic (in this case, syntactic) hypotheses and therefore face a potential hazard reminiscent of the one discussed above in connection with the Strong UG hypothesis. An account of an observed transfer effect in strongly theory-bound terms may find its foundation shattered if those terms are redefined or rejected as syntactic theory evolves. The general point here again is that the extent to which any type of L2 acquisition research is tied to the particular technicalities of specific linguistic analyses is the extent to which it risks being undercut by a better theory around the corner.

The purpose of this chapter then is, first, to illustrate just how the revisions in linguistic theory can fundamentally affect the conclusions drawn in generative L2 acquisition research, and second, to argue nevertheless that there is a way to bypass the changing tides of linguistic theory and still address sophisticated theoretical questions in L2 development. In the second section we consider three studies which we believe have essentially defined significant positions regarding the role of UG and/or L1 transfer in L2 acquisition. As we shall see, in each of the three cases, the particular version of syntactic theory assumed led the authors to conclusions about the role of UG and/or L1 transfer that would not be warranted under alternative syntactic assumptions. In the third and fourth sections, we illustrate how generative L2 acquisition research can lead to conclusions which stand independent of particular versions of syntactic theory. In the third section we discuss generative L2 studies which investigate well-defined poverty-of-the-stimulus problems, ones which will have to be accounted for by UG, whatever their precise analyses may be. In the fourth section we briefly turn to the use of comparative Interlanguage studies as a tool in investigating the role of transfer in L2 development. The fifth Section consists of some concluding remarks.

Honey, I Shrunk the Conclusions!

Clahsen and Muysken (1986)

We first consider the important study by Clahsen and Muysken (1986), which looked at the naturalistic L2 acquisition of German by adult native speakers of Italian, Portuguese and Spanish. The basic SOV surface pattern of German ((1a)) is obscured through the verb-second (V2) phenomenon in main clauses ((1b)):

(1) a. Hans glaubt, dass ich früher den Mann <u>kannte</u>
         Hans believes that I   earlier the man   knew
         "Hans believes that I used to know the man"
     b. Früher <u>kannte</u> ich den Mann
         earlier knew   I   the man
         "I used to know the man"

   The Romance L1s in this study exhibit neither the verb-second nor the verb-final properties of German. Rather, as illustrated in (2) with Spanish, all three languages have surface SVO order with, importantly, the possibility for Adjunct-S-V-O order in both embedded and main clauses:

(2) a. Juan cree   que <u>antes</u> yo conocía a este hombre
         Juan believes that before I   knew   to this man
         "Juan believes that I used to know the man"
     b. <u>Antes</u> yo conocía a este hombre
         before I   knew   to this man
         "I used to know the man very well"

   The acquisition path of the L2 acquirers (henceforth L2ers) in Clahsen and Muysken (1986) is sketched in (3):

(3) a. Stage 1: S (Aux) V O
     b. Stage 2: (AdvP/PP) S (Aux) V O
     c. Stage 3: S $V_{[+fin]}$ O $V_{[-fin]}$
     d. Stage 4: XP $V_{[+fin]}$ S O
     e. Stage 5: S $V_{[+fin]}$ (Adv) O
     f. Stage 6: <u>dass</u> S O $V_{[+fin]}$

The subjects start off with Romance-like SVO order in Stage 1 and Adjunct-S-V-O order in Stage 2. In Stage 3 nonfinite verbal elements begin to occur clause-finally (in both main and embedded clauses). So-called "subject-verb inversion" first appears in Stage 4. (Stage 5 will not be considered here.) In Stage 6 the finite verb in embedded clauses begins to occur in clause-final position.

Clahsen and Muysken argue that this developmental sequence demonstrates that L2 acquisition is not constrained by UG. Their conclusion derives from an analysis which attributes to the L2ers (a) an underlying VO order throughout, and (b) beginning at Stage 3, rightward movement of nonfinite verbs and particles. At this third stage there is no evidence for V2 – thus, no evidence that the finite verb moves to Comp. Unlike later researchers, Clahsen and Muysken do not assume the existence of an independent IP projection. Consider their tree for German main clauses (1986:96, (8)), consistent with the assumptions about V2 in Germanic syntax at that time (see, e.g., Platzack, 1986):

(4)

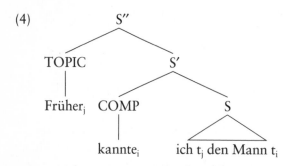

Note that in (4) there are only two head positions available for the verb: V (inside S) and Comp. As a consequence, an analysis for the Interlanguage at Stage 3 which is underlyingly verb-final with a rule moving the finite verb leftward is simply unavailable, since within Clahsen and Muysken's assumptions there is no landing site (other than Comp) on the left (but the L2ers do not have V2 yet); in short, there is no Infl. Thus, they conclude that nonfinite verbal elements move rightward. Since the rightward movement rule they posit was not consistent with UG as understood at that time, Clahsen and Muysken conclude that L2 acquisition is not constrained by UG.

However, if one assumes the existence and independence of Infl and Comp projections (Chomsky, 1986; Travis, 1984), alternative analyses of each of the Interlanguage stages, all consistent with particular (independently motivated) versions of syntactic theory, can be made (duPlessis, Solin, Travis and White 1987; Schwartz and Tomaselli 1990). Exploiting the Infl position as a landing site for finite verbs, duPlessis et al. (1987) were the first to posit a reanalysis at Stage 3 such that the VP is underlyingly head-final. As shown in (5), it is claimed that the finite verb moves leftward to the Infl position; and, as is possible in the L1s, the Adverb adjoins to IP:

(5)

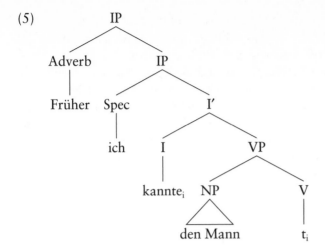

At Stage 4 the topicalized XP moves to Spec, CP and the finite verb moves to Comp (C), as illustrated in (6):

(6)

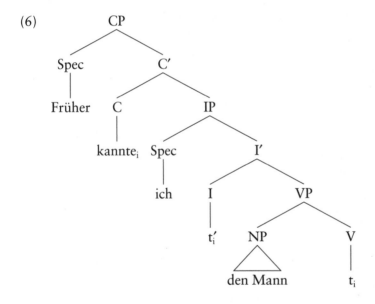

DuPlessis et al. (1987) and Schwartz and Tomaselli (1990) diverge in their treatment of Stage 6 in ways that need not concern us here. What is crucial to our point is that with the introduction of a full-fledged IP projection into syntactic theory, analyses of each of the Interlanguage stages consistent with UG became available. The consequence of this for L2 acquisition theory was that data which had seemed to indicate that Interlanguage is not constrained by UG became data arguing for the opposite view, namely: UG does constrain Interlanguage development. The L2ers pass through several distinct stages, but each of these stages lies within the bounds set by UG.

The discussion above was intended to illustrate how independently motivated revisions of syntactic theory can refine our understanding of the class
of languages allowed by UG – which in this case, moreover, had the further
effect of removing a potential empirical argument against the Strong UG
hypothesis as applied to adult L2 acquisition. In the next section we turn to
an example from the transfer debate of the mid-1990s. This time we will see
how a shift in the understanding of the possible locus of cross-linguistic
variation has consequences for the role of the L1 grammar in UG-based
models of L2 development. Our point again will be to illustrate the fragility
of models of L2 acquisition that depend crucially on fine details of syntactic
theory.

Vainikka and Young-Scholten (1994, 1996)

The Minimal Trees hypothesis of Vainikka and Young-Scholten (1994, 1996)
claims that lexical projections and their linear order transfer from L1 to
Interlanguage, but functional projections do not. Their evidence comes from
what are apparently the earliest stages of word order development in Korean–
German and Turkish–German Interlanguage. Both Korean and Turkish exhibit
verb-final word order in surface syntax, with no trace of the V2 phenomenon
of German. Unlike the Romance speakers discussed in the preceding section,
Korean and Turkish speakers acquiring German begin with verb-final word
order in surface syntax. Vainikka and Young-Scholten suggest that this L1-
differentiated L2-German difference stems from the difference in the structure of VP between Romance, on the one hand, and Korean and Turkish, on
the other. Consider the tree in (7), illustrating what transfers from Korean
and Turkish, according to Vainikka & Young-Scholten:

(7)

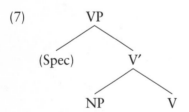

Note that under such an account, verb movement will arise only when verb-
ally related functional projections are added. Verb movement will not be
possible in the initial L2 state, because in (7) there is no position for the verb
to move to.

Vainikka and Young-Scholten make the assumption (which had long been
standard in generative grammar) that linear orientation within phrases – i.e.,
the relative order of head and complement and of head and specifier – is
subject to parameterization. Thus, Vainikka and Young-Scholten interpret the

fact that Korean and Turkish speakers acquiring German initially produce
(S)OV word order as an instance of the transfer of a lexical category (VP)
and its linear orientation (Spec-initial and head-final).

However, under Kayne's (1994) *Antisymmetry* theory, all languages are
underlyingly specifier–head–complement, i.e., SVO. Any OV order arises by
moving the direct object to the specifier of the object agreement head (Spec,
AgrOP), shown in (8):

(8)

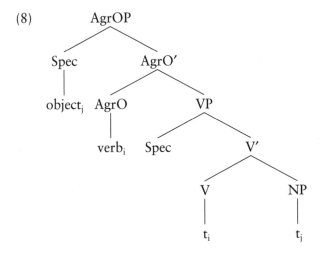

In other words, coupled with the basic assumptions of Chomsky's (1993)
Minimalist Program, complement–head order is a direct indication that the
complement has undergone movement to the specifier of a functional head
(before Spell-Out). Thus, as Schwartz (1998) has pointed out, under such
syntactic analyses, these early data from Korean and Turkish acquirers of
German exhibiting the OV order point to the conclusion diametrically opposed
to that offered by Vainikka and Young-Scholten, viz., that functional projections must be present in their earliest Interlanguage.

However, a still more recent development in syntactic theory suggests
yet another analysis of these same data, this time using the formalism of
Chomsky's (1995) Minimalist Program, in which a different version of the
VP-internal Subject Hypothesis is assumed, and in which the AgrO projection and hence its specifier have been excised. First, Chomsky (1995:315–16)
adopts the hypothesis that the subject of all (active) clauses (except those
with unaccusative predicates) is introduced into the tree not in the "traditional" Spec, VP position, but rather as the specifier of a phrase headed by a
light verb, *v*, which takes the VP as its complement. Furthermore, Chomsky
(1995:348–67) eliminates Agr (both AgrS and AgrO) on the grounds that
among the proposed functional categories Agr, T, C and D, only Agr consists
exclusively of [– Interpretable] formal features. He argues for replacing the
earlier Agr-based theories with one that allows for multiple specifiers. The

underlying positions of subject and object on this theory are sketched in (9) (Chomsky, 1995:352, (182)):

(9)

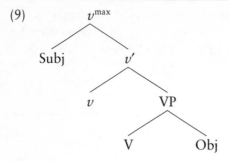

Under this proposal, to derive OV order, the direct object moves not to Spec, AgrO (for case-feature checking), as in (8), but to a second verbal specifier position. However, this is not the Spec, VP position, but rather the inner specifier of the Vb, the category that arises when V raises and adjoins to v, as in (10) (cf. Chomsky, 1995:356, (188)):

(10)

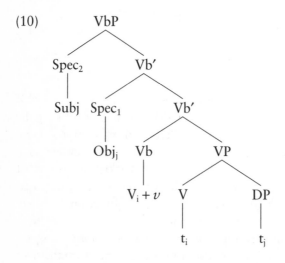

It is far from obvious that as an account for the early (S)OV order in the Interlanguage German data, (10) would be compatible with the letter, let alone the spirit, of the Minimal Trees hypothesis. First of all, one would have to assume that it is not just the VP, but also the vP, that transfers from Korean and Turkish. Yet, the status of v is unclear from the perspective of Minimal Trees: should it be viewed as a lexical category (and thus subject to transfer) or not? Even if vP is subject to transfer, it should be stressed that while (10) may appear to "derive" the SOV order, it does not suffice to ensure a convergent derivation within Chomsky's framework. This is because the subject in (10) must still undergo movement to the specifier position of T for feature checking (Chomsky, 1995:352, 358, etc.). In other words, (10) cannot represent the complete structure for an SOV clause in Korean–German or Turkish–German Interlanguage (if we assume the syntactic framework of Chomsky, 1995), because then there will have to be additional structure which unambiguously belongs to the functional domain.

On a more general theoretical level, however, the Minimal Trees hypothesis seems to lose even further ground within Chomsky's (1995) theory. This is because the adoption of this theory makes it very difficult to evaluate the claim that functional categories are absent from a grammar. If the set of functional categories is in fact limited to those whose role is to "provid[e] 'instructions' at either or both interface levels" for which there is "fairly direct evidence from interface relations" (Chomsky, 1995:349), their absence from early L2 stages would suggest a very serious discontinuity in Interlanguage development. In particular, the roles of at least T, C and D at the interpretive interface in natural language grammars would certainly place a formal system lacking these elements outside the range of grammars permitted by UG – a result which Vainikka and Young-Scholten would certainly not endorse.

In short, under more current views of syntactic theory, the position for which Vainikka and Young-Scholten argued is no longer viable. Furthermore, the data crucial for their contention that only lexical categories (VP, NP) are transferred from the L1 grammar not only fail to support their view (and the variants of it sketched above), but actually suggest that the strength of features is directly transferred; otherwise, the observed initial (S)OV order in the German of these Korean and Turkish speakers would simply be impossible.[1]

Eubank (1993/1994)

This last point suggesting the transfer of feature strength has been disputed by Eubank (1993/1994), our third case study. In Eubank's view, it would be illogical to suppose that the strength of features associated with functional heads transfers in L2 acquisition, since the morphology itself does not transfer, and, following Rohrbacher (1992), it is on the basis of inflectional morphology that feature strength is determined. Thus for Eubank, while functional categories do transfer (*contra* Vainikka and Young-Scholten), the strength of the features associated with them does not.

The most direct evidence in Eubank (1993/1994) for this position comes from studies by Gerbault (1978) and Tiphine (1983, no date) on the acquisition of English by French-speaking children, specifically their word order in the very early stages. Here we focus on the negation data. These spontaneous production data indicate the categorical absence of *no(t)* following thematic verbs. Rather, one finds early utterances such as (11):

(11) Early French–English Interlanguage
    a. I not love you (M)   (from Gerbault, as in Eubank
                                        1993/1994:191, (8a))
    b. you not understand (J-M)   (from Tiphine, as in Eubank
                                        1993/1994:192, (11c))
    c. Joel no knows bike (P)   (from Tiphine, as in Eubank
                                        1993/1994:192, (12b))

   Data as in (11) appear to be in sharp contrast with French, which requires
verb raising (Emonds, 1978; Pollock, 1989), i.e., the negator *pas* must follow
the finite verb, as in (12), schematized in (13):

(12) French
      tu   ne comprends pas
      you ne understand not
      "You don't understand"

(13) French (cf. (12))

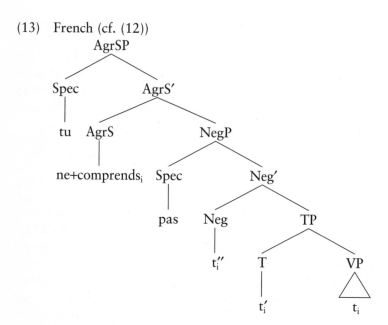

   Given the aims of this chapter, a full exposition of Eubank's analysis is not
necessary (we refer the reader to his article). Essentially, he argues that in the
absence of a verbal paradigm in very early Interlanguage, the L2er has no
way of choosing between the values [weak] (no overt verb movement) and
[strong] (verb raising) for AgrS and thus settles temporarily on the value
[nonfinite], which for Eubank implies the absence of verb raising, as sketched
in (14):

(14)   Eubank's (1993/1994) analysis of (11b)

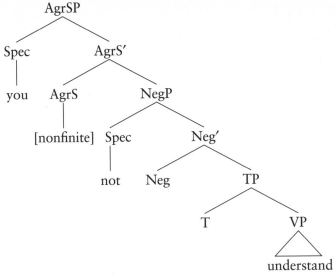

For Eubank, following Chomsky (1991), overt verb movement is driven by affixation, associated with overt verbal morphology. More specifically, in the spirit of Rohrbacher's (1992, 1994) work on adult grammars, Eubank assumes that strength of inflection is determined by an algorithm which takes into account overtly distinct forms and syncretisms in verbal paradigms. Assuming such an approach, Eubank is able, at least in part, to motivate his proposed analysis.

However, overt affixation does not play the same role in Chomsky's (1995) Minimalist Program; here, movement (of any kind) is driven by feature checking, where the principles of Procrastinate (delay movement as long as possible) and Full Interpretation determine the level at which any given movement must take place: [strong] features must be checked before Spell-Out, whereas [weak] features must be checked after Spell-Out. Importantly, Chomsky adopts no algorithm in terms of inflectional paradigms for determining whether V-features are [weak] or [strong]. Indeed, we have argued elsewhere (Schwartz and Sprouse, 1996; Sprouse, 1998) that the presence or absence of overt raising cannot be derived from paradigms, *contra* Rohrbacher (1992, 1994) and Vikner (1995), once, in addition to verb movement, subject and object movement are also considered. Thus, assuming the Minimalist Program, there is no reason why the strength of morphological features could not be transferred from the L1, since they do not depend on overt paradigms.

In Schwartz and Sprouse (1996), we offer an alternative analysis of the data considered by Eubank. We suggest, in essence, that the transfer of the [strong] V-feature from French forces the L2er to (mis)analyze the English negator *no(t)* as a clitic head, analogous to French *ne*. Under such an analysis, even with verb raising, one would not expect utterances in which the verb precedes the negator. When the verb moves from V via T into Neg, *no(t)* (like *ne* in French) procliticizes to the verb, as sketched in (15):

(15) Schwartz and Sprouse's (1996) analysis of (11b) (cf. (13), for French)

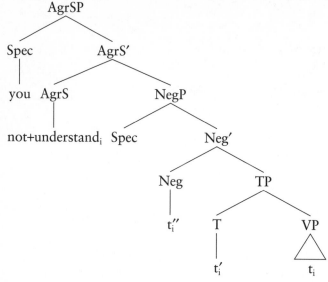

Our analysis is consistent with the view that the syntax of the initial state in L2 acquisition is equivalent to the syntax of the steady state of L1 acquisition,[2] including the specification of the strength of inflectional features, *contra* Eubank. Crucially, feature strength is treated as an abstract morphological property, which is in principle independent of overt morphological paradigms. This approach adopts the innovations of Chomsky (1993), superseding the theoretical proposals of Chomsky (1991). Thus, again we see that changes in syntactic theory have powerful consequences for the conclusions drawn in generativist L2 acquisition research.

Poverty of Stimulus in L2 Acquistion

We believe that one clear point emerges from even this brief review of the three important L2 investigations discussed in section 2: since our understanding of the technicalities of UG is provisional, the conclusions of L2 acquisition studies that depend directly on those technicalities will necessarily also be provisional. While recognizing rigorous syntactic frameworks as absolutely indispensable tools in L2 acquisition research, we advise extreme caution in regard to theoretical conclusions that are deeply embedded within easily revisable details of particular hypotheses of specific syntactic theories. In addition, we advocate the careful examination of Interlanguage data in search of UG-derived poverty of stimulus phenomena (not directly exhibited in the respective L2 acquirers' L1 grammar) if one is seeking to identify the role of UG in (adult) L2 acquisition. Likewise, we advocate extensive comparative Interlanguage research in the study of the role of the L1 grammar in L2 development. Pursuing these research strategies will allow for the characterization of Interlanguage cognitive states in a manner relatively independent of the frequent revision of syntactic theory.

In this section our goal is to illustrate the point that the concern with poverty of the stimulus is compatible with a variety of methodological designs and with the investigation of various aspects of L2 grammatical knowledge. To begin, an exposition of the poverty of the stimulus in language acquisition is in order.

Contextualizing the poverty-of-the-stimulus problem

An especially clear (and we would argue, perspicuous) statement of the poverty of the stimulus in language acquisition is found in Crain and Thornton (1998):

> [M]any aspects of grammatical knowledge are represented as constraints, that is, as sanctions against linguistic analyses of one kind or another. Constraints are negative statements. It is safe to assume that not all children, perhaps no children, encounter evidence pertaining to constraints. The pertinent evidence would be information about which linguistic expressions and meanings are prohibited in the target language. It follows from the absence of such negative evidence in children's experience that knowledge encoded by constraints is not learned from experience. If not, then this aspect of linguistic competence must be innately specified, as part of Universal Grammar. This is the familiar argument from the poverty of the stimulus. (Crain and Thornton, 1998:283)

The emphasis on "constraints" in the quotation above is important. Linguistic constraints restrict the possible realizations a language can take. A grammar without constraint K will be more permissive, that is, will allow more sentences or allow more sentence-meaning pairs, than a grammar with constraint K. By definition, direct evidence for constraint K cannot be part of primary linguistic data (since ungrammatical utterances *qua* ungrammatical sentences or ungrammatical meanings lie outside primary linguistic data). Thus, knowledge of K at any point in the course of acquisition is a poverty-of-the-stimulus effect.

Typically, the poverty of the stimulus is framed in view of the target grammatical system.[3] But logically, this need not – in fact cannot – be so. Linguistic knowledge that arises in the absence of evidence is, to use the phrasing of Hornstein and Lightfoot (1981), the logical problem of language acquisition. And this logical problem does not change over the course of development: there is never (again, by definition) overt evidence for constraint K in the input, and so if knowledge of K arises, even if only temporarily, then this constitutes a poverty-of-the-stimulus effect.[4]

That the poverty-of-the-stimulus argument is traditionally conceived with an eye to the Target Language (TL) grammar is perfectly understandable. This is because the logical problem of language acquisition is devised within the context of L1 acquisition, and (normal) L1 acquisition converges in the end on the TL grammar, on the final-state grammar of the input providers. However, one need only consider the acquisition of sign language by deaf children of non-signing parents (e.g., Goldin-Meadow and Mylander, 1990) to see immediately that it is misguided in principle to take underdetermined knowledge relative to the TL grammar as the unique benchmark of the poverty-of-the-stimulus argument.

Needless to say, examples of what we shall label "developmental" poverty-of-the-stimulus effects have also been identified in less atypical language acquisition (Schwartz, 1998; Schwartz and Sprouse, 1998). Children create intermediate grammars that rule out what their input tells them is possible; this is to say, L1 children pass through stages that evince syntactic and semantic phenomena that are not solely input driven. Consider, first, an example in the purely syntactic domain, Schönenberger's (1995, 1996) L1 acquisition study on verb placement in embedded clauses in Lucernese Swiss German. Similar (but not identical) to German, Lucernese has requirements on the finite verb occurring in final position in embedded clauses, schematized in (16):

(16)   Lucernese Swiss German (Schönenberger 1995, 1996)
    a.   ... complementizer S X $V_{[+fin]}$
    b.   * ... complementizer S $V_{[+fin]}$ X

Schönenberger's two young L1 acquirers of Lucernese, however, consistently fail to place the embedded finite verb in this position when required, despite the robust evidence for it in their input. In over a thousand embedded utterances, the children use the obligatory verb-final pattern only 3.3 percent of the time, producing instead (even with overt complementizers) raised finite verbs of the pattern in (16b), well into the fifth year. What the children do is clearly in disregard of their input: they require what is impossible in the Target Language and disallow what is required.

Another example, this time in the realm of the meanings children assign to sentences, comes from the experiment carried out by Boster and Crain (1994) on L1 acquisition of English. They investigated, as illustrated in (17), quantified sentences, where the subject is modified by *every* and the VP contains a disjunction (viz. *or*):

(17)   Every ghostbuster will choose a cat or a pig

In order for (17) to be true, all that would be necessary is for each ghostbuster (assume there are three, A, B and C) to pick at least a cat, or at least a pig, or (at least) one of each. So, for example, (18) lists some of the circumstances under which (17) is true:

(18) a. ghostbusters A and B each choose a cat, and C chooses a pig
      b. ghostbusters A, B and C all choose a cat (or all three choose a pig)
      c. ghostbuster A chooses a cat, B a pig, and C both
      d. all three pick both a cat and a pig

There are of course circumstances that would make (17) false – for instance, when one of the three ghostbusters fails to make a choice or when one of them selects only animals other than a cat or a pig (only a lion, for example).

Boster and Crain became interested in interpretations (18a) and (18b), which they called, respectively, the "distributed outcome" and the "exclusive outcome". Using a modified truth-value judgment task (Crain and McKee, 1985), Boster and Crain discovered that in situations depicting either the "distributed" interpretation like in (18a) or the "exclusive" interpretation like in (18b), adults responded to test sentences like in (17) as predicted (i.e., they said "yes"), but children between the ages of 3;6 and 6;0 did something different. The behavior of 14 of the 15 children[5] fell into two groups: ten children (mean age 4;7), Group A, readily accepted sentences like (17) in the "distributed" situation but more often than not either rejected it (i.e., they said "no") or didn't know what to do with it in the "exclusive" situation; in stark contrast, the other four children (mean age 4;11), Group B, all accepted as true sentences like (17) in the "exclusive" situation, but in the "distributed" situation mostly rejected the sentence or didn't know what to do with it.

To summarize, 14 of the 15 children tested have systematic, nonadult-like interpretations of expressions like (17). In particular, all 14 place more severe restrictions than adults do on the interpretive possibilities of sentences such as (17): the larger group, Group A, requires that for sentences like (17) to be true, one of each object named in the disjunction (e.g., *a cat or a pig*) be picked at least once; Group B children require instead that the same named object be chosen by every actor. In other words, although children in Group A have a grammar distinct from those in Group B, they all have a constraint in their grammars that adult native English speakers do not have.

Importantly, as Boster and Crain demonstrate, it is nevertheless clear that for each group the respective other meaning adults assign to (17) is learnable. Encountering a sentence such as *Every boy is eating a cookie or a muffin* in contexts where all the boys are eating only cookies is what's needed to falsify and extend Group A's hypothesis, whereas what's needed to falsify and extend Group B's hypothesis is hearing it in contexts where both cookies and muffins are being eaten by the boys. Therefore, each group is predicted to be able to abandon their respective (nontarget-like) constraint and converge on the other interpretation as well.

Let us reiterate the main points of this subsection: The poverty of the stimulus in language acquisition refers to linguistic knowledge – stated in the Crain and Thornton (1998) quotation above in terms of the (negative) constraints of Universal Grammar – for which no external evidence (i.e., input) is available. This linguistic knowledge can but need not be in reference to the Target Language grammar. As we have argued above, non-TL-defined poverty-of-the-stimulus problems can also (provisionally) characterize L1 development as it unfolds what we have termed "developmental" poverty-of-the-stimulus effects; these are additional to those poverty-of-the-stimulus effects that (permanently) characterize the final-state grammar.

It is important to note that strictly speaking, the distinction drawn between "developmental" and "final-state" poverty-of-the-stimulus effects is wholly artificial: they represent one and the same phenomenon in that they are both underdetermined linguistic knowledge whose source can only be internal to the language acquirer (whose source is hence assumed to be UG). Despite this artifice, for the sake of clarity we will continue to make this distinction in our discussion of poverty of stimulus in the (adult) L2 acquisition context, the topic to which we now turn.

Schwartz and Sprouse (1994)

Our first case study is our own (1994) longitudinal study of the acquisition of German word order by Cevdet, an adult native speaker of Turkish. Cevdet displayed an interesting if somewhat unexpected developmental pattern in regard to verb placement. This development is schematized in (19), and sample utterances from each of the three stages are given in (20)–(22):

(19) a. Stage 1 (1;0 to 1;4): (X)SVO
      b. Stage 2 (1;8 to 2;7): (X)SVO; XVS$_{[+pron]}$ . . .
      c. Stage 3 (2;10): (X)SVO; XVS$_{[\pm pron]}$ . . .

(20) Stage 1: (X)SVO
      jetzt er hat Gesicht [das is falsches Wagen]
      now he has face   that is wrong   car
      "now he makes a face (that) that is the wrong car"   (1;4)

(21) Stage 2: (X)SVO; XVS$_{[+pron]}$ . . .
      a. (X)SVO
          in der Türkei der Lehrer kann den Schüler schlagen
          in the Turkey the teacher can   the pupil   beat
          "in Turkey the teacher can hit the pupil"   (1;9)
      b. XVS$_{[+pron]}$ . . .
          dann trinken wir bis   neun Uhr
          then drink   we until nine o'clock
          "then we will drink until nine o'clock"   (2;1)

(22)   Stage 3: (X)SVO; XVS$_{[\pm pron]}$ · · ·
  a.   (X)SVO
         später der Charlie wollte   zum   Gefängnishaus
         later   the Charlie wanted to-the prison
         "later Charlie wanted to go to the prison"   (2;10)
  b.   XVS$_{[\pm pron]}$ · · ·
         das hat eine andere Frau   gesehen
         that has an   other   woman seen
         "another woman saw that"   (2;10)

(23) provides a frequency breakdown of the different patterns for each stage.

(23)   Declarative main clauses with two or more nonverbal constituents
        (excluding copular and existential-presentative clauses) (from Schwartz
        and Sprouse, 1994:339, table 5)

PRONOMINAL SUBJECTS

	pre-verbal		post-verbal	
Stage	SVX	XSV	...VS	Total
1	18 (86%)	3 (14%)	0 (0%)	21 (100%)
2	109 (50%)	38 (18%)	69 (32%)	216 (100%)
3	48 (41%)	2 (2%)	67 (57%)	117 (100%)

NONPRONOMINAL SUBJECTS

	pre-verbal		post-verbal	
Stage	SVX	XSV	...VS	Total
1	11 (92%)	1 (8%)	0 (0%)	12 (100%)
2	93 (78%)	26 (21%)	1 (1%)	120 (100%)
3	46 (75%)	7 (11%)	8 (13%)	61 (100%)

What is crucial here is Stage 2. At this stage, which lasts approximately
one year, Cevdet exhibits "subject–verb inversion" with pronominal subjects,
but not with nonpronominal subjects (see the highlighted figures in (23)). In
our 1994 paper we account for this asymmetry by appealing to Rizzi and
Roberts' (1989) theory of inversion in French, which also exhibits an asymmetry between pronominal and nonpronominal subjects in inversion structures. In brief, Rizzi and Roberts claim that in regard to subjects, French
adopts two of three mechanisms UG makes available for satisfying the Case
Filter: (a) Spec-head agreement and (b) incorporation of subject clitics into
the finite verb in C. Spec-head agreement accounts for non-inverted word
order, as in (24a), and incorporation accounts for inversion with subject
clitics, as in (24b). The nominative case mechanism required for inversion
with nonpronominal subjects (as in German) is government, as in (24c), but
by hypothesis this is not available in French.

(24) a. Spec-head agreement: non-inverted word order (SVO)

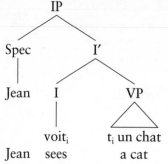

Jean   sees   a cat

  b. Incorporation: inversion with subject clitics only $((X)VS_{[+pron]}O)$

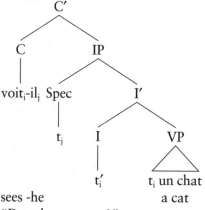

sees -he   a cat
"Does he see a cat?"

  c. Government: inversion possible with all subjects (genuine "V2")

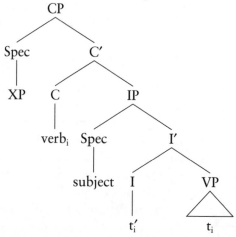

Thus, in French, nonpronominal subjects cannot occur in Spec, IP when I (containing the verb) has moved to C. In our study we assumed that Cevdet's Interlanguage at Stage 2 reflects a similar state of affairs with respect to nominative case: Spec-head agreement and incorporation, but not government. This is summarized in (25):

(25)

	Spec-Head	Incorporation	Government
Turkish	+	−	−
Cevdet's Stage 1	+	−	−
French	+	+	−
Cevdet's Stage 2	+	+	−
German	+	(?)	+
Cevdet's Stage 3	+	(?)	+

Now, it is evident that this analysis would have to be recast in order to become compatible with more recent theoretical developments within mainstream generative grammar. In particular, one could no longer appeal to the government option as the mechanism crucially differentiating Cevdet's Stage 2 from his Stage 3 – or crucially distinguishing French from German, for that matter.

However, we believe that one aspect of this study will remain of interest, regardless of the changing tides of syntactic formalism. In regard to the asymmetry between pronominal and nonpronominal subjects with respect to inversion, it is clear that Cevdet's Interlanguage has not inherited this asymmetry from Turkish, the L1, nor does German, the TL, exhibit it either. Furthermore, it is rather implausible that general problem solving would lead Cevdet to this distinction in his Interlanguage on the basis of his exposure to German.[6] In short, there is a poverty of stimulus problem here, in the sense that neither the L1 grammar nor the L2 surface patterns can account for a property of this Interlanguage system. This poverty of the stimulus is not, as we said, one that characterizes the TL grammar; it is nevertheless linguistic knowledge arising in the absence of direct experience. So far, then, this example appears to be conceptually very similar to what we termed, in the context of L1 acquisition, "developmental" poverty-of-the-stimulus effects. There is, however, one more decisive step to take in the argument.

Central to our claim that this analysis of the L2 data constitutes an argument for the Strong UG hypothesis is the fact that the inversion asymmetry is mirrored in at least one natural language grammar, viz., French. This observation is crucial because no matter what mechanisms syntactic theory may offer in the future to account for the asymmetry in French, these same mechanisms can be relied on to account for Cevdet's Stage 2 data. We therefore conclude that regardless of the precise formulation of syntactic theory, Cevdet's Interlanguage behavior can be accounted for only by assuming that his Interlanguage hypotheses are guided by UG. This is because it instantiates a UG-derived poverty-of-the-stimulus problem. Not to put too fine a point on this: imagine that it were the case that the asymmetry in Cevdet's Interlanguage were reversed such that he allowed inversion only with nonpronominal subjects. Assuming that no natural language grammar has such a system, this asymmetry – while also not inherited from the L1 nor inferable from the surface patterns of the input – not only would fail to be evidence for the Strong UG hypothesis in (adult) L2 acquisition, but would in fact be evidence against it.

Martohardjono (1993)

The case study considered in the previous subsection involved the discovery of a relatively simple asymmetry in distributional syntax from a corpus of naturalistic production data. Discovering and documenting such UG-derived poverty-of-the-stimulus effects in especially naturalistic corpora is in part a matter of luck, and it is unlikely that the phenomena themselves will be particularly subtle. If one wishes to probe knowledge of UG-derived poverty of the stimulus problems in L2 systems, one will generally have to design experiments precisely for this purpose. In this subsection we consider some-what more complex asymmetries in distributional syntax, this time devised in terms of the TL final-state grammar and tested for explicitly as well. We review the results of Martohardjono's (1993) study of L2ers' knowledge of various constraints on (the output of) wh-movement.

Martohardjono's focus was on strong vs. weak violations of grammatical principles, as defined within the framework of Chomsky (1986). Strong violations strike native speakers as substantially "worse" than weak violations. Extractions from relative clauses ((26a)), adjunct clauses ((26b)) and sentential subjects ((26c)) were categorized as strong violations; weak violations included "simple" *that*-trace violations ((27a)) as well as extractions from noun complement clauses ((27b)) and wh-islands ((27c)).

(26) Examples of strong violations   (see Martohardjono 1993:172–6)
    a. Extraction from Relative Clause
       *Which mayor did Mary read the book that praised?
    b. Extraction from Adjunct Clause
       *Which soup did the man leave the table after the waiter spilled?
    c. Extraction from Sentential Subject
       *Which job did getting help the graduate student?

(27) Examples of weak violations   (see Martohardjono 1993:172–6)
    a. "simple" *that*-trace violation
       ?*Which medicine did John think that cured his illness?
    b. Extraction from Noun Complement Clause
       ?*Which game did Anne hear the news that the British team won?
    c. Extraction from wh-Island
       ?*Which parcel did Amy wonder why the boy had brought?

Martohardjono administered an acceptability judgment task on ungrammatical wh-extraction of these types as well as on grammatical wh-extraction to four different groups: native speakers of Indonesian, Chinese and Italian all learning English, and native English speakers. Martohardjono notes that these four languages differ with respect to wh-movement and to constraints on it. Indonesian and Chinese both lack wh-movement in questions, but Chinese relative clauses involve movement of a null operator. English and Italian exhibit wh-movement in questions and relative clauses; however, Italian, unlike English, allows extractions from wh-islands. Martohardjono concluded that because of such differences, native speakers of Indonesian, Chinese and Italian would face distinct challenges in acquiring constraints on wh-movement in English. She therefore considered the performance of the three L2 groups individually.

Martohardjono's hypothesis was that UG guides L2 acquisition, and hence, despite differences across groups, within any given L1 group there should be a statistically significant difference in the rejection of strong vs. weak violations. Such a distinction is indeed reflected in the results, summarized in (28) (cf. Martohardjono, 1993:124, table 18):

(28) Combined Mean Rejection of Ungrammatical Wh-constructions

	Indonesian	Chinese	Italian	English
Strong	87%	76%	89%	94%
Weak	42%	38%	61%	79%

Notice, first, that the native English speakers display a (statistically significant) distinction in their rejection of strong vs. weak violations; while individual thresholds for rejecting an ungrammatical sentence may vary, there is nevertheless a measurable difference between rejection of strong vs. weak violations. As for the L2ers, Martohardjono concludes that while there is a noticeable effect of the L1 on their absolute performance level, within each of the three groups, there is clear evidence of knowledge of the distinction between strong and weak violations.

The point we wish to stress is the following. Martohardjono (1993) based her study on Chomsky's (1986) framework, which included notions like the Empty Category Principle (ECP) and the Constraint on Extraction Domains (CED), which have subsequently been superseded by other principles in, e.g., Chomsky's (1995) framework. However, this is totally irrelevant for the acquisitional hypothesis tested by Martohardjono – because the conceptual problem remains the same. No matter how the constraints on extraction are framed, there is a clear poverty-of-the-stimulus problem involved in acquiring the distinction between strong and weak violations, since they both refer to essentially non-occurring syntactic patterns. Thus, any adequate theory of UG will have to account for this distinction.[7] The fact that Martohardjono's L2 acquirers display knowledge not only of the unacceptability of strong violations, but also of the distinction between strong and weak violations, is a very strong indication that L2 development is constrained by UG.

Dekydtspotter, Sprouse and Anderson (1997)

The first two case studies considered in this section have involved poverty of the stimulus in Interlanguage distributional syntax, the domain to which the vast bulk of generative research on L2 acquisition has been devoted. Although the underdetermination effect at issue in this subsection is, like in Martohardjono (1993), framed in relation to the TL final-state grammar, this time we look at a relatively new approach to the establishment of UG-derived poverty-of-the-stimulus problems in L2 development: the investigation of the syntax–semantics interface in Interlanguage. The purpose here is to determine whether L2 acquirers end up with knowledge about interpretive restrictions associated with particular syntactic forms, for which there is no (direct) input or instruction.

The study we summarize is by Dekydtspotter, Sprouse and Anderson (1997) (henceforth DSA) who investigated the interpretation of French dyadic nominals by native speakers of English acquiring French in a tutored setting. French and English differ in that French, but not English, allows dyadic nominals with both Agent and Theme in post-nominal position and with both Agent and Theme marked by a semantically contentless preposition (*de/ of*). This difference is illustrated in (29):

(29) a. la   version de la   9ème de Karajan   French
      b. ?*the version of the 9th   of Karajan   English

Although French syntax allows two post-nominal *de*-phrases, a crucial semantic condition is imposed: the nominal must have a result interpretation, not a process interpretation (Valois, 1991). Thus, (29a) (= (30a)) contrasts with (30b), because the noun *destruction* in (30b) can only be understood as a process, and this interpretation is not allowed when both Theme and Agent are marked by the preposition *de*.

(30) a. la   version de la   9ème de Karajan
          the version of the 9th   of Karajan   RESULT
      b. *la destruction de Tokyo de Godzilla   (Godzilla = Agent)
          the destruction of Tokyo of Godzilla   PROCESS

It should be noted that such facts are never mentioned in French language proficiency courses and (as DSA show) are not directly transferable from English.

The question DSA posed was whether English-speaking learners of French would be sensitive to the process/result distinction (i.e., ungrammatical/ grammatical) in dyadic nominals with two post-nominal *de*-phrases. Their experiment was a judgment task, where each test item consisted of a paragraph (in English) followed by a French sentence, the acceptability of which the students were asked to judge. In the case of the experimental items, the French sentence contained a dyadic nominal with two post-nominal *de*-phrases. Since many nouns can in principle refer either to a process or to a result, the contextualizing paragraph was included so that for each item either a process or a result interpretation was clearly established. There were ten grammatical result nominals (such as (31)) and twelve ungrammatical process nominals (such as (32)) (as well as fillers).

(31) La description du   Lake District de Wordsworth est très touchante.
      the description of-the Lake District of Wordsworth is very touching

(32) L'extraction de l'or   des   mineurs est interdite. (* in French)
      the extract   of the gold of-the miners is forbidden

   Note that the contexts also established as clearly as possible that, e.g., in (31) Wordsworth is to be understood as the describer of (not a visitor in) the Lake District and in (32) that the miners are the extracters (not the owners) of the gold.
   The results clearly show that all the learner groups as well as the native French control group are sensitive to the process/result distinction in French dyadic nominals. This is shown in the table in (33), where "yes" responses indicate acceptance of a dyadic nominal in either a result or a process context, as indicated.

(33) "Yes" responses on dyadic French nominals with two *de*-phrases

	Beginners/Intermediate (n = 70)	Advanced (n = 20)	Native (n = 48)
Result	70.29%	63.50%	50.42%
Process	51.43%	24.17%	15.65%

The distinction between result and process nominals is statistically very highly significant for all three groups. Note that although the Native group's performance confirms the distinction in grammaticality between result and process nominals as discussed in the literature (Grimshaw, 1990; Valois, 1991), it also reflects the observation that even the result nominals are considered stylistically awkward by native French speakers (Milner, 1982:87). Nevertheless, knowledge of the distinction on the part of even second-semester US college French students is clearly in evidence in (33).
   It is important here to realize that the English-speaking classroom learner of French is faced with an extreme poverty-of-the-stimulus problem in the acquisition of the knowledge of any distinction between dyadic process nominals and result nominals. Recall that these facts are neither the topic of instruction nor transferable from English. Furthermore, dyadic nominals of this sort are typical of fairly abstract discourse and hence relatively

infrequent in the input. What is more, even when an appropriate context for the use of a dyadic nominal arises, it is clear that native French speakers do not particularly care for the use of *de*-marked Agents in the relevant dyadic nominals.

But most importantly, it is far from clear how one could in principle (without the aid of UG) deduce that the surface pattern N-*de*-DP-*de*-DP is permissible only with result interpretations. To understand why, let us consider the interpretations of the sentences in (34).

(34)
a.   La démonstration du théorème par le professeur était très intéressante.
     the proof of-the theorem   by the professor was very interesting
b.   La démonstration du théorème du   professeur était très intéressante.
     the proof of-the theorem   of-the professor was very interesting

The simple noun *démonstration* ("proof") can express either a result or a process. In (34b), however, because the Agent, *le professeur*, is marked by the preposition *de*, the entire nominal can have only a result interpretation. By contrast in (34a), the Agent is instead marked by *par*. Thus, in (34a) the entire nominal is not subject to the restriction that it have only a result interpretation and is in fact perfectly ambiguous between a process and a result interpretation.

Consider now the input that a learner might receive. A sentence like (34a) could occur in both process and result contexts, while a sentence like (34b) could occur only in result contexts. What might help the learner come to know that (34b) is not a simple variant of the more robust (34a) with both process and result interpretations? Suppose that s/he tries to keep track of which dyadic nominals occur in process contexts and which ones occur in result contexts. This of course requires the ability to systematically distinguish result contexts from process contexts, but this is itself a difficult task. Using (34) as illustration, note that in many situations where the resulting proof was interesting, the process of arriving at the proof was interesting as well. In other words, the already small number of opportunities to analyze the semantics of (34b) uttered appropriately in context will be even further diminished by the fact that the context often will not necessarily exclude a process interpretation. And it is hearing (34b) in a context that necessarily excludes the process interpretation that is required in order for the learner even to have a shot at simply inferring the relevant interpretive restriction. This would require a situation in which the process of arriving at the proof was tedious, but the resulting proof itself was interesting. In short, even if the learner were somehow keeping track of whether each dyadic-nominal utterance occurs in a process or a result context, the learner would still have to be able to identify the result contexts in the first place.

As noted by Chierchia (1994) for L1 acquisition, the poverty of the stimulus at the syntax–semantics interface is so severe, the phenomena so subtle, and the relevant mapping from syntax to interpretation so idiosyncratic that acquisition of the actual interpretive properties of natural languages can proceed only if the hypothesis space is narrowly limited by UG. Thus, if adult L2ers exhibit sensitivity to the relevant interpretive distinctions, this can only come about through the operation of UG in L2 acquisition (see also Dekydtspotter, Sprouse and Thyre, 1998). All of this is entirely independent of the precise formulation of the formal system responsible for syntax–semantics correspondences.

Comparative Interlanguage Development

The point of the preceding section was to show the following: In work investigating the role of UG in L2 acquisition, the establishment of clear UG-derived L2 poverty-of-the-stimulus problems serves as an antidote to changes in syntactic theory. In this section we briefly turn to our suggestion for similarly immunizing the investigation of L1 transfer.

It seems to us that much of the Transfer Debate has suffered from insufficient appreciation of the logic at the heart of the issue and the type of empirical findings that can arbitrate. On the one hand, proponents of No Transfer seem to fear that finding evidence for transfer in L2 development somehow constitutes a threat to the role of UG in L2 development. On this approach, transfer is seen as antithetical to the Strong UG hypothesis. Needless to say, this reasoning eludes us entirely. On the other hand, proponents of Partial Transfer attempt to account for the limited performance observed in early Interlanguage through some specific syntactic deficit (such as the absence or underspecification of functioal categories). But such approaches overlook the extremely limited L2 lexicon as well as the underdeveloped processing and production routines in this early phase.

We hold that the key to investigating the extent of transfer is comparative Interlanguage research. For whatever linguistic domain of interest, the logic is completely straightforward: In the acquisition of some phenomenon P in a given Target Language, compare the developmental paths of L2ers whose L1s are, with respect to P, typologically distinct. If one finds divergence in developmental paths (regardless of the L2ers' potential ultimate attainment), one has evidence for transfer in that domain – because there is nothing in the L2ers' input (at least, in their primary linguistic data) which could account for such divergence. If, on the other hand, one finds a uniform developmental path with respect to P, one has evidence against transfer. Note that the success of such research for informing us about the extent of L1 influence in L2 development depends not at all on the fine points of linguistic theory.

Concluding Remarks

We wish to emphasize that we are absolutely not advocating the abandon-
ment of detailed syntactic analyses of Interlanguage data. Rather, what we
have tried to suggest here is that as L2 acquisition researchers we should
perhaps more frequently take a step back from the technicalities of our
particular framework *du jour* and ask two broader questions: (a) Have we
discovered genuine UG-derived Interlanguage poverty-of-the-stimulus effects
(which cannot be attributed to the L1)? These are the phenomena that by
their very nature will necessitate an account that implicates UG in (adult) L2
development.[8] (b) Holding the Target Language constant, have we found
convergent or divergent L2 developmental routes among (groups of) L2ers
with (typologically) distinct L1s? This is what will tell us the extent to which
transfer exerts itself in the development of Interlanguage knowledge. We
believe that L2 acquisition research that rigorously attends to (a) and (b) will
ride the shifting tides of syntactic formalism and will furnish the key to the
etiology and epistemological status of Interlanguage, thereby establishing
beyond any doubt why Interlanguage should be of interest to linguistics as
part of cognitive science.

Acknowledgments

Leads (and weeds) for this paper sprouted (and withered) out of various portions of
talks over the last four years, and we therefore thank those who listened and especially
those who provided feedback at: Linguistic Society of America (New Orleans, January 6,
1995); Language Acquisition Research Symposium (Utrecht, May 12, 1995); University of
York (June 8, 1995); University of Massachusetts, Amherst (October 13, 1995); Keio
University (March 30, 1998); the First Durham Postgraduate Conference in Theoretical
and Applied Linguistics (June 13, 1998); and Second Language Research Forum (Honolulu, October 17, 1998). The first author extends her sincere appreciation in particular to
Kevin Duffy and Yukio Otsu for their gracious hospitality, to the University of Durham
for travel grants to (almost) all the venues outside England, to the Linguistics Department
at the University of Maryland for a conducive work environment, and to the Arts and
Humanities Research Board for making possible the timely final revision through a 1999
Research Leave Award for Term II. For helpful comments on the full written draft, we are
grateful to two anonymous reviewers and to especially Kevin Gregg. Finally, for supporting this paper, one way or another, we would also like to thank: John Archibald, Laurent
Dekydtspotter, Alec Marantz, Silvina Montrul and Martha Young-Scholten. Of course,
no one other than us two is responsible for errors.

Notes

1   It is important to realize here that (contrary to one reviewer's comments) we are not
    condemning Vainikka and Young-Scholten as "out of touch" because their analysis

does not reflect "the very latest from Cambridge." Quite the opposite, because we would offer the very same line of critique of an analysis that depended crucially on the formalisms of the Minimalist Program, or for that matter, of Lexical Functional Grammar, Head-Driven Phrase Structure Grammar, Optimality Theory, or Space Grammar. More specifically, we are not saying here that the fact that early Korean–German and Turkish–German Interlanguages exhibit surface OV order "proves" that functional categories are present in the initial state of L2 development. Rather, we merely point out that the distinction drawn between the role of lexical categories and the role of functional categories is theory-dependent, and moreover, that conclusions at the heart of L2 acquisition research stand or fall as a consequence. To reiterate, the point of this discussion is that L2 researchers are in general better off to avoid this position in the first place by relying not on formal mechanisms but on mid-level generalizations, the acquisition of which involves a poverty-of-the-stimulus problem. (The general thrust of these remarks applies to the following subsection as well.)

2   or to the current state of L1 development, in the case of child L2 acquisition.

3   Consider, for example, the now classic formulation by Hornstein and Lightfoot (1981:9): "People attain knowledge of the structure of their language for which *no* [emphasis original] evidence is available in the data to which they are exposed as children."

4   It is simple to see how in principle constraint K can be subsequently overridden: Accommodating input consisting of utterances that show K to be inoperative. Thus, learnability is not threatened. See below.

5   One child, age 5;7, performed perfectly, just like the 12 adult controls tested.

6   One reviewer seems to suggest that the pattern observed in Cevdet's Stage 2 may somehow arise from frequency effects in the input. Note, however, that even if German input contains more instances of inversion with pronominal subjects than inversion with nonpronominal subjects, an account of the distinction between Cevdet's grammar at Stage 2 and his grammar at Stage 3 is still required. In other words, this observation about frequency in the input in no way undermines or detracts from the necessity of having a grammatical account of Cevdet's Stage 2 system – which, recall, lasts for over a year – where inversion with nonpronominal subjects seems to be prohibited.

7   A helpful reviewer reminds us that the publication of individual as well as aggregate results in studies of this sort encourages and facilitates reanalysis under new syntactic models.

8   The importance of the difference between finding a "UG-compatible" account of a given set of L2 data and finding a UG-derived L2 poverty-of-the-stimulus effect cannot be overemphasized. It is only the latter that necessarily argues for UG constraining (adult) L2ers' hypotheses. The value of UG-compatible analyses of Interlanguage data is at its highest when those very same data have been claimed to be UG-incompatible, as in the case of the L2 German data discussed in the second section. On the other hand, UG compatibility of L2 data is, we believe, of questionable value when the research design takes the following form: Start with a grammatical phenomenon – hence a phenomenon known to be compatible with UG – and then show that it exists in Interlanguage; such a demonstration is especially pointless when the phenomenon at issue exists in Interlanguage in exactly the same form as it exists in the Target Language (as in the experiment conducted by Epstein, Flynn and Martohardjono, 1996). In short, UG compatibility is necessary but not sufficient when arguing for the Strong UG hypothesis in (adult) L2 acquisition; establishing UG-derived

poverty-of-the-stimulus effects in (adult) L2 acquisition is, by contrast, sufficient for inferring that UG is the cause.

References

Boster, C. and Crain, S. (1994) On children's understanding of *every* and *or*. *Early Cognition and the Transition to Language*. Austin: University of Texas, Austin.

Chierchia, G. (1994) Syntactic bootstrapping and the acquisition of noun meanings: The mass-count issue. In B. Lust, M. Suñer and J. Whitman (eds.), *Syntactic Theory and First Language Acquisition: Crosslinguistic Perspectives Vol 1: Heads, Projections, and Learnability*, pp. 301–18. Hillside, NJ: Lawrence Erlbaum.

Chomsky, N. (1995) *The Minimalist Program*. Cambridge, MA: MIT Press.

—— (1993) A minimalist program for linguistic theory. In K. Hale and S. J. Keyser (eds.), *The View from Building 20: Essays in Linguistics in Honor of Sylvain Bromberger*, pp. 1–52. Cambridge, MA: MIT Press.

—— (1991) Some notes on the economy of derivation and representation. In R. Freidin (ed.), *Principles and Parameters in Comparative Grammar*, pp. 417–54. Cambridge, MA: MIT Press.

—— (1986) *Barriers*. Cambridge, MA: MIT Press.

Clahsen, H. and Muysken, P. (1986) The availability of Universal Grammar to adult and child learners: A study of the acquisition of German word order. *Second Language Research* 2: 93–119.

Crain, S. and McKee, C. (1985) Acquisition of structural restrictions on anaphora. In S. Berman, J.-W. Choe and J. McDonough (eds.), *Proceedings of the North Eastern Linguistic Society (NELS) 16*, pp. 94–110. Amherst, MA: GLSA.

—— and Thornton, R. (1998) *Investigations in Universal Grammar: A Guide to Experiments on the Acquisition of Syntax and Semantics*. Cambridge, MA: MIT Press.

Dekydtspotter, L., Sprouse, R. A. and Anderson, B. (1997) The interpretive interface in L2 acquisition: The process–result distinction in English–French Interlanguage grammars. *Language Acquisition* 6: 297–332.

——, —— and Thyre, R. (1998) Evidence for Full UG Access in L2 acquisition from the interpretive interface: Quantification at a distance in English–French Interlanguage. In A. Greenhill, M. Hughes, H. Littlefield and H. Walsh (eds.), *Proceedings of the 22nd Annual Boston University Conference on Language Development Vol. 1*, pp. 141–52. Somerville, MA: Cascadilla Press.

duPlessis, J., Solin, D., Travis, L. and White, L. (1987) UG or not UG, that is the question: A reply to Clahsen and Muysken. *Second Language Research* 3: 56–75.

Emonds, J. (1978) The verbal complex V'–V in French. *Linguistic Inquiry* 9: 151–75.

Epstein, S., Flynn, S. and Martohardjono, G. (1996) Second language acquisition: Theoretical and experimental issues in contemporary research. *Behavioral and Brain Sciences* 19: 677–758.

Eubank, L. (1993/1994) On the transfer of parametric values in L2 development. *Language Acquisition* 3: 183–208.

Gerbault, J. (1978) *The Acquisition of English by a Five-year-old French Speaker*. Unpublished MA thesis, UCLA.

Goldin-Meadow, S. and Mylander, C. (1990) Beyond the input given: The child's role in the acquisition of language. *Language* 66: 323–55.

Grimshaw, J. (1990) *Argument Structure*. Cambridge, MA: MIT Press.

Hornstein, N. and Lightfoot, D. (1981) Introduction. In N. Hornstein and D. Lightfoot (eds.), *Explanation in Linguistics: The Logical Problem of Language Acquisition*, pp. 9–31. New York: Longman.

Kayne, R. (1994) *The Antisymmetry of Syntax*. Cambridge, MA: MIT Press.

Martohardjono, G. (1993) Wh-movement in the Acquisition of a Second Language: A Cross-linguistic Study of Three Languages with and without Overt Movement. Unpublished Ph.D. dissertation, Cornell University, Ithaca, NY.

Milner, J.-C. (1982) *Ordres et Raisons de Langue*. Paris: Editions du Seuil.

Platzack, C. (1986) COMP, Infl, and Germanic word order. In L. Hellan and K. Christensen (eds.), *Topics in Scandinavian Syntax*, pp. 185–234. Dordrecht: Reidel.

Pollock, J.-Y. (1989) Verb movement, Universal Grammar, and the structure of IP. *Linguistic Inquiry* 20: 365–424.

Rizzi, L. and Roberts, I. (1989) Complex inversion in French. *Probus* 1: 1–30.

Rohrbacher, B. (1994) The Germanic VO Languages and the Full Paradigm: A Theory of V to I Raising. Unpublished Ph.D. dissertation, University of Massachusetts, Amherst.

—— (1992) English AUX^Neg, Mainland Scandinavian AUX^Neg and the theory of V to I raising. MS., University of Massachusetts, Amherst.

Schönenberger, M. (1996) Why do Swiss-German children like verb movement so much? In A. Stringfellow, D. Cahana-Amitay, E. Hughes and A. Zukowski (eds.), *Proceedings of the 20th Annual Boston University Conference on Language Development*, vol. 2, pp. 658–69. Somerville, MA: Cascadilla Press.

—— (1995) Embedded V-to-C in "early" Swiss German. In C. Schütze, J. Ganger and K. Broihier (eds.) *MIT Working Papers in Linguistics* 26: 403–50.

Schwartz, B. D. (1988a) Back to Basics. Paper presented at the 18th Second Language Research Forum (SLRF), University of Hawaii at Manoa, 17 October. MS., University of Durham.

—— (1998b) On two hypotheses of "Transfer" in L2A: Minimal Trees and Absolute L1 Influence. In S. Flynn, G. Martohardjono and W. O'Neil (eds.), *The Generative Study of Second Language Acquisition*, pp. 35–59. Mahwah, NJ: Lawrence Erlbaum.

—— and Sprouse, R. A. (1998) Back to Basics in generative second language acquisition research. MS., University of Durham/Indiana University (http://mitpress.mit.edu/celebration).

—— and —— (1996) L2 cognitive states and the Full Transfer/Full Access model. *Second Language Research* 12: 40–72.

—— and —— (1994) Word order and Nominative Case in nonnative language acquisition: A longitudinal study of (L1 Turkish) German Interlanguage. In T. Hoekstra and B. D. Schwartz (eds.), *Language Acquisition Studies in Generative Grammar: Papers in Honor of Kenneth Wexler from the 1991 GLOW Workshops*, pp. 317–68. Amsterdam: John Benjamins.

—— and Tomaselli, A. (1990) Some implications from an analysis of German word order. In W. Abraham, W. Kosmeijer and E. Reuland (eds.), *Issues in Germanic Syntax*, pp. 251–74. New York: Mouton de Gruyter.

Sprouse, R. A. (1998) Some notes on the relationship between inflectional morphology and parameter setting in first and second language acquisition. In M. Beck (ed.), *Morphology and its Interfaces in L2 Knowledge*, pp. 41–67. Amsterdam: John Benjamins.

Tiphine, U. (1983) The Acquisition of English Statements and Interrogatives by French-Speaking Children. Unpublished Ph.D. dissertation, University of Kiel.

—— (no date) The acquisition of English negation by four French children. MS., University of Kiel.

Tomaselli, A. and Schwartz, B. D. (1990) Analysing the acquisition stages of negation in L2 German: Support for UG in adult SLA. *Second Language Research* 6: 1–38.

Travis, L. (1984) Parameters and Effects of Word Order Variation. Unpublished Ph.D. dissertation, MIT.

Vainikka, A. and Young-Scholten, M. (1996) Gradual development of L2 phrase structure. *Second Language Research* 12: 7–39.

—— and —— (1994) Direct access to X′-theory: Evidence from Korean and Turkish adults learning German. In T. Hoekstra and B. D. Schwartz (eds.), *Language Acquisition Studies in Generative Grammar: Papers in Honor of Kenneth Wexler from the 1991 GLOW Workshops*, pp. 265–316. Amsterdam: John Benjamins.

Valois, D. (1991) The Internal Structure of DP. Unpublished Ph.D. dissertation, UCLA.

Vikner, S. (1995) V^0-to-I^0 movement and inflection for person in all tenses. *Working Papers in Scandinavian Syntax* 55: 1–27.

White, L. (1989) *Universal Grammar and Second Language Acquisition*. Amsterdam: John Benjamins.

6

An Overview of the Second Language Acquisition of Links between Verb Semantics and Morpho-syntax*

Alan Juffs

1 Introduction

This chapter provides an overview of research into the way adult learners of second languages acquire knowledge of the relationship between verb meaning and morpho-syntax. For example, if learners of English as a second language know that both *fall* and *drop* mean "to move downwards", do they also know that "the apple fell to the ground", "the apple dropped to the ground", and "Sandy dropped the apple" are possible English sentences, but "*Sandy fell the apple" is not? The first part of the chapter reviews one approach to verb semantics and how it accounts for mapping from the lexicon to morpho-syntax. The second part of the chapter discusses research into the developmental processes in second language acquisition in this sub-domain of grammar: The questions that are addressed are familiar ones in a Principles and Parameters approach to SLA: (a) is there a logical problem of acquisition? (b) are L2 grammars constrained in the way that first language grammars are constrained even if they do not look exactly like those of native speakers? and (c) what is the role of the first language in interlanguage representations?

* I am grateful to the National Science Foundation Grant #SBR-9709152 for support for this research.

1.1　The place of verb semantics in syntactic theory

The study of the syntax of human languages focuses to a large degree on clause structure and the constraints governing the interpretation and the ordering of constituents within and across clause boundaries. It has been argued that some of the constraints must be part of a species-specific linguistic endowment – namely Universal Grammar (UG) (Chomsky, 1981, 1986; papers in Hornstein and Lightfoot, 1981), because adult speakers know more about the clause structure and meanings of their native language than they could possibly have induced from the input they receive.[1]

Verbs play a particularly important part in a clause because it is thought that they determine the number of NPs and other constituents that are required, and can affect the ordering or position of these constituents within the clause: This property of a verb has been referred to as its "argument structure" or "subcategorization requirements". Although much of the lexicon is idiosyncratic (di Sciullo and Williams, 1987; Chomsky, 1995), verb subcategorization has been held to be constrained by UG at least since the inception of the Principles and Parameters (P&P) framework (Chomsky, 1981:11; Grimshaw, 1981). In standard P&P theory, the central role of the verb in clause structure was captured by constructs such as Theta Theory, the Projection Principle (Chomsky, 1981:29) and the Universal Thematic Alignment Hypothesis (Baker, 1988). (In the Minimalist Program, "lexical resources" remain as the source of derivations, Marantz, 1995.) Theta theory proposed a list of semantic or *theta roles*, e.g., causer of action = Agent, experiencer of action = Experiencer, undergoer of action = Theme, and location of destination of the action = Goal. Theta roles were not an unordered list but existed in a *thematic hierarchy*, where Agent and Experiencer are higher than Theme which in turn is higher than Goal: Agent > Experiencer > Theme > Goal (c.f. Grimshaw, 1990; Larson, 1988). Noun phrases bearing thematic roles are assigned to syntactic positions in accordance with that hierarchy, so that Agent is assigned to the highest position, i.e., that of syntactic Subject [NP, IP], the Theme to the Direct Object, and Goal to the Indirect Object. Verbs were assumed to have a *theta grid* which stated the semantic roles associated with the predicate (Stowell, 1981). To illustrate, the verb *put* is assumed to subcategorize for, or require an Agent, a Theme, and a Goal. The projection principle required that the syntax had to reflect a theta grid and the theta criterion states that an NP can only receive one theta role. If any one of the requirements just discussed is violated, the result is ungrammatical, as illustrated in (1).

(1)　a.　John put the book on the table.
　　　b.　*John put the book.
　　　c.　*John put the table.
　　　d.　*John put the table with the book.[2]
　　　e.　*John put the book the magazine on the table.

In order to strengthen the links between thematic relations and syntax, Baker (1988) proposed the Uniformity of Theta Assignment Hypothesis (UTAH). The UTAH states that "identical thematic relationships between items are represented by identical structural relationships between those items at D-structure" (Baker, 1988:47). He illustrates this idea with the following pairs of sentences:

(2) a. Julia melted the ice-cream into mush.
     b. The ice-cream melted into mush.

(3) a. [s Julia [vp melted [the ice-cream] into mush]]
     b. [s e [vp melted [the ice-cream] into mush]]

The D-structures in (3) reflect the fact that the thematic relation between *melt* and *ice-cream* is the same in both (2a) and (2b), even though it is a syntactic object in (2a) and a syntactic subject in (2b); the ice cream is the thing that changes state in both cases and this identity is reflected in the same relationship at D-structure in (3).

Verbs that have similar meanings often exhibit similar syntactic behaviour. For example, "dissolve" behaves like "melt" and not like "put" in that the Agent can be omitted and the Theme can appear as the syntactic subject. In order to explain such regularities in the lexicon and some mismatches in the mapping stated by the thematic hierarchy and the syntactic position of arguments, researchers modified early P&P theta theory and increasingly appealed to the semantic properties of verbs (Levin and Pinker, 1991; Pinker, 1989). The key questions are why verbs have the theta grids they do, and how children acquire the knowledge that certain verbs are associated with, or express, particular thematic relations? Answers to these questions are by no means obvious, and considerable disagreement remains as to (a) the status of lexical knowledge in relation to the mapping of semantic roles to syntactic positions and (b) whether such knowledge is of the same kind as abstract principles in UG such as the Empty Category Principle. The next subsection thus addresses the issue of the learnability of verb semantics and its relation to morpho-syntax.

1.2 A learnability problem? Verbs and their syntax

One of the most powerful arguments for UG is that, despite the lack of relevant evidence, adult native speakers of a language possess a highly complex grammatical system that includes not only knowledge of what is possible in their language, but also knowledge of what is *not* possible (Chomsky, 1986; see White, 1989 for a review of this issue in SLA). Both Gleitman (1990) and Pinker, (1984, 1989:5–9), while they differ in their approaches, have both argued that knowledge of the relationship between a verb's semantics and its morpho-syntax is guided in part by UG because adult grammars go beyond the input available and that therefore such knowledge is covered by standard poverty-of-the-stimulus arguments (Chomsky, 1986).

However, it can be argued that the learning problems of the lexicon are somewhat different than those involved with acquisition of constraints on the movement and interpretation within and across clause boundaries. This difference has at least three sources. First, children receive a good deal of information from the input for the acquisition of argument structure because they are constantly exposed to scenes where verbs are used with NP arguments in the correct position (Bowerman, 1988, 1990; Pinker, 1989); presumably the child is able to learn a great deal about meaning from observation, a process Naigles (1991) calls "ostension." Gleitman (1990) points out at least two problems children face if they rely on input alone: one is that children hear verbs in the input where the action described by the verb is not taking place, hence they must be quite tolerant of mismatches between input and the scenes they observe; second, for some verbs, e.g., of mental activity *think*, *believe*, there simply is not a scene to observe, so acquisition cannot proceed on the basis of matching input and activity. In these two senses, then, the input severely underdetermines the knowledge children end up with.

Second, examples of *errors of overgeneralization* with argument structure and syntax are well-documented in the first language acquisition literature (Pinker, 1989, provides a summary), whereas they are much rarer or absent with knowledge of other sub-modules of the grammar. Indeed, it is claimed that children make few, if any, errors with some constraints which are held to be universal principles of language (see research by de Villiers and Roeper (1995) for a discussion of young children's knowledge of constraints on wh-movement).[3] Overgeneralization is a problem because language learners must somehow come to terms with productive alternations, but not overgeneralize them to instances where the alternation may not take place (Baker, 1979; Bowerman, 1988; Clark, 1993; Rutherford, 1989; White, 1987). The situation is illustrated in figure 6.1.

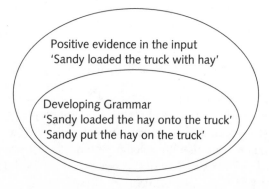

Figure 6.1 Positive evidence for adding to a verb's syntactic frames

If we suppose that the learner knows that both the sentences in the inner circle in figure 6.1 are possible, direct positive evidence, in the outer circle, in the form of sentences in the input can add forms such as "Sandy loaded the truck with hay". The learner who overgeneralizes from this structure to "*Sandy put the truck with hay" is in trouble: once the learner has assumed that a form is possible, absence from the input is not enough to guarantee deletion from the grammar. This is because innumerable sentences are possible that are unattested in the input, and therefore non-occurrence is no reason to exclude a form (Pinker, 1989:14). This logic has led some researchers to believe that learners are constrained by the Subset Principle – a learning principle which requires that a wider grammar not be posited until direct positive evidence is heard (Manzini and Wexler, 1987; White, 1989). However, reports of overgeneralizations indicate that learners do not obey this principle where argument structure is concerned.

A third reason for supposing that the acquisition of links between verb meaning and morpho-syntax might be different from abstract principles is that knowledge of verb meaning seems to interact with other cognitive knowledge which *may* precede the emergence of knowledge of syntax and interact with it (Chomsky, 1995:30–1). Pre-linguistically, the child may have general cognitive constructs such as "Agent-of-an-action" which could help in identifying the Agent in a sentence. Such semantic knowledge relates to semantic properties of verbs (s-selection, Grimshaw, 1981) which may correlate with formal properties of a lexical entry (e.g., whether a verb takes an NP or a CP complement – referred to as "c-selection" by Grimshaw), but do not constitute a one-to-one mapping. When learning the links between a verb's meaning and its morpho-syntax, the child is presented with evidence for both s-selection and c-selection at the same time and may use both kinds of evidence in constructing lexical entries. Hence, unlike the purely linguistic principles that govern syntactic movement and interpretation, the lexicon probably relies on an interface with modules outside the linguistic module (Jackendoff, 1990).[4]

To sum up, the acquisition of the lexicon and principles of mapping to syntax has been claimed to face a similar logical problem that other parts of the grammar face: Namely that adults end up knowing more than they could reasonably be expected to have obtained from the input; however, acquiring the lexicon may also be subject to other learning principles, e.g., the Subset Principle, and interface with knowledge systems that are *not* specifically linguistic.

It is important to first establish a theory of *what* is being acquired before considering *how* that knowledge is acquired (Gregg, 1989). Thus, research efforts have been directed at providing a theory of the knowledge adults have which includes the relationship between a verb's meaning and the syntax of the clause. In the next section, a version of the theory which is adopted in most SLA research is discussed in some detail. Other theories are addressed in section 4.

2   A Theory of Verb Meaning and Links to Morpho-syntax

2.1   Verb classes and lexical decomposition

In SLA research, the most influential account of the observation that verbs of similar meaning have similar syntactic requirements has been that of Pinker (1989) and his colleagues (Gropen et al., 1989; Gropen et al., 1991a, b). Partially in response to the shortcomings of early GB theta theory, they maintain that verbs belong to *verb classes* that are defined by a common decompositional structure, and that this structure determines the number and position arguments in a clause, not an ordered list of theta roles. Hence, the central claim is that verbs' meanings are made up of smaller units of meaning. In addition, linking rules relate semantic configurations which define "Agent-of-action" and "Undergoer-of-action" with syntactic positions such as Subject [NP, IP] and Object [NP, VP] respectively. Hence, in this theory theta roles are not primitive, but emerge from semantic structures.

Juffs (1996a) adopts Pinker's framework in large part but also suggests that in order to provide an adequate decompositional theory of the semantics which affects argument structure, some limits on both the type of unit of meaning and the rules which combine those units are necessary; such constraints are not immediately apparent from Pinker's (1989) book. The type of meaning unit needs to be restricted, since a recurring theme in discussions of the acquisition of the lexicon has been that not all possible semantic distinctions are relevant to argument structure and mapping to grammatical functions. For instance, Talmy (1985) notes that although possible elements such as symmetry, the colour of the actor, etc. do occur as part of a verb's meaning, they are almost never encoded systematically in a verb's meaning. Based on Pinker (1989:172–6) and Talmy (1985:126–7), table 6.1 lists some major meaning units which have syntactic reflexes and may have a basis in UG.

The main meaning units are called main functions and are the major categories of semantic structure. Lexical structure is not *purely* syntactic, but Hale and Keyser (1993:94) argue that it is useful to look to known constraints on syntactic structure to help limit what a possible semantic structure would be. Hence, the usual categories V, A, and P, will not be used, but instead Pinker's labels ACT(±effect): (+effect) for lexically causative verbs, and (−effect) for non-causative, transitive verbs;[5] GO and BE to capture the difference between dynamic and non-dynamic "events", and STATE and PATH may be "complements" of the functions GO and BE.

As table 6.1 suggests, in addition to the main functions, a number of syntactic features can also be associated with the main functions. These include [±effect] for causative and non-causative ACT events, and [±MANNER] for dynamic events. Note that MANNER is a syntactic feature, but does not specify what the *meaning* of the feature is. In Pinker's (1989) theory, the precise

Table 6.1 Building blocks of semantic structure

Building block	Event types	Example
Main Functions		
ACT(+effect)	Causative events. Adds an external argument.	John filled the glass.
ACT(−effect)	Non-causative transitives. Unergatives.	Mary saw a ghost. Jane laughed.
GO + STATE	Unaccusatives (change of state).	The ice melted.
GO + PATH	Unaccusatives (motion).	The ball slid.
BE + STATE	Statives.	A theory exists. John knows the answer.
Features	*Function which the feature is most commonly linked to.*	
±Effect	ACT	kill, (+effect); see (−effect)
±Manner	GO	pour, splash, spill.
Property of the Theme/Agent	THING	ooze: whatever oozes must be liquid but sticky. See Talmy (1985:73).
±Polarity	BE + STATE	*believe*. vs. *doubt*
±Factivity	BE + STATE	*regret* vs. *hope*

semantic value is the basis of certain subclasses of verb: e.g., verbs which involve transfer from one person or place to another may involve *a ballistic manner of motion*, e.g., *throw*, or *continuous motion*, e.g., *push*. These differences may have syntactic consequences and will be discussed further in section 3.

Pinker (1989) does not propose any constraints on rules of semantic structure. In contrast, Hale and Keyser (1993:94) propose that lexical relational structure (LRS) is constrained by X-bar theory (Jackendoff, 1977); in other words, decompositional lexical representations are constrained by principles of syntax. As evidence, they claim that denominal verbs, such as *saddle* and *shelve*, are derived by head movement of an N into an abstract V in lexical structure, and that the constraints on such movement are the same as those observed in syntax, namely the Empty Category Principle and Minimality. They attempt to show that principles such as unambiguous projection and full-interpretation provide powerful constraints on argument structure, e.g., on when arguments are required, and on when additional arguments are prohibited.

To see how this whole system works, consider semantic structures for a member of the class of locative verbs. Locative verbs describe the movement of an object to a destination or location. The issue with locative verbs is that some allow one syntactic pattern, where only the moving object (Theme) can be the direct object in the syntax (4), whereas others allow only the Goal to the direct object (5). Still others allow both patterns (6, 7). Such data clearly pose a problem for the thematic hierarchy, but if it is assumed that the underlying semantic structure of these verbs is in fact different despite the superficial similarities in meaning, then the problem is solved.

(4)   a.   John poured the soup into the bowl.
            [X ACT+effect [Y GO [PATH]]]
      b.   *John poured the bowl with soup.

(5)   a.   John covered the bed with the blanket.
            [X ACT+effect [Y GO [STATE]]]
      b.   *John covered the blanket onto the bed.

(6)   a.   John sprayed insecticide onto the tree.
            [X ACT+effect [Y GO [PATH]]]
      b.   John sprayed the tree with insecticide.

(7)   a.   John loaded the hay onto the truck.
      b.   John loaded the truck with hay.
            [X ACT+effect [Y GO [STATE]]]

Verbs that have the decomposition structure [GO [PATH]] in (4) allow only Theme direct objects; those with meaning components in (5) [GO[STATE]] allow only Goal direct objects. Verbs of either class may allow alternation if they belong to narrow classes within the main classes of (4) and (5), e.g., *spray* belongs to a class which specifies ballistic motion in a specified trajectory, and *load* belongs to a class which involves a mass put onto an object intended for that use. Pinker maintains that verb learning involves acquiring these narrow range classes, and that once these classes are established errors will cease.

2.2   Cross-linguistic differences in verb semantics and argument structure

If this theory is based on UG, then it should be possible to account not only for patterns found in English, but also for cross-linguistic similarities and differences among languages. In particular, differences should be describable in the way the meaning components can be combined in a root morpheme and/or derivational morphology. Juffs' (1996a) analysis of locative verbs in Chinese showed that Chinese does not allow the conflation of a STATE meaning component into root morphemes which also has both the functions ACT(+effect) and GO components. Therefore, the representation in (5) cannot be a possible semantic structure for a *root* morpheme in Chinese, and indeed most equivalents of non-alternating container verbs, *speckle*, *stud*, *ripple*, etc. simply do not exist in Chinese. Chinese conflates PATH most naturally into a locative verb. In order to create a caused locative verb which unambiguously indicates change of state, Chinese uses a resultative verb compound which adds a STATE morpheme to the root. This is one reason resultative verb compounds are so frequent in the language. These facts are illustrated in (8).

(8) a. ??Zhang San yong tanzi gai le   chuang.
         Zhang San use blanket   cover ASP bed
         "Zhang San covered the bed with a blanket."
     b. Zhang San wang chuang shang gai le tanzi.
         Zhang San to bed   on cover ASP blanket
         "Zhang San covered the blanket onto the bed."
         (Ungrammatical in English, but fine in Chinese)
     c. Zhang San   yong tanzi gaiZHU le   chuang.
         Zhang San use blanket   cover-complete ASP bed
         "Zhang San covered the bed with a blanket."

The claim that Chinese does not have [ACT+effect [GO [STATE]]] predicts that caused change of state verbs should not be productive at all in the language and not just with locatives. This does in fact turn out to be correct, as can be observed in table 6.2. The claim here is that knowledge of possible

Table 6.2   Root morpheme CAUSE/STATE conflation parameter

√[ACT(+effect) [GO [STATE]]]	*[ACT(+effect) [GO [STATE]]]
Transitive psych verbs	(i) *Nei ben shu shiwang le Zhang San
(i) The book disappointed Mary.	That CL. book disappoint Asp Zhang San.
Transitive change of state	(ii) ?? Taiyang rong(hua) le xue.
(ii) The sun melted the ice.	Sun melt ASP snow
Container locative verbs	(iii)
(iii)	? Zhang San yong tanzi gai le chuang.
John covered the bed with a blanket.	Zhang San use blanket cover ASP bed
(iv)	"Zhang San covered the bed with a blanket."
*John covered the blanket onto the bed.	(iv)
	Zhang San wang chuang shang gai le tanzi.
	Zhang San to bed on cover ASP blanket
	"Zhang S. covered the blanket onto the bed."
e.g., English, Romance, Bulgarian, Russian.	Chinese, Tagalog, Japanese, Chechen. German (??).

semantic structures in V root morphemes is subject to limited parametric variation. In this case, it is a parameter on the possible combinations of features in a lexical head which is a verb root.[6]

Such semantic patterns are the basis of conflation classes. If a language does allow (5), then it will have many root verbs of caused change of state, (e.g., melt), causative psych verbs (e.g., bore, disappoint), and change of state locatives (e.g., cover and fill). If not, additional morphology will be required to indicate causation, and without extra stative morphology most locative verbs will allow only one pattern in (13). Nichols (1984:194, 197) notes that the kind of alternation in locative verbs in English and Russian is simply not possible in Chechen-Ingush, which is consistent with it having the same parameter setting as Chinese. Other languages which do allow alternation also require additional morphology, presumably added in the syntax as in Chinese.

Morphology and the ordering of NPs within the VP has also been the focus of work by other researchers. For example, Kim, Landau and Phillips (1999) make similar proposals to Juffs (1996a) based on a survey of ten languages. In their survey, they point out that Korean, Chinese and Thai allow Theme objects in cases where English locative verbs do not. They relate this finding with the availability of productive verb serialization patterns in these languages. Hence, they also propose a single property can account for cross-linguistic differences in the behaviour of locative verbs.

In addition, Snyder (1995, 1996) and Snyder and Stromswold (1997) have proposed that a range of structures may be acquired together and depend on one morphological property. They argue that children acquire English datives, verb-particle constructions, put-locatives, and causative/perceptual constructions all as a group. These are illustrated in (9), (= Snyder 1996, (1));

(9) a. John painted the house red. (Resultative)
     b. Mary picked the book up / picked up the book. (Verb particle)
     c. Fred made Jeff leave. (Make causative)
     d. Fred saw Jeff leave. (Perceptual report)
     e. Bob put the book on the table. (Put locative)
     f. Alice sent the letter to Sue. (To dative)
     g. Alice sent Sue the letter. (Double object dative)

Snyder (1996) proposes a parametric model of acquisition in which the acquired knowledge is not construction-specific; and the favored analysis is that all the constructions belong to a single syntactic class. Snyder and Stromswold (1997) argue that acquisition of the entire class depends on the acquisition of parametric properties. These properties allow the grammar to generate double object datives, causative/perceptual constructions, put-locatives, and V-NP-Particle constructions. V-Particle-NP constructions and to-datives may depend on the combination of two properties. The precise nature of the parameter(s) could be related to compounding (Snyder, 1996), or more abstractly to a morpheme related to telicity and aspect (Snyder, 1995; Slabakova, in press), but the aim is clearly compatible with a view that parameters underlie the relationship between verbs and syntax. Clearly, more extensive investigation of these issues is warranted.

In this section, we have only dealt with the implications of (lexical) parameters across a variety of verb classes in order to sketch out what the principal components of the theory are. More extensive descriptions will be included in the section on second language acquisition as they relate to the issues raised in each section.

3 Verb Semantics, Morpho-syntax, and Second Language Acquisition Research

A large literature exists on the L1 acquisition of semantics–syntax correspondences beginning with Baker (1979) and Bowerman's (1982a, b) seminal work; Pinker (1989) provides an overview of the issues, and a more recent collection of papers can be found in Gleitman and Landau (1994). Rutherford (1989) and White (1987) lay out some of the learning issues in second language acquisition, but the SLA of verb semantics and morpho-syntax has only really attracted more detailed attention in the 1990s. This increase in interest was due in large part to Pinker (1989)'s important work. The beginning of the paper raised the questions: (a) Is there a logical problem of acquisition? (b) Are L2 grammars constrained in the way that first language grammars are constrained or are they "wild" grammars? (c) What is the role of the first language in interlanguage representations? (See Schwartz and Sprouse, 1996, for a recent discussion of transfer and access to UG). SLA researchers initially investigated only one L1/L2 pair and one class of verbs, but more recently links have been made between semantic structure and a broad range of verb classes (e.g., Juffs, 1996a; Montrul, 1997, in press; Slabakova, 1997, in press).

3.1 The dative alternation

Dative verbs are verbs that involve the transfer of some object to or for another person or location. "Alternation" refers to the possibility that the NP which is the object of the preposition in (10a) can move to a position directly adjacent to the verb in (10b) along with the deletion of the preposition (in English). However, not all verbs permit this alternation, as (11) shows.

(10) a. Kim sent a letter to Sandy.
      b. Kim sent Sandy a letter.

(11) a. Sandy donated the money to the poor people.
      b. *Sandy donated the poor people the money.

The dative alternation was the topic of some of the earliest work in syntax and lexical alternations (see for example, Akmajian and Heny, 1975:183–6; Levin, 1993:45–8, for comprehensive references) and first language acquisition research (e.g., Mazurkewich and White, 1984; Gropen et al., 1989). Akmajian and Heny (1975) assumed that dative movement was a purely syntactic operation involving a re-ordering and then a deletion operation. They noted that this process was constrained by lexical marking on individual verbs, but they acknowledge that such marking did not explain why certain verbs allowed dative movement and some do not. Cross-linguistically, some languages do not permit the dative alternation, e.g., French (White, 1987), in (12):

(12) a. Henri a donné   des fleurs   à Lucie.
          Henri AUX given some flowers   to Lucie
          "Henri gave some flowers to Lucie."
      b. *Henri a donné Lucie des fleurs.

Some languages allow a re-ordering within the VP, but maintain the morphology regardless of which argument is adjacent to the verb, e.g., Japanese in (13), (Inagaki, 1997). (See also Dryer, 1986, for a discussion of cross-linguistic variation and details from other languages where morphology does change.)

(13) a. John-ga   Mary-ni   hon-o   atae-ta
          John-Nom Mary-DAT book-ACC give-PAST
          "John gave the book to Mary."
      b. John-ga   hon-o   Mary-ni   atae-ta
          John-Nom book-ACC Mary-DAT give-PAST
          "John gave Mary the book."

In head-final languages such as Turkish and Japanese, the case marking may help keep track of grammatical and semantic relations after scrambling (Saito, 1987).

In early SLA research, the learning issues involved transfer and the Subset Principle, discussed in the first section. White (1987, 1991b) investigated whether English-speaking learners of French as a second language assumed that French also allowed dative alternation when in fact it does not. White found that transfer did indeed occur, that the L1 formed the basis of their hypotheses about datives in the L2, and concluded that second language learners do not obey the Subset Principle in the case of dative verbs. She suggests that in order to retreat to a narrower grammar, explicit negative evidence in the form of correction and other instruction would be required (see Juffs, 1996a, and White, 1989 for more detailed summaries of work prior to 1990).

More recent research has been based on a finer-grained analysis of the dative alternation using Pinker's verb class approach, which is a semantic rather than a syntactic solution to the problem of learning verb meaning–syntax correspondences. A summary of these studies is provided in table 6.3.

Pinker (1989) provides one explanation for why certain dative verbs allow alternation and others do not. In his framework, dative verbs have the basic semantic conflation class illustrated in (14a). Conflation classes can be converted via Broad Range Rules (BRR) which convert one conflation class to another, e.g., (14b). This BRR rule is subject to the constraint that the recipient be a potential (animate) possessor (14c). (Examples from Sawyer, 1996.)

(14)   a.   Mary sent a letter to John.
            [X CAUSE Y TO GO TO Z]
       b.   Mary sent John a letter.
            [X CAUSE Z TO HAVE Y]
       c.   Mary sent a package to the house/ ?? Mary sent the house a
            package.

However, according to Pinker, dative verbs may also fall into more narrow conflation classes, some of which permit the alternation, such as verbs which specify a MANNER of *ballistic* motion in (15), and some of which do not, as in (16), which specify a *continuous* motion.

(15)   a.   John tossed the ball to Mary
            [X CAUSE Y TO GO TO Z [MANNER = ballistic motion]]
       b.   John tossed Mary the ball.

(16)   a.   Jan pushed the ball to Jay.
            [X CAUSE Y TO GO TO Z [MANNER = continuous motion]]
       b.   *Jan pushed Jay the ball.

The features that define narrow range conflation classes are held to be language-specific, whereas constraints on Broad Range Rules, such as the animate possessor constraint, are held to be universal. Bley-Vroman and Yoshinaga (1992) investigated whether learners have access to the narrow range conflation rules as well as the Broad Range Rules. At issue is whether the learners can access UG in the development of constraints or whether the Interlanguage is constrained by constraints available only through the first language. If L2 learners show sensitivity to narrow range rules that are not in the L1, such sensitivity would constitute evidence for access to UG.

Bley-Vroman and Yoshinaga (1992) chose Japanese learners of English as participants because Japanese appears not to have the dative alternation – the differences in word order are often attributed to scrambling. They carried out two experiments on Japanese learners of English L2 in the USA. In their

Table 6.3 Studies of the dative alternation in SLA in the 1990s

Study	L1	L2	Number and level of subjects	Tasks	Main findings
Bley-Vroman and Yoshinaga (1992)	Japanese	English	64–85 Japanese TOEFL: 500–670	Stories and GJ task. Real and made-up verbs.	Real verbs are acquired. Made-up verbs do not show sensitivity to narrow range rules in L1.
Sawyer (1996)	Japanese	English	33 Japanese TOEFL 380–550	Based on Gropen et al. (1989). Elicited production with real and made-up verbs.	Found subjects showed sensitivity to narrow range rules in L1.
Inagaki (1997)	Japanese Chinese	English	32 Japanese (508–650 TOEFL) 32 Chinese (500–650 TOEFL)		Mixed results.
Slabakova (1997, in press)	Bulgarian	English	122 Bulgarian (Cloze test)	GJ tasks.	Dative acquired at same time as other parts of to aspect parameter.

experiments, they use first real verbs and then made-up verbs. Made-up verbs are used to try and test for a rule rather than test learners' knowledge of individual verbs they may have seen or heard in the input. Findings from the first experiment suggest that the Japanese speakers show "comparable sensitivity" to the animate possessor constraint in the L2 to that of native speakers. The second experiment tests the learners' knowledge of the narrow range constraints, specifically the hypothesis that "after the native grammar is fixed, the adult learner no longer has access to that universal list of linguistically relevant manners and properties." The results show that native speakers are sensitive to the constraints even with made-up verbs. The Japanese subjects were able to distinguish the dativizable verbs from the non-dativizable real verbs. For made-up verbs, however, the learners show no such difference. The authors conclude that their results show that where there is exposure (to real verbs) the constraints can be learned from input frequency/pattern association, but where novel verbs are concerned, the crucial test of a productive rule, the learners are different from the native speakers. The authors maintain that this result is predicted by the Fundamental Difference Hypothesis (Bley-Vroman, 1989).

Sawyer's (1996) study also involved the use of made-up verbs. Using a methodology based on Gropen et al. (1989), he showed that L2 learners were sensitive to the animacy constraint on the BRR. In addition, Sawyer found that his Japanese participants also showed a sensitivity to the ballistic vs. continuous motion distinction illustrated in (15) and (16) even though no such distinction exists in Japanese. These results contradict those of Bley-Vroman and Yoshinaga (1992). The results are striking for two reasons: (i) the learners showed sensitivity to narrow range rules with made-up verbs, and (ii) the learners' proficiency level is lower than the learners in Bley-Vroman and Yoshinaga's study. However, Sawyer used a production task and not a judgment task which means that a direct comparison is difficult to make.

Inagaki (1997) also investigated knowledge of the constraints on dative movement by Japanese and Chinese learners of English. Inagaki maintains that in fact Japanese does show some differences in the use of the dative structure in *throw* vs. *push* type datives, with *push* type datives being ungrammatical in the dative construction if the possessor is the head noun of the direct object NP. Hence, Japanese learners should be sensitive to the narrow range constraint in (15) and (16). Inagaki's participants also provided mixed results: Japanese were sensitive to difference in MANNER narrow range rules in verbs of speech which do not exist in Japanese (e.g., *tell* vs. *whisper*), but not *throw* vs. *push* type verbs. The latter result is surprising for Inagaki because even the dative form with "-ni" is ungrammatical for the "push" type prepositional datives in Japanese. The Chinese learners were sensitive to the difference between the *tell* vs. *whisper* verbs – not surprising since the constraint also operates in Chinese – but not to the *throw* vs. *push* difference which does not exist in Chinese. Inagaki suggests that frequency in the input could explain some of these results because even with the made-up verbs participants reported making an analogy with a verb they already knew, but unfortunately measuring the frequency in L2 input is difficult since so few analyses of input corpora for L2 learners exist (Juffs, 1998). He also suggests that typological factors may mean that the Japanese learners do not perceive the dative structures as related to the L1 which is why they accept the datives which are not possible in the L1.

Finally, the most recent research to include the dative alternation is that of Slabakova (1997). Slabakova was primarily interested in aspect in L2 acquisition, but it has been suggested that the existence of the dative alternation in a language is part of a larger parameter of aspect (Snyder, 1995, 1996; issues relating to this aspect will be developed in section 4). Slabakova (1997, in press) reports on knowledge of datives in a grammaticality judgment (GJ) task in relation to knowledge of datives and a parameter of aspect with Bulgarian learners of English illustrated in (17):

(17) a. The native men and women waited out the crisis.
          (Verb + particle)
      b. *George loves out eggplant and basil pizza.
      c. Steven nailed all the top floor windows shut. (Resultative)
      d. *My friend Pamela fears dinosaurs senseless.
      e. Simon gave Jenny a red scooter and a red hat. (Double object)
      f. *Sharon taught French the children in the neighbourhood.

She found sensitivity to the key aspects of the parameter she was investigating and the datives appeared to pattern together with the other two structures under investigation. Hence, under this analysis, the acquisition of the dative alternation is part of a larger parameter which relates to compounding and/or aspect. However, Slabakova does not investigate whether or not the learners are sensitive to constraints on the alternation of the kind investigated by researchers such as Bley-Vroman and Yoshinaga. Clearly, research that combines a parametric approach while controlling for whether the verbs which are used in the experiment are able to alternate is called for.

Our understanding of L2 learners' knowledge of dative movement is perhaps the most detailed, but still incomplete. It is clear that learners overgeneralize (White, 1987), but there is at least some evidence that suggests that more proficient learners seem able to acquire even narrow range rules that are not available in their L1s. For logistical reasons, most of the studies discussed here rely on relatively few tokens of each type/class of verb and with relatively small numbers of learners. As it stands, however, most evidence seems to indicate that the initial hypothesis for knowledge of syntactic frames is the L1. Narrow range features which are not part of the L1 grammar seem very difficult to acquire. However, if narrow range features which constrain alternation are idiosyncratic rather than being part of UG, then suggestions that they are acquired through input, and that indirect negative evidence helps pre-empt errors, are reasonable and imply that acquisition of these features cannot be used to argue for or against access to UG. (See White, 1989 for a discussion of *indirect* negative evidence.) Finally, as the summary in table 6.3 shows, exact replication studies are rare – much more carefully controlled replications are necessary before any real conclusions can be made.

3.2   The locative alternation and lexical parameters

Locative verbs pose a very similar learning problem to the datives because of differences in the way locative verbs behave cross-linguistically. Juffs (1996a) shows that Chinese-speaking learners of English are faced with a learnability problem similar to that faced by English learners of dative movement in French. As the data in (18) show, Chinese permits verbs which are non-alternating container locative verbs in English to have a Theme as the direct object unless they are part of a resultative construction.

(18)   a.   ??Zhang San yong tanzi gai le   chuang.
            Zhang San use blanket cover ASP bed
            "Zhang San covered the bed with a blanket."
       b.   Zhang San wang chuang shang gai le tanzi.
            Zhang San to bed on   cover ASP blanket
            "Zhang San covered the blanket onto the bed."
            (Ungrammatical in English)
       c.   Zhang San   yong tanzi gaiZHU le   chuang.
            Zhang San use blanket cover -complete ASP bed
            "Zhang San covered the bed with a blanket."

If Chinese transfer the L1 pattern to the L2, and fail to notice differences in morphology, they will overgeneralize and assume *all* locative verbs may take the theme object, or alternate in their argument structure.

As discussed earlier in section 2, Juffs (1996a) suggests that the absence of the *cover/fill* type locative verbs is related to lack of causative unaccusatives and stimulus psych verbs: Underlying all three classes is the possibility to have (ACT [+effect]) combined with CHANGE of STATE meaning components in a *root* morpheme. English allows this, and therefore has caused change of state locatives (cover, etc.), causative unaccusatives (*melt*, etc.), and stimulus psych verbs (*convince, anger*). Chinese has none of them in a root morpheme. For L2 acquisition, sensitivity to causative meaning components in the causative versions of unaccusatives, stimulus psych verbs, plus the frequent positive evidence of direct Goal objects in container locatives, should *together* alert learners to the different semantic organization of the L2, and thereby the different syntactic possibilities.

Thus, Juffs is suggesting that the need for negative evidence suggested by White (1987) may be obviated by the resetting of a lexical parameter: Pre-emption of "*John covered the blanket onto the bed" can occur through the lexical parameter. Without sensitivity to the new conflation *class* which captures a generalization across more superficial verb classes, Chinese learners who accept "*John covered the blanket onto the bed" should not be able to retreat from the false assumption that such sentences are possible.

Juffs (1996a) investigated these hypotheses with a pool of participants in China: 120 learners of English from beginner to very advanced. Results of both an oral elicitation task and a Grammaticality Judgment task show that the learners start off with a wider grammar for non-alternating locative verbs and reject the causative psych verbs. However, the very advanced learners accept psych verbs used causatively in an NP–V–NP pattern and end up with a narrower grammar than they start out with and reject sentences such as "*John covered the blanket onto the bed". These results are interpreted as evidence that new conflation classes can be acquired that can help learners retreat from overgeneralizations.

Thepsura (1998) in a replication study of Thai students learning English as a second language argues that Thai also behaves like Chinese: It allows Theme objects where they would be prohibited in English, but does not allow lexical causatives. Thepsura had his participants do several tests which were as similar to Juffs (1996a) as possible – although the elicitation task that he used was a written one rather than an oral one. The results he obtained were remarkably like those of Juffs (1996a) with the exception that his most advanced group did not retreat from accepting sentences such as "*John covered the cloth onto the table". Thepsura interprets these results as being consistent with the Fundamental Difference Hypothesis, namely that the Thai learners were not able to reset the parameter and that they can only access the knowledge of lexical structure via the L1. However, Thepsura (personal communication) does not think that his advanced group is comparable with Juffs' advanced group and suggests that more data from very advanced Thai speakers are necessary.

3.3 The causative/inchoative alternation and split intransitivity

The dative and locative verbs showed alternations *within* the VP. The verb classes in this section raise the issue of alternation and projection in the direct object/subject positions which are VP internal and external respectively (e.g., Levin and Rappaport-Hovav, 1995). One alternation is illustrated in (19) and (20):

(19) a. Sandy melted *the chocolate*.
       b. *The chocolate* melted.

(20) a. Sandy closed *the door*.
      b. *The door* closed.

The problems for learners concern alternations in mapping of NPs with certain semantic roles, e.g., Agent and Theme, with different syntactic positions. Verbs like *melt* and *close* can appear with the Theme as Subject, as in (19b) and (20b). This is not a possibility for *put*, nor for *read* and *write*, as the ungrammatical examples in (21) show. (The construction in (21d), known as "the middle voice" (Levin, 1993:25), usually requires an adverb. Unlike English, many languages of the world mark the middle voice morphologically.)

(21) a. *The book put on the shelf.
      b. *The letter wrote.
      c. *The book read.
      d. The book reads well.

The reason for the difference between transitive verbs like *put* and *write* and verbs such as *melt* (*end*, *freeze*, etc. are other examples, Levin, 1993: 27) is that verbs like *melt* entail a caused change of state as part of their meaning, whereas verbs such as *put*, *read*, and *write* do not. One can read a book without the book being affected by the reading, but one cannot melt chocolate without a change of state (solid to liquid). Other verbs which allow the Agent to be omitted, and the Theme to appear as a Subject, are verbs of directed motion such as *slide*. The alternation between Theme as Object and Theme as Subject is called the causative/inchoative alternation (Levin, 1993:27). English does not mark the difference in syntactic position in (19) and (20) by changes in morphology on the verb, but other languages do (Haspelmath, 1993). Consider the example from French in (22). In (22a), both the Agent and the Theme are present in Subject and Object positions respectively; however in (22b), the Theme is in Subject position, and there is a corresponding change in morpho-syntax: the morpheme *se* has been attached to the auxiliary and the auxiliary itself has changed from *avoir* "to have" to *être* "to be".[7]

(22) a. *Sandy a   cassé   la   fenêtre*
          Sandy AUX break-PAST DET window
          "Sandy broke the window."
      b. *La   fenêtre s'est   cassée*
          DET window   AC-AUX break-PAST-FSO
          "The window broke."

Thus in French, when a causative verb appears with only one NP, namely the Theme, a change in morphology is often required. In contrast, Mandarin Chinese and many other languages, require causativity to be indicated in the sentence morpho-syntactically. This is shown in the example in (23) with the Chinese verb *chen* "sink".

(23) a. *chuan chen ru　le　he di*
boat　sink-enter PERF river bottom
"The boat sank to the bottom of the river."

b. *Di　ren **shi**　chuan chen ru　le　he　di*
enemy person CAUS boat　sink-enter PERF river bottom
"The enemy **made** the boat sink to the bottom of the river."

c. **Di　ren chen ru　le　chuan dao he di*
enemy person sink-enter PERF boat　to river bottom
"The enemy sank the boat to the bottom of the river."

In (23a), in which the single NP is a Theme in Subject position, the verb appears without morphology; the causative version is in (23b), with the morpheme *shi* "make"; (23c) shows that without the morpheme *shi* "make", the sentence with both Agent/Subject and Theme/Object is ungrammatical. Chinese is thus the opposite of French in the way that causativity is encoded in causative/inchoative alternators. Haspelmath (1993) suggests that the inchoative form is by far the most common – the French type anticausative perhaps being an Indo-European feature.

The alternations described in (18) through (23) are made more complex by another set of facts involving intransitive verbs. One group of verbs that are also intransitive, like the example in (24), but that do not alternate as the structures in (19), are verbs such as *happen*, *appear*, and *arrive*.

(24) a. Several guests arrived by taxi.
b. *The taxi arrived several guests.
c. There arrived several guests dressed in strange clothing.
d. *The driver arrived the guests.
e. $[_S e [_{VP} [_{NP}]]]$. C.f. (3b).

Verbs of the type illustrated in (24) are grouped together because they denote "coming into and out of existence" (e.g., *appear*, *die*, *happen*), and "undirected motion" (e.g., *arrive*, *fall*). These verbs are termed *unaccusative* (Perlmutter, 1978). Syntactic reflexes of this type of verb include the ability to appear with a pleonastic (or "dummy") Subject in (24c), as well as in Subject position (24a). The NPs associated with these verbs are understood to undergo change (either of state or location) *without* external causation; hence, clauses containing these verbs do not have an Agent/Subject, but instead they have a Theme/Subject. This class of verbs is assumed to have a D-structure which is the same as the inchoative version of the causative/inchoative alternators (23e and 3b); some have a morphologically unrelated transitive counterpart, for example, *die* is an unaccusative verb, whereas *kill* is a causative version of *die* (but see Fodor (1970) for arguments against too close a relation between these lexical entries), but others, e.g., *disappear*, *arrive*, do not.

Perlmutter (1978) distinguishes unaccusatives from other intransitive verbs. Example (25b) shows that a verb like *laugh* cannot be used causatively: the cause of the children's laughter, *the clown*, may only appear in a prepositional phrase (25a) or as the object of *make* in (25c).

(25) a. The children laughed (at the clown).
  b. *There laughed three clowns in red noses.
  c. The clown made the children laugh.
  d. *The clown laughed the children.
  e. [s NP [vp]]. C.f. (23e).

Laugh is in a class of verb which is termed *unergative*; unergative verbs are said to describe an event which is internally caused (*sing, shout, cry, sweat, smile, blush* are also members of this class). These verbs are therefore assumed to be associated with one NP which is an Agent that must appear in Subject position (25a) and have a deep structure as in (25e). The difference in Deep structure between unaccusatives and unergatives is claimed to derive from a difference in semantic structure, where the semantic structure of unaccusatives is [GO [STATE]], e.g., *disappear*, or [GO [PATH]], e.g., *slide* whereas unergatives are either pure [ACT] events or at least events with an [ACT] component for causer (see Montrul, 1997, for arguments that unergatives are bi-eventive). Acquisition presumably involves gaining the knowledge of the semantic structure which links to the syntax.

Although English does not distinguish between unergatives and unaccusatives morphologically, many languages do. For example, in Romance, unaccusatives are frequently associated with the auxiliary verb *to be* rather than the verb *to have* for compound tenses, as well as some types of clitic placement; unergatives typically select the *to have* auxiliary (Sorace, 1993, 1995). Hence, acquisition of semantics–syntax correspondences for these verb classes may pose problems for learners of English in the same way that acquisition of the causative/inchoative alternation may be difficult because (a) class membership is not marked morphologically and (b) there is a potential for overgeneralizing or confusing the inchoative/causative alternators with pure unaccusatives because they share the same D-structure in some sentences (c.f. 24e and 3b); as a result, learners may assume that pure unaccusatives can also be causative.

The general acquisition questions for these classes of verbs for second language learners involve: (i) do learners know the semantic constraints on verb class membership in the L2, i.e., do they know change of state verbs are unaccusative whereas verbs of emission of sounds can be unergative? (ii) can they add conflation patterns to the inventory of possible verb classes (e.g., can Chinese learners of English add lexical causatives to a class of non-alternating inchoatives?), but not overgeneralize this to unaccusatives and unergative verbs that do not alternate; (iii) once a conflation class has been acquired or transferred from the L1, can correct morpho-syntactic reflexes be acquired in the L2?

Research on the SLA of these alternations and of the subtle distinction between causative/inchoative alternators, pure unaccusative verbs and unergative verbs has really only taken off in the 1990s. In a useful overview of the topic, Oshita (in press) highlights questions raised by Kellerman (1978) who noted that the Dutch subjects did not fully transfer the L1 structure from Dutch to English because they were reluctant to accept sentences such as "the cup broke" even though they are fine in Dutch. Yip (1994) reports similar failures to transfer. Adjémian (1983) had noted errors of transfer of so-called reflexive morphology by francophone learners of English in his work in lexical transfer.

Zobl (1989) was the first to discuss second language learners' pattern of verb use and syntax in terms of split intransitivity. In a study of production data from English compositions written mainly by Japanese-speaking learners of English, he noticed that he could explain a pattern of errors such as those in (26) by appealing to the split between unaccusative verbs and unergative verbs: Learners only used passive morphology with unaccusatives (Zobl, 1989:204):

(26) a. *The most memorable event of my life *was* happen*ed* 15 years ago.
      b. *My mother *was* died when I was just a baby.

Hirakawa (1995) has also investigated Japanese learners' knowledge of unaccusativity in English. Hirakawa elicited judgment of sentences with inchoative/causative alternators (*melt, break, continue, dry, increase, spill*), unaccusatives which do not take part in the alternation (*appear, die, fall, arrive, happen, disappear*), and transitives (*hit, cut, see, read, build, need*). With the alternators, Hirakawa found significant differences between the controls and the learners on sentences such as *the snow melted*, and a similar difference on causative structures such as *the sun melted the snow*. Although Hirakawa does not use these terms, there were no significant differences in verbs which are transitive, but not causative, e.g., *Bill hit* versus *they hit Bill*. If one focuses on the difference in semantics between the causative change of state semantic structure of a verb like *melt* and the non-change of state structure of a verb like *hit*, a possible reason for the rejection of *the snow melts* is perhaps because learners' interlanguage grammar is changing from allowing conflation of CAUSE into change to unaccusative state verbs. Morphology is crucial here. Hirakawa notes that with the exception of the passive most of the alternations which involve unaccusatives are *not* marked morphologically in English, as is shown in (27). In Japanese, and indeed in many other languages, these differences must be marked morphologically.

(27) a. The vase broke.   (Unaccusative)
      b. The vase broke easily.   (Middle)
      c. John broke the vase easily.   (Causative)
      d. The vase **was** broken by John.   (Passive)

One can speculate that Japanese learners' difficulties with both syntactic environments of the *melt* type derive from their uncertainty concerning the way English encodes causativity in the L2 and its relationship to the morphology of the language.

Research by Yip (1994) and Balcom (1997) suggests a similar pattern of results to those of Zobl (1989). Learners seem to latch on to passive morphology as a way of marking a Theme in Subject position with unaccusatives, but not with unergatives. Oshita's (1997, in press) examination of learner corpus data seems to confirm this hypothesis, but he also notes that learners whose L1 background is Romance also use null expletive and expletive constructions, e.g., "(it) happened a tragic event", significantly more than speakers of east Asian languages. Such a finding also indicates some L1 influence since Romance languages allow null expletives and "post-verbal Subjects".

Sorace (1993, 1995) has investigated knowledge of the semantic and syntactic properties of Italian unaccusatives by English-speaking and French-speaking learners. Sorace points out that *purely* syntactic approaches fail to distinguish unaccusatives from unergatives adequately, but in Italian there is a very close correlation between the "themehood", or affected argument, and the selection of the auxiliary *essere* "to be"; passives, reflexives, and unaccusatives all select *essere* "to be", and their syntactic subjects may all be D-structure objects. Sorace (1995:159) identifies a semantic hierarchy of unaccusatives and unergatives, with those classes of verbs higher on the hierarchy more likely to exhibit syntactic reflexes of unaccusativity and unergativity respectively:

Unaccusativity Hierarchy:
(i)   Change of location
(ii)   Change of condition
(iii)   Continuation of condition
(iv)   Existence of condition
Paired Unaccusatives:
(v)   With a transitive alternant (e.g., *aumentare* "increase" – i.e., causative/
        inchoative alternators)
(vi)   With an atelic alternant (e.g., *telic correre* "run" = move to a place)

Unergative Hierarchy:
(i)   Non-motional activity (e.g., *dormire* "sleep")
(ii)   Motional activity (e.g., *nuotare* "swim")
Paired Unergatives:
(iii)   With telic alternant
        e.g., *correre* "run" (atelic = engage in an activity)

In Italian, all unaccusative verbs may appear with the auxiliary *essere* "to be". French is somewhat different from Italian, with only a subset of unaccusatives taking the auxiliary *être*, namely change of location verbs and some change of condition verbs. English has few if any syntactic reflexes of unaccusativity (with the exception perhaps of *there* insertion). English and Italian are said to be in parametric variation for having a lexical, versus a syntactic rule, of Unaccusative formation, respectively (Sorace, 1993:30).

Sorace (1993) tested English and French near-native speakers of Italian on several structures, (1) auxiliary selection and (2) optional auxiliary change in several types of construction with modals, raising verbs, etc. She found that although intuitions were different from native speakers, both learner groups are sensitive to the semantics of the hierarchy, and the French being superior in their judgment of the syntactic reflexes where clitics are concerned. She concludes (1993:43) that "the relevance and the salience of positive evidence may be a matter of degree and . . . other things being equal – some learners may be in a more favourable position to notice the relevance of the L2 input and to incorporate it into their developing grammar." Not whether a learner's L1 has a property P or not, but how P interacts with the whole system, is considered crucial. In the (1995) overview, Sorace reports increasing sensitivity to the hierarchy in a cross-sectional study of English-speaking learners of Italian. However, she reports that for Italian-speaking learners of French, the subjects seem to have difficulty in restricting the range of verbs that may be conjugated with "être". This last set of results confirms findings in other areas of the lexical acquisition in this domain: When the L1 is a less restrictive grammar than the L2, learners have difficulties in retreating from the wider grammar.

Montrul (1997, in press) and Toth (1997, in press) have independently investigated acquisition of the semantics and morpho-syntax of causatives and unaccusativity in Spanish by English-speaking learners. Both authors find evidence of L2 grammars being constrained by the L1 grammar in addition to showing evidence of constraints derived from Universal Grammar. Montrul (1997) investigated both the acquisition of English and the acquisition of Spanish as second languages. She finds evidence that no matter what the L1, learners seem to start off with a Subject–verb–Object pattern which leads her to suggest that L2 learners may begin in much the same way as first language learners. This finding could explain the rejection by some learners of the inchoative form with such sentences as "the cup broke". She also found that Spanish learners showed evidence of L1 in that Spanish learners of English seemed more likely to require an anti-causative morpheme with inchoatives.

Toth (in press) found that his learners overgeneralized the use of "se" in Spanish (c.f. the French example in (22)), but only with pure unaccusative verbs and not with unergatives. If L2 grammars were wild grammars, we would not expect that "se" would be restricted in this way. Indeed, it seems that English learners of Spanish use the morpheme "se" to mark NP movement, or a Theme in subject position, in much the same way that learners of English use the passive morphology to mark NP movement, as suggested by Zobl (1989) and Oshita (1997).

To sum up, the causative/inchoative alternation, unaccusatives, and unergatives have provided the second largest set of data with regard to the acquisition of semantics–syntax correspondences. So far, it is clear that advanced learners do seem able to converge on a native-like grammar with these verbs, but that the development is not direct: It proceeds with both guidance from Universal principles and with interference from the L1 morpho-syntax. In contrast to studies of the dative alternation, there has been a greater variety of language pairs investigated. A summary of these studies is provided in table 6.4. However, different methodologies used make it difficult sometimes to compare studies and the results can really only be treated as preliminary at this point. Far greater numbers of subjects and more carefully controlled judgment and guided production data are needed before any firm conclusions can be drawn.

3.5 Psych verbs

Psychological predicates are a class of verbs which describe mental and emotional states, for example, *fear* and *frighten*, *like* and *hate*, *disappoint* and *excite*. The problem is that despite the parallel syntax in (28) and (29), in (28a) *Bill* is the locus of the emotion of *worry*, whereas in (29a) it is *John* who *knows*. However, in both the (b) examples, *John* is the locus of emotion and knowledge. In particular, the semantic roles of *John* in (28a) and (28b) seem to be different (causing Bill to worry in (28a) and being worried by Bill in (28b), but the grammatical function (GF) is the same, namely the subject.

(28) a. John worries Bill.
      b. John worries about Bill.

(29) a. John knows Bill.
      b. John knows about Bill.

Moreover, the truth conditions of (30a) and (30b) are the same, a fact that implies that at some level the meaning is the same, even though the grammatical functions are reversed.

(30) a. I liked the play.
      b. The play pleased me.

Hence, psych verbs pose a problem in acquisition because the meanings that they describe have very similar truth conditions, but different predicates require the semantic roles involved to be projected in different surface syntactic positions. Early Principles and Parameters analyses of psych verbs suggested that such verbs fell into two classes: Subject experiencer verbs like *fear* and object experiencer verbs like *frighten*. The other argument is assumed to be

Table 6.4 Studies involving transitivity alternations and the unergative/unaccusative distinction

Study	L1	L2	Level of subjects	Tasks	Main findings
Zobl (1989)	Japanese and others	English	90 of various levels	Production data from essays	Sensitivity to the unaccusative vs. unergative split.
Sorace (1993)	English French	Italian	24 English 20 French Near native	Preference task contrasting verb and aux. selection and use of clitics. Magnitude estimation used to analyze results.	Hierarchy of use of "essere" with unaccusatives very close to native Italians, but not the same.
Sorace (1995)	English	Italian	Cross-section Numbers not reported.	Preference task, similar to above.	Increasing sensitivity to semantic restrictions on use of auxiliary.
Yip (1994)	Various L1s	English	10 Advanced	Pre-test, instruction, and post-test	Transfer cannot account for many errors.
Hirakawa (1995)	Japanese	English	22 Intermediate	GJ Task; production tasks	Low acceptance of alternators with Theme subjects.
Oshita (1997, in press)	Various	English	Unknown	Corpus search of the Longman Learners' Corpus	Ungrammatical use of passive signals NP movement with pure unaccusatives for Japanese/Korean learners. Some evidence of L1 influence in use of structure of expletives.
Toth (1997, in press)	English	Spanish	91 Low intermediate	GJ Task, Free and guided production in pre, immediate post and delayed post	Evidence for learning of "se" constrained by UG, explicit instruction and transfer.
Montrul (1997, in press)	Spanish Turkish English	English Spanish	18 Turks/ESL 29 Spanish/ESL (Cloze) 19 Turks/Spanish SL 15 English/Spanish SL (Cloze)	GJ Task with pictures.	Evidence for UG in developing grammars. Beginning learners show pattern similar to L1 speakers but also evidence of L1 transfer.

a Theme; in the case of object experiencer verbs, the Theme is assumed to move to Subject position from D-structure, e.g., [Spiders (Theme) ᵢ [frighten [Mary (Experiencer)] [t ᵢ]]], because Experiencers are projected higher than Themes at D-structure. Therefore, although the issues are not quite the same as the alternations inside the VP with datives and locatives or VP internal Theme/object or Theme/Subject in inchoative alternators, they can nevertheless pose a serious problem for learners, especially in the light of some cross-linguistic differences described below.

The analyses used by SLA researchers for these verbs has not been a semantic one based on a decompositional semantics described by Pinker (1989) and Juffs (1996a). Rather, researchers have stuck to unanalyzed theta role labels and the thematic hierarchy described in section 2. Specifically, White (1995) and White et al. (in press) adopt Pesetsky's (1995) syntactic account of knowledge of psych verbs. Pesetsky (1995) maintains psych verb Theme subjects are also causers. He claims that there are in fact three psych theta roles in the following hierarchy of mapping from theta role to grammatical function (GF): Causer, Experiencer, and Target/Subject Matter. These roles are illustrated in (31). He further argues that clauses with Causer subjects have a phonologically null causative morpheme.

(31) a. The severe winter worried Bill. (Theme = Causer)
      b. Bill worried about the severe winter. (Theme = Subject Matter)
      c. *The severe winter worried Bill about global warming.
      d. The severe winter made Bill worried about global warming.

Armed with these assumptions, it is then necessary to explain why Bill cannot be the target of the worry in (31c), but in (31d) he can. Pesetsky claims that (31c) is ruled out because raising of the causer/theme to the subject position in the null causative head would violate the head movement constraint (Travis, 1984, see Pesetsky for details). Presumably such knowledge is subtle and rather arbitrary and hence part of UG. Japanese appears not to have the T/SM restriction because it does not have root causative psych verbs, but French does. Hence, L1 influence may contribute to what the learners know about these constructions.

Thus, White (1995) set out to investigate whether learners know that English allows stimulus psych verbs, but not with the target subject matter of the stimulus in a separate PP as in (31c). Participants in the study were 29 French-speaking learners and 14 Japanese-speaking learners. In a grammaticality judgment task administered aurally based on scale of acceptability from (–2 completely impossible to +2 completely possible), White found that the Japanese learners only marginally accepted sentences such as (31a) (consistent with Juffs', 1996a, findings for beginning–intermediate Chinese learners), and treated sentences such as (31c) the same as those in (31d). The French learners knew (31a) was possible but reacted in the same way as the Japanese to (31c). The native controls also treated (31c) differently from other control ungrammatical stimuli. White concludes that there are no L1 effects, and there is still insufficient reason to believe that the L1 and L2 are fundamentally different.

The L1s of White (1995) learners were French, Japanese, and Malagasy. In this study, the authors note that Japanese and Malagasy lack root version of the stimulus type. Therefore, the main problem they will have will be with the causative type (*frighten*), not those versions where the experiencer is the subject (the *fear* type). With the exception of one verb, ironically *fear*, which altered results somewhat, White et al.'s predictions that stimulus psych verbs will be the ones to cause problems are borne out. Another point is that the learners do not have problems with verbs which are merely transitive, and not causative, a point which indicates that it is the causative aspects of stimulus psych verbs which is the problem. Another factor which White and her colleagues mention is that the subjects may be uncomfortable with *non-animate* Subjects with stimulus psych verbs. The issues of animacy and the relationship of learners' knowledge of psych verbs with causativity in other verb classes remains to be sorted out, and suggests that the interface with other cognitive aspects of the learners' knowledge of language may be involved (cf. Harrington, 1987).

Montrul (1998) considers the acquisition of psych verbs by English and French learners of Spanish as a second language. In her study, she considers the acquisition of the dative case marking in Spanish with verbs such as those illustrated in (32) (= Montrul, 1998, 15):

(32)   La música *(le)   gusta a Juan.
       The music to-him   like   to Juan
       A Juan   *(le) gusta la música.
       "Juan likes music."

Spanish differs from English in that dative case is assigned to the experiencer, not nominative, Case assignment – in English it is agreement with Infl, but in Spanish it is agreement with a dative experiencer clitic that is in Infl, and the need for this overt clitic which "doubles" the dative subject, "le", in (32). French shares with Spanish the dative case assignment, but does not allow clitic doubling. Despite the assignment of dative case, dative experiencers nevertheless behave like syntactic subjects in a variety of tests, for example control of PRO in adjunct clauses. Montrul investigated the knowledge English- and French-speaking learners of Spanish had of structures such as (32). Two main test instruments were used: An interpretation task and a preference task. Montrul's design and the syntactic tests are too complex to yield to a simple summary; however, it is clear that there are differences based on the first language, with anglophones being inferior to francophones, but the learners also seem to be guided by UG to some degree.

4 Summary and Directions for Future Research

4.1 Summary

Learning certain aspects of the lexicon, and verbs in particular, poses a problem for children if they have no restriction for the hypothesis space. Although input is available, it underdetermines what children end up knowing about verb meaning and the links between verb meaning and morpho-syntax: Hence, UG must be involved to some extent although to be sure not in the same way as other, more abstract principles of syntactic computation where no input seems to be available.

From the SLA studies that have been considered in this chapter, L1 effects appear strong in this area of the grammar: Based on their L1, learners transfer and overgeneralize in dative movement and the locative alternation; they show a preference for morphology for inchoatives; learners are helped if their L1 has certain features which are also in the L2: French learners seem more accurate than English learners in their acquisition of the morpho-syntactic reflexes of unaccusativity in Italian (Sorace, 1995), and French learners are helped with Spanish psych verbs because French has dative Case, whereas English does not (Montrul, 1998). Despite overgeneralizations and somewhat different developmental paths based in part on L1, advanced learners seem able to recover from overgeneralizations in some instances and rely perhaps on positive evidence from verbs which may superficially seem unrelated to the class of verbs they are facing difficulties with but which nevertheless share the same semantic conflation class (Juffs, 1996a).

However, some evidence of universal patterns of development is also apparent. Learners from a variety of backgrounds seem to use passive morphology for NP movement in English L2 with pure unaccusatives, and English-speaking learners of Spanish seem to use *se* selectively for the same purpose even when it is not required with unaccusative verbs (Toth, 1997). Where causativity is concerned, the picture is a little more complex. Montrul (1997) finds evidence for an initial hypothesis that all verbs can have a default transitive template, allowing an SVO structure in English even with pure unaccusatives and unergatives. Hence, learners seem to overgeneralize causativity in root morphemes much as children acquiring their first language do. However, some learners also seem reluctant to accept psych verbs and alternators in a causative syntactic frame (Hirakawa, 1995; Juffs 1996a; White, 1995) – a result which seems to indicate that despite a tendency to allow transitive structures with verbs that do not allow it, the L1 can limit hypotheses about causativity in the L2.

Absent in the literature are arguments that learning of verb semantics – argument structure links is completely unconstrained and remains unconstrained. Even Bley-Vroman and Yoshinaga (1992) find sensitivity to some constraints, even if narrow range features are not clearly available in their data.

4.2   Future research

Despite recent advances, much research remains to be done in the acquisition of verb meaning and the way such knowledge relates to syntax. First, much more cross-linguistic data are needed. As with many aspects of SLA, our understanding of the acquisition of this sub-domain of the grammar is hampered by the lack of detailed descriptive studies of the links between verb semantics and morpho-syntax in non-Indo-European languages and the corresponding lack of L1 developmental data. Such research will take some time because it requires painstaking data collection from large numbers of verbs in a variety of syntactic environments.

Second, theoretical development based on cross-linguistic data is required. Theoretical linguists still cannot agree on the precise nature of the domain broadly labeled "thematic relations" (Dowty, 1991). Some accounts emphasize syntax over semantics, and vice versa. This lack of agreement is due in part to the complexity of the problem: On the one hand there is a problem of developing a theory of representations that can do justice to what speakers know about meaning; on the other hand, a theory of how that meaning links to syntax is required (Jackendoff, 1990).

In the SLA literature, syntactic accounts have dominated in some areas, e.g., psych verbs, but a semantic focus has been adopted for others, e.g., recent investigations of datives and locatives. As Sorace (1995) points out, a purely syntactic account of this domain will not work and SLA researchers need to guard against taking an oversimplified syntactic approach to the problem of meaning. I believe that the approach of Hale and Keyser (1993) is correct to deny the validity of the thematic hierarchy and require constraints on semantic representations, but incorrect in assuming that semantic structures are the same as those in "surface" syntax because they cannot account for the problem of meaning and hierarchies of the kind described in Sorace's research. Moreover, SLA researchers should now abandon theta role labels; eliminating theta role labels would avoid the need to make the counter-intuitive claim that the theta role of "John" is a Theme in a sentence like *John scared Mary*. It is clear that in such sentences the Subject is an Agent – or causer as Pesetsky (1995) points out – and behaves as such with regard to a range of tests (Van Valin and La Polla, 1997: 97). To persist in calling such arguments "Themes" – the definition of which is "undergoer" or object moving – is to carry on the tradition of using theta roles as "wild cards" (Jackendoff, 1987).

Finally, we need a much better worked-out account of the relationship between semantic structure and *morphology* as well as syntax. This is because the SLA literature shows that it is morphology which is the fragile component *across the board* in L2 grammatical development, at least at the beginning (Adjémian, 1983; Larsen-Freeman and Long 1991:254–5, 262); this domain is no exception as the overgeneralization of passive shows. An observation is that morphology is not merely omitted – as Oshita (in press) and Toth (1997) show, morphology is selectively *added* to some classes of verbs.

Pending advances in our knowledge of data and theory, more studies with pairs of languages with different lexical parameter settings such as those developed by Juffs (1996a), Slabakova (1997), and Snyder (1995) are needed: For example, we need to know whether Thai and Japanese learners of Chinese do better than speakers of Indo-European languages with the morphology required for causatives and resultative verb compounds as a result of their sharing a parameter setting with Chinese.

In addition, more information on the relationship between input and acquisition, with attention being paid to input frequency, is important, especially where narrow range conflations classes are concerned (Inagaki, 1997). Debate continues in the first language acquisition literature as to the role of input frequency, or absence of input, in developing children's L1 knowledge of this area (see discussion of Bowerman, 1990; Gordon and Chafetz, 1990 in section 4.4), and SLA researchers need to rule out, or accept, alternative explanations based less on internal contributions and more on data which is available to the learner. Input cannot be ruled out as a key factor until we have some idea of the input available. As Gleitman (1993) pointed out in the Human Language video series, the question is: What parts of language are learned and what parts are derived from input? We cannot know the answer to the latter question through linguistic theory alone but only through looking at what data are available.

4.3   Other theories of semantics–syntax correspondences[8]

More recently, the verb-class approach has been challenged by some scholars who believe that the verb-class approach lacks both descriptive and explanatory adequacy (Rosen, 1996). Some researchers who challenge the verb-class approach are making claims about the influence of lexical semantics on the *position of arguments in the syntax*, rather than the lexical representation *per se* (Tenny, 1994). In other words, they do not deny lexical decomposition or that verbs may share elements of meaning that can be captured by a theory of lexical decomposition (Tenny, 1994:190), but they do question the role of verb classes and their part in the determination of how arguments are assigned to syntactic positions. For instance, Dowty (1991) points out that the basic government and binding (GB) function of theta roles was that of argument indexing – assuring a one-to-one mapping of theta roles to arguments, and maintaining a consistent interpretation of an argument's semantic role after the application of Move α. Dowty contrasts this approach with that of Jackendoff and Pinker, whose focus, he states, is more on lexical and syntactic patterns, and what they reveal about conceptual structure. In other words, the decompositional meaning of a predicate, according to Dowty

(1991), is in principle separable from the way NP arguments are projected in the syntax, that is linked to syntactic positions.

Rosen (1996) points out a problem with the verb-class approach: If a verb's syntactic frame is determined by its semantics, then verbs of similar meaning should all have the same syntax, but that this situation does not hold. She also argues that some verbs do not rigidly belong to one class, and their syntactic behaviour is variable and "context-dependent." Instead of verb classes, Rosen (1996:194) holds that "event structure determines the mapping of arguments into the syntax, and . . . event structure must reside outside the lexicon, as a separate level of representation." The theory of event structure is quite new and not yet very explicit; however, Rosen posits three event roles that are related to "universal mapping principles":

1   Causer maps to the external argument position
2   Measure maps to the direct internal argument position
3   Delimiter maps to an internal argument position – direct if it measures the event, indirect if it does not.

These constructs are aspectually based and are related to Tenny's (1994) Aspectual Interface Hypothesis. In Tenny's (1994:95) theory, the "measure" aspectual role "is assigned to an argument of the verb, which (in the event described by the verb) either undergoes some internal change or motion . . . ; or provides a scale or parameter without undergoing change or motion; that measures out the temporal extent of the event." The "delimiter" refers to the argument that defines when the end-point of the event has been reached: "delimitedness refers to the property of an event's having a distinct, definite and inherent end point" (Tenny, 1994:4). Hence, event structure theory is in many senses temporal rather than related to the lexical decomposition of the verb.

Rosen presents the following data as evidence (a) that verbs' syntactic frames are *not* determined by their inherent semantics and (b) that their behaviour can be explained by principles such as those in (1)–(3). (Judgments are those given in Rosen, 1996):

(33)   a.   Sue danced.
     b.   The horse jumped.
     c.   Bill walked.

(34)   a.   *Bill danced Sue.
     b.   ??The trainer jumped the horse.
     c.   *Sue walked Bill.

(35)   a.   Sue danced across the room.
     b.   The horse jumped over the fence.
     c.   Bill walked home.

(36) a. Bill danced Sue across the room.
     b. The trainer jumped the horse over the fence.
     c. Sue walked Bill home.

The verb-class theory accounts for the differences in (33) and (36) by arguing that when the goal argument is added to the examples, the verbs switch from being unergative to unaccusative. The event structure approach claims that the sentences without the PP are activity verbs and hence atelic – that is, a verb that has no specified end; in contrast, a verb which is used to describe a means of reaching a location is actually a telic verb – one that has a delimited event. Since causitivable verbs are delimited events, and the goal phrase provides the event with an end point, these verbs are able to be causitivized. Rosen extends this to say that verbs that can never be delimited will never permit causativization.

The second set of verbs that Rosen seeks to make the theory work for are the verbs that take part in the locative alternation: *spray/load* and those that do not, e.g., *fill* and *pour*, which were discussed above. Rosen recalls that since Anderson (1971) many scholars have noted that when the Goal is the object of a locative verb it is interpreted as completely affected. Advocates of the event structure approach suggest that the alternating verbs describe events where both the moving object and the goal can measure out the event – that is (2). For example, in (37a), when all the hay is gone the event is over, and in (37b) when the truck is full the event is over.

(37) a. John loaded the hay onto the truck.
     b. John loaded the truck with hay.
       [X ACT+effect [Y GO [STATE]]]

In Rosen's view, in the verb-class theory verbs belong to one category and they are fixed. She notes, however, that this is not the case as the examples in (38) show:

(38) a. The children taped the pictures on the wall.
     b. *The children taped the wall with pictures.
     c. The children taped up the wall with pictures.
     d. *The children taped up the pictures on the wall.

According to Rosen (1996), *tape* should not allow a Goal direct object – but the particle *up* – which has event structure properties – changes the aspectual nature of the verb to one in which the location can measure the event (38c), but not the Theme (38d). Rosen's account is somewhat less forceful when it comes to other non-alternators and actually makes use of a representation like Pinker (1989) for *fill*. Yet she does point out that event structure can bypass the lexicon for special uses – hence even *fill* can allow a Goal object when the Goal can measure out the event as in "Fill the mixture into the zucchini" (Pinker, 1989).

The learning mechanism that Rosen assumes is that children know how arguments are mapped into syntax by the role they play in the event denoted by the verb not the semantics of the verb. Children still have to learn verbs' meanings, but the mapping principles are innate. Unfortunately, Rosen does not address the issue of overgeneralization and unlearning, nor is there much cross-linguistic data presented.

Since Rosen (1996) does appeal to some verbal semantics and does not develop her acquisition account very clearly, her conclusion that verb classes "have no cognitive or linguistic reality in the presentation or operation of the linguistic system" is probably too strong for now. This chapter is not the place to engage in a lengthy discussion of the pros and cons of the event structure approach *vis-à-vis* verb classes, but clearly Rosen's discussion needs to be addressed by advocates of the verb-class approach in both first and second language acquistion. Her review of particle constructions with locatives, as well as that of Tenny (1994), is directly relevant to the claims regarding aspect and the role of derivational morphology in constraining the placement of arguments by Juffs (1996a), Slabakova (1997), and Snyder (1995).

Moreover, as Juffs (1996a:204) pointed out, a verb like *pour* which is most often discussed as a "locative" verb, also takes part in the dative alternation, and the causative/inchoative alternation, as shown in (39):

(39) a. Chris poured the whisky into the glass.
          ([X ACT+effect) [Y GO [PATH]]]
      b. *Chris poured the glass with whisky.
      c. The whisky poured onto the floor.
          [Y GO [PATH]]
      d. Chris poured a drink for Sandy.
          [X ACT+effect [Y GO Z]]
      e. Chris poured Sandy a drink.
          [X ACT+effect [Z HAVE Y]]

Clearly, *pour* does not belong to one class alone – indeed the whole point of Juffs' (1996a) parameter is that verbs that appear to be in different classes may in fact share key aspects of semantic structure that determine mapping of arguments into syntax. However, we can say that (39 a and e) would share part of a decompositional structure that like [GO [PATH]] in (39c) and [ACT+Effect [GO[PATH]]] in (39a and c). Whether (39d, e) are related to (39a, c), and how a theory of polysemy could account for the relationship between *pour* = causative/inchoative and *pour* = dative is an issue that remains to be investigated. A theory of event structure could provide a range of testable hypotheses and structures which second language researchers should take advantage of in their search for a reasoned relationship between semantic structure and aspectual structure (see Tenny, 1994, for more detailed discussion).

4.4   Verb classes and input

Bowerman's view (1982b, 1988, 1990) attributes more importance to the input a child receives and hence to learning verbs individually. Hence, her view is closer to that of Baker (1979), who assumed that children were conservative learners. Bowerman (1982b:334) holds that children begin by recording verb-argument structures one by one, and that they only later perceive the semantic correlates among them which "serve to organize and transform what the child already 'knows' on a piecemeal basis into an integrated system." Overgeneralizations are based on the child's sensitivity to the statistically preponderant patterns, at least in the case of locative verbs (Bowerman, 1982b:341) and psych verbs (Bowerman, 1990:1285). For the locatives, Bowerman claims that there are more content verbs than container verbs in the input, and that this ratio is the source of overgeneralizations of content verb-argument structure (e.g., *pour* in (4)) to container locatives (e.g., *cover* in (5)). The no negative evidence problem is resolved by allowing errors to peter out over time (Bowerman, 1982b:342). Additional evidence for the one-by-one approach to verb-argument structure acquisition is research by Gordon and Chafetz (1990), who show that although children's treatment of passive action verbs had been interpreted as demonstrating a class effect, in fact it can be accounted for better as a verb-by-verb effect.

Bowerman seems reluctant to concede any more details of the acquisition process than absolutely necessary to innate structures. This is of course not to say that she does not accept *any* role for innateness (Bowerman, 1994): Children quite quickly home in on properties of the ambient language, as shown by the contrasting patterns of Korean children and English children. "Children could not learn language specific spatial meanings as quickly as they do unless they have some good ideas about what to look for" (Choi and Bowerman, 1991:118). But specifically linguistic, abstract constructs are not the first line of argument for Bowerman, or for functionalists. Their position is that languages have only certain tendencies where conflation patterns are concerned (Talmy, 1985), and would be cautious about claims to be made for a specifically linguistic parameter-setting model in this area. To my knowledge, no studies have been conducted that compare the input second language learners receive with the output that they produce in terms of the verb classes that have been discussed in the first acquisition literature.

4.5   Pedagogical implications

Theoretical research should not be required to have classroom applications and indeed few studies exist that attempt to apply results of the SLA studies cited in this chapter to classroom research in the way that White (1991a) did with the verb movement parameter. Exceptions to this are Carroll and Swain (1993), who conducted a study of Spanish-speaking learners' responses to different types of feedback of the dative alternation. They found that feedback (both explicit and implicit) of any kind was useful to the learners, but explicit feedback was most beneficial. Yip (1994) attempted some consciousness-raising activities in her pilot study, but the number of participants make it impossible to draw any firm conclusions. Toth (1997) found an effect for the type of instruction on the production frequency, but not with the judgment accuracy, in a classroom study of the acquisition of the use of *se* in Spanish as a second language.

However, the knowledge that has been discussed in this chapter lends itself very well to classroom studies because we have known for a long time that learners face overgeneralization problems (Burt and Kiparsky, 1972). Moreover, acquisition of these properties is dependent on input to some degree, unlike more abstract principles, so that classroom intervention may be appropriate and necessary (White, 1987). However, simple classroom studies should not just ask questions such as whether enhanced input will have an effect – we know it will at least in the short term (White, 1991a). The questions that need to be answered are what *kind* of instruction is best – input flood, explicit correction – and just as importantly how such knowledge can best be *sustained*. In addition, Juffs (1998) has suggested that knowledge of the issues discussed in this chapter can help teachers understand developmental stages in this domain and also help materials writers provide the right kind of input – input that appears to be lacking in some materials.

5   Conclusion

Research on the way verb semantics influences the acquisition of morphosyntax is a rapidly developing field of inquiry in linguistic theory as well as in first and second language acquisition. We are only beginning to discover properties of the lexicon and event structure that may or may not constrain the acquisition of second languages. The newness of this field makes it a challenging, but rewarding, field of inquiry as the range of theoretical positions offers a variety of testable hypotheses for second language researchers to explore.

Notes

1   See Karmiloff-Smith (1994) for challenges to generative assumptions concerning learnability and modularity.
2   This sentence is ungrammatical on the reading that the book moves, and not on a reading where the table is put *next to* the book.

3   However, they do make errors with interpretation, for instance with Principle B of the Binding Theory (e.g., Grimshaw and Rosen, 1990).
4   I am assuming that linguistic knowledge is separate from, or "encapsulated", other higher cognitive abilities. This view remains highly controversial.
5   Talmy notes that there may be more than just two types of ACT, etc., but many of his cause types seem to be multi-clause sentences with more than one main predicate.
6   See Juffs (1996b) for a comparison of features in Functional Categories and features in major lexical categories.
7   Abbreviations used in this chapter are as follows:
    AUX = Auxiliary verb.
       AC = Anti-causative marker: A morpheme which indicates that the verb does not assign an Agent semantic role. In Romance, this morpheme is homophonous with the reflexive morpheme.
    DET = Determiner, e.g., "the", "a", etc.
    FSO = Feminine Singular Object.
    CAUS = Causative verb.
    PERF = Perfective marker.
8   A reviewer makes clear that a range of theories now exist and that they are not compatible with the verb-class approach. Much of the work the reviewer mentioned could not be found in data base searches and incomplete bibliographic information was provided. Moreover, none of these theories has been used in SLA research to my knowledge. I therefore only deal with the Event Structure approach here.

References

Adjémian, C. (1983) The transfer of lexical properties. In S. Gass and L. Selinker (eds.), *Language Transfer in Language Learning*, pp. 250–68. Rowley, MA: Newbury House.

Akmajian, A. and Heny, F. (1975) *An Introduction to the Principles of Transformational Syntax*. Cambridge, MA: MIT Press.

Anderson, S. R. (1971) On the role of deep structure in semantic interpretation. *Foundations of Language* 6: 197–219.

Ard, J. and Gass, S. (1987) Lexical constraints on syntactic acquisition. *Studies in Second Language Acquisition* 9: 233–52.

Baker, C. L. (1979) Syntactic theory and the projection problem. *Linguistic Inquiry* 10: 533–81.

Baker, M. C. (1988) *Incorporation: A Theory of Grammatical Function Changing*. Chicago, IL: University of Chicago Press.

Balcom, P. (1997) Why is this happened? Passive morphology and unaccusativity. *Second Language Research* 13: 1–9.

Bley-Vroman, R. (1989) What is the logical problem of foreign language learning? In S. Gass and J. Schachter (eds.), *Linguistic Perspectives on Second Language Acquisition*, pp. 41–68. Cambridge: Cambridge University Press.

—— and Yoshinaga, N. (1992) Broad and narrow constraints on the English dative alternation: some fundamental differences between native speakers and foreign language learners. In *University of Hawai'i Working Papers in ESL*, vol. 11, pp. 157–99. University of Hawai'i at Manoa.

Bowerman, M. (1994) Learning a semantic system: What role do cognitive dispositions play? In P. Bloom (ed.), *Language Acquisition: Core Readings*, pp. 329–63. Cambridge, MA: MIT Press.

—— (1990) Mapping thematic roles onto syntactic functions: Are children helped by innate "linking rules"? *Linguistics* 28: 1253–89.

—— (1988) The "No negative evidence problem": How do children avoid constructing an overly general grammar? In J. Hawkins (ed.), *Explaining Language Universals*, pp. 73–101. Oxford: Basil Blackwell.

—— (1982a) Evaluating competing linguistic models with language acquisition data: implications of developmental errors with causative verbs. *Quaderni di Semantica* 3: 5–66.

—— (1982b) Reorganizational processes in lexical and syntactic development. In E. Wanner and L. R. Gleitman (eds.), *Language Acquisition: The State of the Art*, pp. 319–46. Cambridge: Cambridge University Press.

Burt, M. and Kiparsky, C. (1972) *The Gooficon: A Repair Manual for English*. Rowley, MA: Newbury House.

Carroll, S. and Swain, M. (1993) Explicit and implicit negative feedback: an empirical study of the learning of linguistic generalizations. *Studies in Second Language Acquisition* 15: 357–86.

Choi, S. and Bowerman, M. (1991) Learning to express motion events in English and Korean. *Cognition* 41: 83–121.

Chomsky, N. (1995) *The Minimalist Program*. Cambridge, MA: MIT Press.

—— (1981) *Lectures on Government and Binding*. Dordrecht: Foris.

—— (1986) *Knowledge of Language*. New York: Praeger.

Clark, E. (1993) *The Lexicon in Acquisition*. Cambridge: Cambridge University Press.

de Villiers, J. and Roeper, T. (1995) Relative clauses are barriers to Wh-Movement for young children. *Journal of Child Language* 22: 389–404.

di Sciullo, A. M. and Williams, E. (1987) *On the Definition of Word*. Cambridge, MA: Massachusetts Institute of Technology Press.

Dowty, D. (1991) Thematic proto-roles and argument selection. *Language* 67: 547–619.

Dryer, M. (1986) Primary objects, secondary objects, and anti-dative. *Language* 62: 808–45.

Fodor, J. (1970) Three reasons for not deriving kill from cause to die. *Linguistic Inquiry* 1: 429–38.

Gleitman, L. (1993) Interview comments, *The Human Language Series. Part two: Acquiring the human language*. New York: Ways of Knowing Inc.

—— (1990) The structural sources of verb meaning. *Language Acquisition* 1: 3–55.

—— and Landau, B. (eds.) (1994) *The Acquisition of the Lexicon*. Cambridge, MA: MIT Press. (Reprinted from *Lingua* 92).

Gordon, P. and Chafetz, J. (1990) Verb-based versus class-based accounts of actionality effects in children's comprehension of passives. *Cognition* 36: 227–54.

Gregg, K. (1989) Second language acquisition theory: the case for a generative perspective. In S. Gass and J. Schachter (eds.), *Linguistic Perspectives on Second Language Acquisition*, pp. 15–40. Cambridge: Cambridge University Press.

Grimshaw, J. (1990) *Argument Structure*. Cambridge, MA: MIT Press.

—— (1981) Form, function and the language acquisition device. In C. L. Baker and J. J. McCarthy (eds.), *The Logical Problem of Language Acquisition*, pp. 163–82. Cambridge, MA: MIT Press.

—— and Rosen, S. T. (1990) Knowledge and obedience: The developmental status of Binding Theory. *Linguistic Inquiry* 21: 187–222.

Gropen, J., Pinker, S., Hollander, M. and Goldberg, R. (1991a) Affectedness and direct objects: the role of lexical semantics in the acquisition of verb argument structure. *Cognition* 41: 153–95.

——, ——, —— and —— (1991b) Syntax and semantics in the acquisition of locative verbs. *Journal of Child Language* 18: 115–51.

——, ——, ——, —— and Wilson, R. (1989) The learnability and acquisition of the dative alternation in English. *Language* 65: 203–57.

Hale, K. and Keyser, S. J. (1993) On argument structure and the lexical expression of syntactic relations. In K. Hale and S. J. Keyser (eds.), *The View from Building 20: Essays in Linguistics in Honor of Sylvain Bromberger*, pp. 53–110. Cambridge, MA: MIT.

Harrington, M. (1987) Processing transfer: Language-specific processing strategies as a source of interlanguage variation. *Applied Psycholinguistics* 8: 351–77.

Haspelmath, M. (1993) More on the typology of inchoative/causative verb alternations. In B. Comrie and M. Polinsky (eds.), *Causatives and Transitivity*, pp. 87–120. Amsterdam: Benjamins.

Hirakawa, M. (1995) L2 acquisition of English unaccusative constructions. In D. MacClaughlin and S. McEwen (eds.), *Proceedings of the 19th Boston University Conference on Language Development*, 1, pp. 291–302. Somerville, MA: Cascadilla Press.

Hornstein, N. and Lightfoot, D. (eds.) (1981) *Explanation in Linguistics: the Logical Problem of Language Acquisition*. London: Longman.

Inagaki, S. (1997) Japanese and Chinese learners' acquisition of the narrow-range rules for the dative alternation in English. *Language Learning* 47: 637–69.

Jackendoff, R. S. (1990) *Semantic Structures*. Cambridge, MA: MIT Press.

—— (1987) The status of thematic relations in linguistic theory. *Linguistic Inquiry* 18: 368–411.

—— (1977) *X′-syntax: A Study of Phrase Structure*. Cambridge, MA: MIT Press.

Jaeggli, O. and Safir, K. J. (eds.) (1989) *The Null Subject Parameter*. Dordrecht: Kluwer.

Juffs, A. (1998) ESL materials and the acquisition of semantics syntax correspondences. *Language Teaching Research* 2: 93–123.

—— (1996a) *Learnability and the Lexicon: Theories and Second Language Acquisition Research*. Amsterdam, Philadelphia, PA: John Benjamins.

—— (1996b) Parameters in the lexicon, language variation, and language development. In A. Stringfellow, D. Cahana-Amitay, E. Hughes and A. Zukowski (eds.), *Proceedings of the 20th Annual Boston University Conference on Language Development*, 1, pp. 407–18. Somerville, MA: Cascadilla Press.

Karmiloff-Smith, A. (1994) Innate constraints and developmental change. In P. Bloom (ed.), *Language Acquisition*, pp. 563–90. Cambridge, MA: MIT Press.

Kellerman, E. (1978) Giving learners a break: native language intuition as a source of predictions about transferability. *Working Papers in Bilingualism* 15: 59–92.

Kim, M., Landau, B. and Phillips, C. (1999) Crosslinguistic differences in children's syntax for locative verbs. *Proceedings of the 23rd Boston University Conference on Language Development*. Somerville, MA.

Larsen-Freeman, D. and Long, M. H. (1991) *An Introduction to Second Language Acquisition Research*. London: Longman.

Larson, R. K. (1988) On the double object construction. *Linguistic Inquiry* 19: 335–91.

Levin, B. (1993) *English Verb Classes and Alternations: A Preliminary Investigation*. Chicago: University of Chicago Press.

—— and Pinker, S. (1991) Introduction to special issue of Cognition. *Cognition* 41: 1–7.

—— and Rappaport-Hovav, M. (1995) *Unaccusativity: At the Syntax-lexical Semantics Interface*. Cambridge, MA: MIT Press.

Manzini, R. and Wexler, K. (1987) Parameters, binding theory, and learnability. *Linguistic Inquiry* 18: 413–44.

Marantz, A. (1995) The Minimalist Program. In G. Webelhuth (ed.), *Government and Binding Theory and the Minimalist Program*, pp. 351–82. Oxford: Blackwell.

Mazurkewich, I. (1984) The acquisition of the dative alternation by second language learners and linguistic theory. *Language Learning* 34: 91–109.

—— and White, L. (1984) The acquisition of the dative alternation: Unlearning overgeneralizations. *Cognition* 16: 261–83.

Montrul, S. A. (in press) Causative errors with unaccusative verbs in L2 Spanish. *Second Language Research* 15.

—— (1998) The L2 acquisition of dative experiencer subjects. *Second Language Research* 14: 27–61.

—— (1997) Transitivity alternations in second language acquisition: a crosslinguistic study of English, Spanish and Turkish. Unpublished Ph.D. dissertation, McGill University.

Naigles, L. (1991) Review of Pinker 1989. *Language and Speech* 34: 63–79.

Nichols, J. (1984) Direct and oblique objects in Chechen-Ingush and Russian. In F. Plank (ed.), *Objects: Towards a Theory of Grammatical Relations*, pp. 183–210. London: Academic Press.

Oshita. H. (in press) The unaccusative trap and the development of the L2 lexicon. *Proceedings of the 34th Regional Meeting of the Chicago Linguistics Society*, Chicago.

—— (1997) "The unaccusative trap": L2 acquisition of English intransitive verbs. Unpublished Ph.D. dissertation, University of Southern California.

Perlmutter, D. M. (1978) Impersonal passives and the Unaccusative Hypothesis. In *Proceedings of the Fourth Annual Meeting of the Berkeley Linguistics Society*, pp. 157–89. Berkeley: University of California.

Pesetsky, D. (1995) *Zero Syntax: Experiencers and Cascades*. Cambridge, MA: MIT Press.

Pinker, S. (1989) *Learnability and Cognition: The Acquisition of Argument Structure*. Cambridge, MA: MIT Press.

—— (1984) *Language Learnability and Language Development*. Cambridge, MA: Harvard University Press.

Rosen, S. T. (1996) Events and verb classification. *Linguistics* 34: 191–223.

Rutherford, W. E. (1989) Preemption and the learning of L2 grammars. *Studies in Second Language Acquisition* 11: 441–58.

Saito, M. (1987) Three notes on syntactic movement in Japanese. In T. Imai and M. Saito (eds.), *Issues in Japanese Linguistics*. Dordrecht: Foris.

Sawyer, M. (1996) L1 and L2 sensitivity to semantic constraints on argument structure. In A. Stringfellow, D. Cahana-Amitay, E. Hughes and A. Zukowski (eds.), *Proceedings of the 20th Annual Boston University Conference on Language Development*, 2, pp. 646–57. Somerville, MA: Cascadilla Press.

Schwartz, B. D. and Sprouse, R. (1996) L2 cognitive states and the Full Transfer/Full Access model. *Second Language Research* 12: 40–72.

Slabakova, R. (in press) The parameter of aspect in second language acquisition. *Second Language Research* 15.

—— (1997) Zero acquisition: the parameter of aspect in second language acquisition. Unpublished Ph.D. thesis, McGill University.

Snyder, W. (1996) The acquisitional role of the syntax morphology interface: morphological compounds and and syntactic complex predicates. In A. Stringfellow, D. Cahana-Amitay, E. Hughes and A. Zukowski (eds.), *Proceedings of the 20th Annual Boston University Conference on Language Development* 2 pp. 728–35. Somerville, MA: Cascadilla Press.

—— (1995) Language acquisition and language variation: the role of morphology. Unpublished Ph.D. thesis, MIT.

—— and Stromswold, K. (1997) On the structure and acquisition of the English dative construction. *Linguistic Inquiry* 28: 281–317.

Sorace, A. (1995) Acquiring linking rules and argument structures in a second language: the unaccusative/unergative distinction. In L. Eubank, L. Selinker and M. Sharwood-Smith (eds.), *Current Trends in Interlanguage*, pp. 153–76. Amsterdam/Philadelphia PA: Benjamins.

—— (1993) Incomplete versus divergent representations of unaccusativity in non-native grammars of Italian. *Second Language Research* 9: 22–48.

Stowell, T. (1981) Origins of Phrase Structure. Ph.D. thesis, MIT.

Talmy, L. (1985) Lexicalization patterns: semantic structure in lexical patterns. In T. Shopen (ed.), *Language Typology and Syntactic Description*, pp. 57–149. Cambridge: Cambridge University Press.

Tenny, C. (1994) *Aspectual Roles and the Syntax–semantics Interface*. Dordrecht: Kluwer.

Thepsura, S. (1998) The acquisition of lexical causatives by Thai EFL learners. MS., of MA Paper, Georgetown University.

Toth, P. D. (in press) The interaction of instruction and learner internal factors in the acquisition of L2 morphosyntax. *Studies in Second Language Acquisition*.

—— (1997) Linguistic and pedagogical perspectives on acquiring second language morpho-syntax: a look at Spanish *se*. Unpublished Ph.D. thesis, University of Pittsburgh.

Travis, L. (1984) Parameters and effects of word order variation. Ph.D. thesis, MIT.

Van Valin, R. and La Polla, R. (1997) *Syntax: Structure, Meaning and Function*. Cambridge: Cambridge University Press.

White, L. (1995) Psych verbs and the T/SM restriction: what do L2 learners know? In *Proceedings of the 1995 Canadian Linguistics Association Annual Conference*. University of Toronto Working Papers in Linguistics.

—— (1991a) Adverb placement in second language acquisition: Some effects of positive and negative evidence in the classroom. *Second Language Research* 7: 133–61.

—— (1991b) Argument structure in second language acquisition. *Journal of French Language Studies* 1: 189–207.

—— (1989) *Universal Grammar and Second Language Acquisition*. Amsterdam: John Benjamins.

—— (1987) Markedness and second language acquisition: the question of transfer. *Studies in Second Language Acquisition* 9: 261–86.

—— Brown, C., Bruhn-Garavito, J., Chen, D. and Montrul, S. (in press) Psych verbs in second language acquisition. In E. Klein and G. Martohardjono (eds.), *The Development of Second Language Grammars: A Generative Approach*. Philadelphia: Benjamins.

Yip, V. (1994) Grammatical consciousness-raising and learnability. In T. Odlin (ed.), *Perspectives on Pedagogical Grammar*, pp. 123–39. Cambridge: Cambridge University Press.

Zobl, H. (1989) Canonical typological structures and ergativity in English L2 acquisition. In S. Gass and J. Schachter (eds.), *Linguistic Perspectives on Second Language Acquisition*, pp. 203–21. Cambridge: Cambridge University Press.

7

Representation and Processing in the Second Language Lexicon: The Homogeneity Hypothesis

Gary Libben

1   Introduction

It has been estimated that an average native speaker of English possesses a vocabulary of about 50,000 words (Aitchison, 1994:7). The question of how these words are represented in the mind and how they are accessed in language production and comprehension has occupied a central position in psycholinguistic research. This research domain has served as a place in which psychologists, linguists, and neuropsychologists can share findings, models, and insights that affect our conceptions of human cognition and language ability. There is implicit agreement among researchers that understanding how lexical knowledge is organized is the key to understanding the overall organization of language in the mind because lexical knowledge is at the core of the language system.

This same perspective perhaps also accounts for the centrality of the bilingual lexicon in the study of bilingual cognitive organization.[1] The lexicon has very often served as the primary "concrete example" in the elaboration of theories and models of the organization of two languages in one mind and in the elaboration of the role played by acquisition and use in shaping this cognitive organization.

Although researchers in both the bilingual and monolingual literature on lexical processing often point to the centrality of the mental lexicon within their respective research domains, it is important to note that these domains have until recently remained relatively independent and that mental lexicon research within each domain has maintained a fundamentally distinct character. While this distinctness is of course a natural result of the kinds of questions that need to be addressed within each domain, I argue in this chapter that monolingual and bilingual lexical processing data cannot be considered in isolation. This argument is at the core of the specific proposal advanced in this chapter – *The Homogeneity Hypothesis*.

1.1   Overview of the Homogeneity Hypothesis

The essence of the Homogeneity Hypothesis is that monolinguals, bilinguals, and second language learners possess the same kinds of lexical representations and employ the same kinds of processes in the activation of words in the mental lexicon. Thus, monolingual, bilingual, and second language lexical knowledge can be represented in a single lexical architecture and there is no need to postulate individual lexicons for individual languages.

I argue that this perspective follows from recent developments in the bilingual processing literature in which proposals concerning the bilingual lexicon have been cast within more general models of language and cognitive processing. Examples of such developments include De Bot's (1993) proposal for bilingual production, which is situated in the context of Levelt's (1989) model of speaking, as well as the Bilingual Interactive Activation model proposed by Grainger and Dijkstra (1992) and Dijkstra and Van Heuven (1998) which extends the network architecture of McClelland and Rumelhart's (1981) model of monolingual word recognition. Finally, Green's (1998) proposal concerning bilingual control over language use, which would arguably be expected to require theoretical constructs specific to bilingualism, has been advanced on the foundation of general cognitive principles such as action control (Norman and Shallice, 1986) and script usage (Shank, 1982).

Developments such as these have the advantage of bringing experimentation on bilingual processing into closer methodological and theoretical proximity to the monolingual processing literature only under the assumption that the monolingual and bilingual lexicons indeed share a common architecture. If, however, the architecture of the bilingual and monolingual systems are not homogeneous, then we are in the disadvantageous position of dealing with comparisons between "apples and oranges".

My goal in advancing the Homogeneity Hypothesis is both to bring this assumption of comparability to the foreground and to explore its consequences for modeling the general properties of the bilingual lexicon and the specific characteristics of lexical representations within that lexicon. The hypothesis claims that bilinguals possess a single lexical store and lexical architecture. This claim follows from the suggestion first put forward in Paradis' (1987) Subset Hypothesis that the individual languages of a bilingual form a *de facto* subset of a larger lexical store that emerges from patterns of language use.

The specific characteristics and consequences of the Homogeneity Hypothesis are elaborated in the following sections of this chapter. I begin by situating the hypothesis within an historical perspective on the core debates and models concerning the functional architecture of the bilingual lexicon. This is followed by an elaboration of the consequences of the hypothesis for the modeling of interlingual facilitation and inhibition in bilingual lexical processing and, finally, by an outline of the manner in which the Homogeneity Hypothesis opens up new lines of investigation in the study of the mental lexicon.

2   From Separate Lexicons to Organizational Homogeneity

As presented above, the Homogeneity Hypothesis claims that bilingual lexical knowledge is represented in a single store. This places it in contrast with the modeling tradition in which bilinguals are viewed as possessing separate lexicons which overlap and interact in varying degrees. In this section, I present a brief sketch of developments in the characterization of the bilingual lexicon. This sketch highlights the fact that early models focused on the development of functionally insulated language-specific lexicons whereas later models focused on the manner in which there is cross-language activation and overlap in bilingual lexical processing. I argue that this trend – which itself has been necessitated by an accumulation of experimental evidence – points us rather directly to the view that proficient bilinguals possess a homogeneous lexical architecture.

2.1   Compound and coordinate bilinguals: Focus on interlingual insulation

The separate lexicon tradition was launched by Weinreich's (1953) publication in which he outlined the manner in which word knowledge could be organized in the mind of a bilingual. His postulation of compound bilingualism, coordinate bilingualism, and subordinate bilingualism was based on the relationship between conceptual representations and linguistic representations in the mind of a bilingual. In his framework,[2] a coordinate bilingual is someone who has separate conceptual representations for translation equivalents. A compound bilingual, on the other hand, possesses a single set of conceptual representations onto which different language-specific expressions are mapped. Finally, a subordinate bilingual is someone for whom lexical representations in one language are mediated through both the lexical and conceptual representations in another language and is characteristic of low levels of second language proficiency. These three types of cognitive organization are shown schematically in figure 7.1.

The basic distinctions presented by Weinreich (1953) provided the framework for much of the discussion that followed in the literature on bilingual

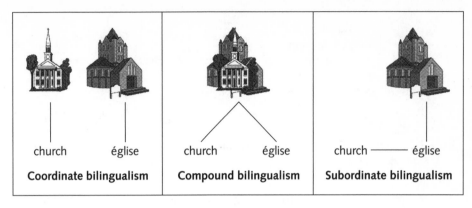

Figure 7.1 Three organizations of bilingual knowledge. In compound bilingualism, the conceptual representations are represented as fused

lexical organization (see De Groot, 1993 for a review). Most notably, his tripartite distinction was dichotomized by Ervin and Osgood (1954) who focused on the differences between compound and coordinate bilingualism. Their dichotomy related differences between bilingual cognitive organizations to the individual's context of acquisition and attached an explicit value judgment to the alternative forms of bilingual cognitive organization such that coordinate bilinguals who develop two language-specific lexicons were seen to have achieved "true" bilingualism.

In various manifestations, discussion and debate over the compound–coordinate dichotomy was ubiquitous in the bilingual literature for the next forty years. Interestingly, the greatest reason for this is that, as a construct, the dichotomy was simultaneously extremely appealing and extremely dissatisfying. The dissatisfaction associated with it is primarily related to two factors: The first, is that it is extremely unlikely that individual bilinguals fall wholly into one category or the other. If we accept (as is urged by Hamers and Blanc (1989:96) among others) that the distinction captures a continuum rather than a dichotomy, then we are left with a model of bilingual organization which claims that practically all organizations are possible and that each is the product of complex factors associated with language acquisition and use.

On the other hand, there is a way in which the appeal of the dichotomy has been almost irresistible. It provides a natural account for interference errors and also provides a metaphor for refinements such as those presented by Paradis (1978) in which it was claimed that language learners and bilinguals can possess compound organization at some levels of linguistic structure (e.g., phonology) but coordinate organization at others (e.g., lexical meaning).

Perhaps most importantly, the dichotomy opened up new issues in the study of bilingual organization. As is shown in figure 7.2, the dichotomy is easily translatable into discussions of whether the single-store organization or the dual-store organization characterizes most bilinguals. In this debate

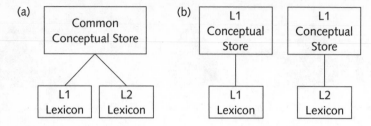

Figure 7.2 Compound and coordinate bilingual organizations as seen at the level of single-store vs. dual-store lexicons

McCormack (1977) argued for the single-store position whereas Kolers and Gonzales (1980) and others including Hummel (1986) presented evidence in favour of the dual-store approach.

Finally, representations of the type displayed in figure 7.2 (b) generated considerable research on the existence of the putative "bilingual language switch" which was postulated to account for the bilingual's ability to switch between languages on the basis of environmental demands (Penfield and Roberts, 1959; MacNamara, 1967; MacNamara and Kushnir, 1971). In the decade of experimentation that followed, however, evidence failed to support the notion that bilingual performance requires the postulation of a switching mechanism between separate language-specific stores (see Hamers and Blanc, 1989:84–90 and Grosjean, 1997:250). This is, of course, what would be predicted by the Homogeneity Hypothesis, because under this hypothesis there are no separate stores between which to switch.

2.2   Later models: Focus on interlingual activation

In 1984, Potter, So, Von Eckardt, and Feldman published a key paper that presented a reformulation of the manner in which bilingual lexical know-ledge could be represented in the mind. The paper returned to Weinreich's original distinctions and presented the alternative organizations of bilingual knowledge in terms of two competing models.

In the Concept Mediation Model, words of both L1 and L2 are linked to amodal conceptual representations. In the Lexical Association Model, on the other hand, words in a second language are understood through L1 lexical representations. As can be seen in figure 7.3, this latter configuration is struc-turally equivalent to Weinreich's subordinate bilingualism.

Potter et al. (1984) tested these alternative organizations in a study that compared translation and picture naming among fluent Chinese–English bilinguals and much less fluent French learners of English as a second lan-guage. They found that the patterns across both groups of subjects were the same for picture naming (which is assumed to obligatorily involve concept mediation) and translation. Accordingly, they concluded that the

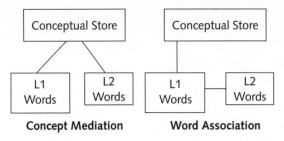

Figure 7.3 The Concept Mediation vs. Word Association models of bilingual lexical organization (adapted from Potter et al (1984)). The difference in size between the L1 and L2 boxes represents the dominance of L1 lexical representations

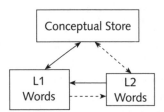

Figure 7.4 Kroll and Stewart's (1994) Revised Hierarchical Model. As in figure 7.3, the L2 lexicon is shown as a smaller box. The dotted lines represent the claim that L2 connections to concepts are weaker and that L2–L1 lexical associations are stronger than L1–L2 associations

Concept Mediation Model characterizes lexical organization across levels of proficiency.

Subsequent studies using similar experimental paradigms, however, found evidence for the view that lexical mediation is associated with low levels of proficiency and for a shift toward concept mediation at higher levels of second language proficiency (Chen and Leung, 1989; Kroll and Curley, 1989). These findings, as well as others using the Stroop technique (e.g., Chen and Ho, 1986; Tzelgov, Henik, and Leiser, 1990), were taken as evidence by Kroll and Stewart (1994) for the need to represent concept mediation and word association not as different models but rather as alternative routes within the same model of bilingual organization. Their Revised Hierarchical Model is presented in figure 7.4.

The Revised Hierarchical Model incorporates elements of both concept mediation and word association. It is assumed that, in the early stages of language learning, comprehension of L2 words is achieved through their translation equivalents. As proficiency increases, direct conceptual links are created between L2 representations and conceptual representations. Even in this case, however, the earlier word association links are not lost and can be activated under specific task demands. The model also predicts that, in translation, conceptual mediation is more likely when going from L1 to L2 than in

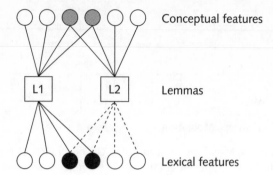

Figure 7.5 The Distributed Lexical/Conceptual Feature Model (adapted from Kroll and De Groot (1997))

the opposite direction. The reason for this is that the L1-conceptual links, formed early in childhood, always remain stronger. This view is supported by the results of Fox (1996) in which cross-language semantic priming effects were found for L1 primes on L2 targets, but not in the opposite direction.

Through the Revised Hierarchical Model, we seem to have come full circle to Weinreich's original proposals for how bilinguals differ in terms of their lexical organization and how this organization is related to second language competence. On the surface, then, this would yield a 1990s' version of how functionally distinct lexical organizations emerge in "true" bilingualism. I argue, however, that this is in fact not the case: By incorporating a single level of conceptual structure and a view of lexical association in which connection strength is variable, the model and recent findings in the bilingual priming literature actually move us toward a more network-like working model and toward the view that there never was any difference between monolingual and bilingual lexical processing in the first place.

This trend is perhaps most clearly evident in Kroll and De Groot's (1997) representation of the organization of the bilingual lexicon. Their Distributed Lexical/Conceptual Feature Model incorporates elements of the Revised Hierarchical Model, represents lexical entries in a more distributed fashion, and employs Levelt's (1989) lemma–lexeme distinction. In the Distributed Lexical/Conceptual Feature Model, translation equivalents are represented as items that have feature overlap at the conceptual level, but distinct representations at the lemma level. As is shown in figure 7.5, the lexeme level is also represented in their model in a distributed fashion and allows for partial overlap that would be characteristic of words that share lexical features.

Casting the process of interlingual activation in terms of feature overlap both at the conceptual level and at the lexeme level, offers an interpretive framework for the findings reported in the literature that concrete translation equivalents show greater ease of interlingual activation than abstract words. The reasoning here is that, while concrete words might show identity at the level of conceptual features, abstract words, because of cultural and interlingual usage differences, would typically show some conceptual non-correspondence (De Groot, 1992). The model, of course, also offers a natural means of representing interlingual homophone activation. Words such as "pain" in English and "pain" (= bread) in French, activate each other because they share surface lexical features. This degree of interlingual activation, however, is less than the activation obtained for cognates which share both lexical features and conceptual features.

In the Distributed Lexical/Conceptual Feature Model, we see beginnings of a homogeneous lexical architecture in which all words that an individual knows are attached to a common level of conceptual and lexical features. In such a model, the manner in which the word "cat" primes the words "dog" and "chien" would be identical. However, the model does maintain the notion of separate lexicons by positing language-specific stores at the level of the lemma. In this way, the model has much in common with the Bilingual Interactive Activation (BIA) Model (Dijkstra, Van Jaarsveld, and Brinke, 1998; Dijkstra and Van Heuven, 1998) which represents the bilingual lexicon as a connectionist model that follows the interactive activation architecture proposed by McClelland and Rumelhart (1981). The BIA model explicitly characterizes the bilingual lexicon as an integrated store in which the initial stages of lexical activation are language non-selective (see figure 7.6). The activation of a single language is achieved through language nodes that receive activation from words of one lexicon and have inhibitory connections to all words of a bilingual's other lexicon.

2.3   So, where are we?

In the sections above, we have seen how the early decades of research in bilingualism were characterized by the desire to identify the psycholinguistic correlates of "good" bilingualism. Because the most desirable form of bilingualism is one in which the bilingual shows no interference in either language, it was assumed that the ideal lexical architecture was one in which the bilingual is in possession of two monolingual lexical systems. Later models of the bilingual lexicon, such as the Revised Hierarchical Model, reflect the fact that the field of bilingual lexical research has become much more associated with the monolingual lexical processing literature in which the tradition has been to investigate word association effects. By definition, these effects reveal much more about how mental representations are connected than about how they are insulated.

This brings us to our current situation. On the one hand, there is considerable experimental evidence that words in the bilingual lexicon activate one another, suggesting an integrated architecture. On the other hand, it is impossible to avoid addressing the fact that a good bilingual is one who is able to produce relatively pure forms of more than one language. Therefore, there

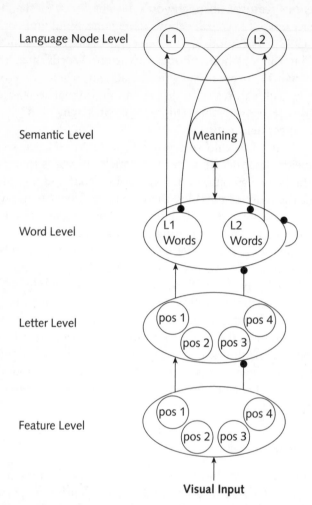

Figure 7.6 The Bilingual Interactive Activation Model (adapted from Dijkstra, Van Jaarsveld, and Brinke (1998))

must also be a way in which elements of individual languages can be selected and deselected in the bilingual lexicon.

These sorts of considerations are addressed in both the Conceptual/Lexical Feature Model and the Bilingual Interactive Activation Model, which attempt to capture interlingual activation and language selectivity by positing language specificity at one level of representation but organizational homogeneity at other levels of representation.

In the following sections of this chapter, I argue that we can go one step further: It is possible to model the spread of activation in the bilingual lexicon as well as the bilingual's ability to function in a single language by positing a lexical architecture that is characterized by homogeneity at all levels of representation. A homogeneous architecture, I argue, can account for the data patterns reported in the recent literature and also opens up some new lines of investigation.

3   Claims and Predictions of the Homogeneity Hypothesis

We may begin our discussion of the claims and predictions of the Homogeneity Hypothesis by considering what we understand to be the fundamental properties of the mental lexicon. Decades of experimental psycholinguistic research have painted a picture of the mental lexicon in which the activation of one element results in the activation of other lexical elements that are related semantically, morphologically and formally (Napps and Fowler, 1987; Napps, 1989; Drew and Zwitserlood, 1995). This activation of associated units is seldom available to consciousness and is seldom under strategic control. Studies of the effects of context on the recognition of ambiguous words have suggested that a word form such as "bug" (to take a rather famous example) will initially activate both the "spy" and "insect" readings even in sentences that bias toward only one reading (e.g., "The spy planted the bug"). Findings such as these suggest that the lexicon is organized so that all representations are initially activated and that subsequent decay of activation or selection at higher levels of processing create the necessary disambiguation. In other words, the lexicon is primarily governed by bottom-up procedures and is relatively unaffected by top-down sources of information.

This same pattern is also found in the processing of multimorphemic words for which it has been shown that multimorphemic word recognition results in the activation of constituent as well as whole-word representations (e.g., Marslen-Wilson et al., 1994; Schreuder and Baayen, 1995; Zwitserlood, 1994). In recent experiments conducted in our lab, it has also been found that the recognition of novel multimorphemic forms involves the automatic and obligatory creation of all possible morphological structures (Libben, 1994; Libben, Derwing and de Almeida, in press). Thus, the novel compound "clamprod," which can be parsed as either "clamp-rod" or "clam-prod" will result in the initial activation of all four morphemes (clam, clamp, prod, and rod) even when participants are unaware of the ambiguous nature of the stimuli. These findings suggest again that the early components of lexical processing are driven by bottom-up procedures, that activation of associated morphemes proceeds automatically and that the lexical system is ill-equipped to limit the activation of representations. To take a concrete example, these principles claim that it would not be possible for the reader of this paragraph to prevent the activation of the "shopping" association to the word "store" in the sentence "Bilinguals possess a single lexical store" even though the present discussion will likely have little to do with shopping. Eventually, however, the appropriate reading of "store" is the one that is integrated into memory, suggesting that processing in the mental lexicon has the following general sequence: (1) activation of a form activates all its constituent representations; (2) all associates of all representations are activated; and (3) contextually inappropriate representations decay or are deselected subsequent to lexical access.

According to the Homogeneity Hypothesis, we should see this same sequence in bilingual lexical processing. Thus, for an individual whose lexicon contains words of more than one language, all representations linked by meaning, sound, or visual form should show activation effects in a priming paradigm (particularly in the early stages of processing).

The fact that this is indeed what has been found in a large number of experimental studies (e.g., Beauvillain and Grainger, 1987; De Groot and Nas, 1991; Grainger and O'Regan, 1992; Gollan, Forster and Frost, 1997; Van Heuven and Grainger, 1998) offers support for the view that the lexicon is characterized by organizational homogeneity (but see Gerard and Scarborough, 1989). Under the Homogeneity Hypothesis, there aren't any language-specific lexicons in the mind and, because the overriding property of the lexicon is that activation spreads, bilingual priming effects are identical in nature to monolingual ones. Language selection and deselection can occur only subsequent to lexical access. This view claims that the underlying mechanisms that account for my knowledge that the English word "salt" has the same meaning as the French word "sel" must be the same as those that account for my knowledge that "salt" has the same meaning as "NaCl" or that "9:45" has the same meaning as "a quarter to ten".

It is important to note, however, that the Homogeneity Hypothesis claims that bilingual priming effects are identical *in nature* to monolingual effects, not that they are equivalent in strength. Because bilinguals very rarely have equal proficiency in both their languages, representations in one language will often have less entrenched representations and show activation thresholds below those expected on the basis of monolingual frequency counts (Grosjean, 1997).

In addition to claiming that a bilingual is in possession of a single lexicon, the Organizational Homogeneity Hypothesis claims that there is no difference between the organization of a bilingual lexicon and the organization of a monolingual one. It follows from this that language tags, which mark for example that the word "dog" is a word of English and the word "chien" is a word of French, must be internal to the lexical representations for these words and not labels for subdivisions within the lexicon. Otherwise, bilingual lexicons would differ from monolingual ones in that the former contain subdivisions. At present, there are two ways to conceive of such language markers. Dijkstra and Van Heuven's (1998) BIA Model contains language nodes which can be considered to be internal to lexical entries in the sense that they form part of a word's distributed representation. Green's (1998) model of bilingual control also posits a language tag as part of a lexical representation. I argue here that although the distinction between word-internal markers and word-external markers may at first appear to be minor, in fact, it has substantial consequences.

The first of these is that it makes it possible to model language selectivity phenomena using simple priming principles. As has been noted by Grosjean (1989, 1998), bilinguals can find themselves in monolingual or bilingual modes, where the latter mode is associated with conversational situations in which more than one language is being used. According to the Homogeneity Hypothesis, the difference between these modes can be modeled by assuming that in the bilingual mode, the use of lexical items of both languages primes items with both language tags and thus lowers their activation thresholds. In the monolingual mode, on the other hand, there is a priming asymmetry. Consider, for example, that the reader of this chapter has encountered about 3,000 words with English markers and only about three words marked for French. It is this priming asymmetry that places the English–French bilingual reader of this chapter in "English Mode".

A good example of how such priming effects work in an experimental setting is evident in the results recently reported by Dijkstra, Van Jaarsveld, and Brinke (1998). Their study of interlingual homograph priming presented evidence that when Dutch speakers of English were presented with Dutch words in a lexical decision task, their response times to Dutch words that had English homographs were non-distinct from those of Dutch control words. In the second experiment of their study, however, the stimulus set was changed so that English words were also presented. Because these words were not words of Dutch, the appropriate lexical decision response was "no." This change in stimulus set resulted in an elevation of both the response times and error rates for interlingual homographs. Finally, in the third experiment of their study, participants were given a "generalized lexical decision task" in which they were required to answer "yes" if the stimulus was either a word of Dutch or a word of English. This task change resulted in response time facilitation for interlingual homographs.

Under the Homogeneity Hypothesis, the results of Dijkstra et al. (1998) would be interpreted in the following manner: In the first experiment, homographs had no effect because the monolingual stimulus set created a priming asymmetry between lexical items with Dutch and English language tags. In the second experiment, because words of both languages were present, interlingual activation occurred. This activation resulted in an inhibition effect for interlingual homographs because the correct answer for the English reading would be "no" and the correct answer for the Dutch reading would be "yes." Crucially, I am claiming that this inhibition results from post-access indecision.

Finally, according to the Homogeneity Hypothesis, the facilitation in the generalized lexical decision task in Experiment 3 of Dijkstra et al. (1998) does not result primarily from the change in instructions to the participants but rather from the bottom-up priming effects obtained when words of both languages are activated. This explanation makes a straightforward

prediction (not tested in their study): If the key factor is the change in instructions, then the facilitation effect should be seen across all trials of the experiment. However, if as the Homogeneity Hypothesis claims, the effect is the
result of language tag priming, then the facilitation effect for items presented
in the second half of the experiment should be greater than that for items
presented in the first half. It should be noted that this prediction holds for all
experiments in which the putative language barrier is opened by the instructions to participants. Because the Homogeneity Hypothesis claims that the
lexicon is governed by bottom-up principles and that the language tag is part
of a morpheme's representation, the lexical elements of more than one language can only be activated through lexical activation that builds during the
course of multilingual stimulus presentation.

This account of homograph priming effects, which I have sketched above,
has three fundamental characteristics: It assumes that lexical processes are
automatic and obligatory, it assumes that they are governed by bottom-up
procedures, and finally, it assumes that language tags are internal to lexical
representations. Together, these assumptions lead us to the view that the
volitional aspects of bilingual performance are governed by procedures that
lie outside the lexical processing system.

Thus, in word translation for example, the Homogeneity Hypothesis claims
that the bilingual does not volitionally select one language and then subsequently search his or her lexicon for an item with a particular meaning.
Rather, the activation of an element of one language automatically and
obligatorily activates its translation equivalents in other languages and, only
subsequent to this, may the bilingual choose to report on the results of the
interlingual activation. If I am asked, for example, how to say "dog" in
French, the word acts as a stimulus which activates the translation equivalent
"chien". By identifying this word as the correct translation equivalent, I am
not making something happen, but rather am reporting what already has
happened.

In more specific terms, I claim that word translation can be modeled through
a mechanism of synonym priming in which the activated elements in the mental
lexicon possess different language tags. An explanation along these lines must
deal, however, with the findings that second language speakers show enhanced
activation of translation equivalents whereas, within languages, synonyms do
not show strong priming effects (Napps, 1989). I suggest that these findings
can be accounted for again by priming effects. Antonyms are more effective
primes than synonyms within a language because they have been linked in
the mental lexicon by patterns of use. Antonyms (e.g., black and white, good
and evil, king and queen) commonly occur together. Synonyms, on the other
hand, rarely occur together. I suggest that translation equivalents may be
organized in the mind much in the way that intralingual antonyms are. Antonyms are lexical items that share all but one semantic feature and frequently

co-occur (particularly during the acquisition of the lexical item) and transla-tion equivalents are lexical items that share semantic features and are distin-guished by their word-internal language tags. They also frequently co-occur in the early second language acquisition context (accounting for the domin-ance of word interlingual links at lower levels of proficiency).

3.1 Monolingual language use in the bilingual lexicon

We now turn our attention to the other side of the coin. Even if it is clear that interlingual lexical activation is automatic and obligatory, we still need some means by which we can model language selectivity. In real life, the bilingual is not completely data-driven and can choose to only speak in English or French. This domain of inquiry has been addressed in Green's (1986, 1998) work. Green (1998) suggests that language selectivity can be modeled through a mechanism of inhibitory control that functions at two levels. Language selectivity can be achieved by suppressing *the output* of activated items with particular language tags and can also be achieved by suppressing *the activation* of items with particular language tags. In his framework, inhibitory control is related to particular task schemata. For example, a monolingual lexical decision task (e.g., Dijkstra's et al. (1998) Experiment 1) would activate one task schema, whereas a generalized lexical decision task (e.g., Dijkstra's et al. (1998) Experiment 3) would activate a different task schema. Green (1998) suggests that inhibitory control can extend into the lexicon itself, so that a monolingual English task can result in the raising of the activation threshold for French words in a French–English bilingual's mental lexicon. This type of inhibitory control, which is based on views expressed in Green (1986) is currently at odds with the Homogeneity Hypothesis. The reason for this is simply that if our overall knowledge of lexical processing is such that opera-tions within the mental lexicon are insulated from the effects of top-down control, then this principle should extend to operations within the bilingual lexicon. Thus, inhibitory control should be able to suppress the output of lexical items with particular language tags, but should not be able to affect their activation. Which of these views is correct is, of course, an empirical question and Green (1998) suggests a number of ways in which the predic-tions of the Interactive Control Model could be tested. It is important to note in this regard that, under the Homogeneity Hypothesis, the relevance of bilingual and monolingual findings for our conceptions of the functional architecture of the mental lexicon is a two-way street. Thus, if task schemata can indeed control lexical activation levels, then this would constitute evid-ence that the mental lexicon is not as computationally encapsulated as we had previously thought. It is this claim of bi-directional theoretical constraint (rather than any particular position on lexical architecture) that is the core feature of the Homogeneity Hypothesis.

4 Summary and Implication for Future Research

In this chapter, I have sketched a view of the mental lexicon in which the representation of words of individual languages does not require special language-specific stores. Under this view, patterns of association and language use priming effects that facilitate the activation of words that share a particular language designation. These priming effects "generate" the surface impression of specific language stores and also the impression of different types of bilinguals. "Coordinate bilingualism" naturally results within this framework from the strong intralingual priming effects generated by non-mixed language use. "Compound bilingualism", on the other hand, is simply another term for a history of interlingual priming and, finally, "subordinate bilingualism" reflects the relatively short-term priming effects associated with an acquisition context in which L2 words are acquired in the context of their L1 equivalents.

The claims of the Homogeneity Hypothesis are thus in direct opposition to those concerning the "true" bilingualism that was at the core of the compound–coordinate dichotomy. It claims that the true bilingual is not someone with dual non-interfering lexicons. Rather, the true bilingual is someone for whom all lexical knowledge is fully integrated and for whom L2 representations have the same types of connections as monolingual ones.

The view also suggests that all volitional aspects of bilingual language use, including translation, language switching, and exclusive languages use are the domain of cognitive processes that occur outside the mental lexicon. The mental lexicon is thus seen as the repository of lexical representations and the locus of automatic processes that act on those representations.

Viewed in this way, the Homogeneity Hypothesis belongs in the family of Occam's Razor-like proposals in that it proposes to restrict the creation of new theoretical constructs. It generalizes the claims of Paradis' (1987) Subset Hypothesis from the issue of how individual languages might be represented in an integrated bilingual lexicon to the issue of whether bilinguals and monolinguals possess the same lexical architecture. In this final section, I discuss the implications of this broader claim for future research.

4.1 Organizational and representational homogeneity

Thus far, our discussion of the functional architecture of the bilingual mental lexicon has been in fairly broad terms. We have reviewed proposals concerning the existence of language-specific stores and proposals concerning how words of individual languages may be linked to conceptual representations and to each other. We have also discussed the question of whether language tags are internal or external to lexical representations and whether lexical representations can be viewed as multi-layered networks. But the details of lexical representations have not been examined beyond these broad terms. We have dealt with what I will now call "organizational homogeneity" but have not explored the consequences of extending the Homogeneity Hypothesis to the domain of "representational homogeneity". Here, I think the Homogeneity Hypothesis opens up some exciting domains of inquiry by forcing us again to view the bilingual lexicon in the same terms as we consider the monolingual lexicon. Below, I list some of these domains.

4.1.1   The unit of representation

The Homogeneity Hypothesis leads us to ask questions concerning whether it is profitable to consider the morpheme rather than the word as the fundamental unit of representation in the bilingual lexicon such that each morpheme would possess its own language tag. If this were the case, we would expect interlingual homograph effects to be seen below the level of the word so that, for example, the English word "bankroll" would affect the processing of the German word "Parkbank" (= park bench) even though they have different forms and meaning at the bimorphemic word level. Extending this question to the level of bound morphemes such as affixes leads us to the question of how the French and English language tags of the prefix "re-" would need to be represented and to the question of whether they show priming effects that are equivalent to those for cognate free morphemes.

4.1.2   Morphological homogeneity

An important issue in the investigation of whether homogeneity extends to the domain of representations is how words of multiple languages would be integrated into a single morphological system. Consider compounding in English, French, and German: If compounds for these languages develop a homogeneous architecture, then we would expect that compounds such as White House and "maison blanche" would be linked to a common node[3] specifying that they are both compounds. However, the integration of compounds for these forms would also require the development of a new node "headedness" for native speakers of English. The reason for this is that all English compounds are right-headed, whereas compounds may be both left-headed and right-headed in French. This consideration also leads to the prediction that *ceteris paribus*, compound priming effects would be greater for English–German compound translation equivalents (which are both always right-headed) than for English–French compounds which show different headedness patterns.

Considerations of this sort lead us to a more general statement concerning the predictions of the Representational Homogeneity Hypothesis: It claims that the lexical homogenization that must occur in the mental lexicon ensures that (to use the formulation of Grosjean's (1989)) the bilingual cannot be two monolinguals in one person. By acquiring a new language, all representations in a native speaker of English's mental lexicon will be modified so that they may include specifications for headedness, grammatical gender, etc.

4.1.3 Parsing homogeneity

As a final example of the potential effects of the Representational Homogeneity Hypothesis on how we model the mental lexicon, consider morphological parsing: The Homogeneity Hypothesis predicts, for example, that if English multimorphemic words are processed through a mechanism in which the whole string is activated while a morphological parse is simultaneously conducted (see Zwitserlood, 1994; Libben, 1994) then this same procedure would be employed by Finnish–English bilinguals when processing Finnish and Chinese–English bilinguals when processing Chinese. This is predicted despite the fact that whole word access might not be the preferred method for accessing Finnish words and that morphological parsing might be largely unnecessary in Chinese. Thus, again, the hypothesis predicts that bilingualism leads to the homogeneity of processes and representations in the mental lexicon.

5 Conclusion

My goal in this chapter has been to bring to the foreground recent developments in the lexical processing literature that lead us to the view that monolinguals and bilinguals are in possession of a single mental lexicon. By doing this, I have endeavored to highlight the fact that our current views of the bilingual lexicon are qualitatively different from those that characterized the early literature in which bilingualism was typically treated as a relatively exotic ability in which an individual could in principle behave as a native speaker of more than one language. In contrast, recent treatments take as their point of departure the fact that more than half of the world's population is bilingual. These bilinguals typically do not have equal proficiency in their languages and do not have separate lexicons. But they do typically know many more words than monolinguals do. The Homogeneity Hypothesis addresses the issue of whether these words are represented in the mental lexicon in a homogeneous manner.

At present, there seems to be strong support for homogeneity at the organizational level. By postulating language tags as the means by which words of different languages are identified, we can model both interlingual and intralingual activation. By assuming that the lexicon is computationally encapsulated, we can model volitional language switching and deselection through extra-lexical systems that monitor and control the output of lexical activation.

The question of whether there is representational homogeneity is more complex. Here, the Homogeneity Hypothesis makes the somewhat counter-intuitive claim that bilingual lexical representations have a single (expanded) architecture that can accommodate morphological differences among languages. It claims that bilinguals develop a single architecture for representing monomorphemic and multimorphemic forms of different languages, that different languages make use of a common set of morphological nodes in the mental lexicon, and that they employ the same set of procedures for parsing complex words of different languages. Whether or not these claims turn out to be supported is of course a matter for future research. However, whatever the result of this research, the Homogeneity Hypothesis offers the opportunity to test to what extent it will be possible to unite models of the bilingual and monolingual mental lexicon.

Notes

1   The term "bilingualism" has been notoriously difficult to define. In this chapter I use the term "bilingual" to refer to people who can produce and understand more than one language. Thus intermediate and advanced second language learners would be considered to be bilinguals as would others who have a functional ability in two or more languages. The use of this relatively unrestricted definition in this chapter allows us to address issues concerning the organization of two languages in one mind as well as issues related to second language development.
2   Weinreich himself expressed his model using the structuralist terminology of de Saussure and did not employ cognitivist terms such as conceptual and lexical representations.
3   It is important here to note that the claim in the Revised Hierarchical Model is based on negative evidence (i.e., not finding significant priming effects). Such failure to find statistical significance in psycholinguistic research is of course always consistent with two conclusions: That the putative connections do not exist or that they do exist but are not detectable in a particular experimental paradigm relative to other stronger effects.

References

Aitchison, J. (1994) *Words in the mind*. Oxford: Blackwell.

Beauvillain, C. and Grainger, J. (1987) Accessing interlingual homophones: Some limitations of a language selective access. *Journal of Memory and Language* 26: 658–72.

Chen, H.-C. and Ho, C. (1986) Development of Stroop interference in Chinese–English bilinguals. *Journal of Experimental Psychology: Learning, Memory, & Cognition* 12: 397–401.

—— and Leung, Y. S. (1989) Patterns of lexical processing in a non-native language. *Journal of Experimental Psychology: Learning, Memory, & Cognition* 15: 316–25.

De Bot, K. and Schreuder, R. (1993) Word production and the bilingual lexicon. In R. Schreuder and B. Weltens (eds.), *The Bilingual Lexicon*, pp. 191–214. Philadelphia, PA: John Benjamins.

De Groot, A. (1993) Word type effects in bilingual processing tasks. In R. Schreuder and B. Weltens (eds.), *The Bilingual Lexicon*, pp. 27–52. Philadelphia, PA: John Benjamins.

—— (1992) Bilingual Lexical Representation: A Closer Look at Conceptual Representations. In R. Frost and L. Katz (eds.), *Orthography, Phonology, Morphology, and Meaning*, pp. 389–412. Amsterdam: Elsevier.

—— and Nas, G. (1991) Lexical representation of cognates and noncognates in compound bilinguals. *Journal of Memory and Language* 30: 90–123.

Dijkstra, T. and Van Heuven, W. (1998) The BIA model and bilingual word recognition. In J. Grainger and A. Jacobs (eds.), *Localist Connectionist Approaches to Human Cognition*. Hove: Lawrence Erlbaum.

—— Van Jaarsveld, H. and Brinke, S. (1998) Interlingual homophone recognition: Effects of task demands and language intermixing. *Bilingualism: Language and Cognition* 1: 51–66.

Drew, E. and Zwitserlood, P. (1995) Morphological and orthographic similarity in visual word recognition. *Journal of Experimental Psychology: Human Perception and Performance* 21: 1098–116.

Ervin, S. and Osgood, C. E. (1954) Second language learning and bilingualism. *Journal of Abnormal and Social Psychology, Supplement* 49: 139–46.

Fox, E. (1996) Cross language priming from ignored words: evidence for a common representational system in bilinguals. *Journal of Memory and Language* 35: 353–70.

Gerard, L. and Scarborough, D. (1989) Language-specific lexical access of homographs by bilinguals. *Journal of Experimental Psychology: Learning Memory and Cognition* 15: 305–13.

Gollan, T., Forster, K. and Frost, R. (1997) Translation priming with different scripts: Masked priming with cognates and noncognates in Hebrew–English bilinguals. *Journal of Experimental Psychology: Learning, Memory and Cognition* 23: 1122–39.

Grainger, J. and Dijkstra, T. (1992) On the representation and use of language information in bilinguals. In R. J. Harris (ed.), *Cognitive Processing in Bilinguals*, pp. 207–20. Amsterdam: Elsevier.

—— and O'Regan, J. (1992) A psychophysical investigation of language priming effects in two English–French bilinguals. *European Journal of Cognitive Psychology* 4: 323–39.

Green, D. W. (1998) Mental control of the bilingual lexico-semantic system. *Bilingualism: Language and Cognition* 1: 67–81.

—— (1986) Control, activation and resource: A framework and a model for the control of speech in bilinguals. *Brain and Language* 27: 210–23.

Grosjean, F. (1998) Studying bilinguals: Methodological and conceptual issues. *Bilingualism: Language and Cognition* 1: 133–49.

—— (1997) Processing mixed language: issues, findings and models. In M. De Groot and J. Kroll (eds.), *Tutorials in Bilingualism*, pp. 225–54. Mahwah, NJ: Lawrence Erlbaum.

—— (1989) Neurolinguists beware! The bilingual is not two monolinguals in one person. *Brain and Language* 36: 3–15.

Hamers, J. and Blanc, M. (1989) *Bilinguality and Bilingualism*. New York: Cambridge University Press.

Hummel, K. (1986) Memory for bilingual prose. In J. Vaid (ed.), *Language Processing in Bilinguals: Psycholinguistic and Neuropsychological Perspectives*. Hillsdale, NJ: Lawrence Erlbaum.

Kolers, P. and Gonzales, E. (1980) Memory for words, synonyms, and translation. *Journal of Experimental Psychology, Human Learning and Memory* 6: 53–65.

Kroll, J. and Curley, J. (1987) Lexical memory in novice bilinguals: The role of concepts in retrieving second language words. In M. M. Gruneberg, P. E. Morris, and R. N. Sykes (eds.), *Practical Aspects of Memory: Current Research and Issues*, vol. 2, pp. 389–95. London: Wiley.

—— and De Groot, A. (1997) Lexical and conceptual memory in the bilingual: mapping form to meaning in two languages. In M. De Groot and J. Kroll (eds.), *Tutorials in Bilingualism*. Mahwah, NJ: Lawrence Erlbaum.

—— and Stewart, E. (1994) Category interference in translation and picture naming: evidence for asymmetric connections between bilingual memory representations. *Journal of Memory and Language* 33: 149–74.

Levelt, W. J. M. (1989) *Speaking*. Cambridge, MA: MIT Press.

Libben, G. (1994) Computing hierarchical morphological structure: a case study. *Journal of Neurolinguistics* 8: 49–55.

—— Derwing, B. and de Almeida, R. (in press) Ambiguous Novel Compounds and Models of Morphological Parsing. *Brain and Language*.

MacNamara, J. (1967) The linguistic independence of bilinguals. *Journal of Verbal Learning and Verbal Behavior* 6: 729–36.

—— and Kushnir, S. (1971) Linguistic independence of bilinguals: the input switch. *Journal of Verbal Learning and Verbal Behavior* 10: 480–7.

Marslen-Wilson, W., Tyler, L. K., Waksler, R. and Older, L. (1994) Morphology and meaning in the English mental lexicon. *Psychological Review* 101: 3–33.

McClelland, J. L. and Rumelhart, D. E. (1981) An interactive activation model of context effects in letter perception, Part 1: An account of basic findings. *Psychological Review* 88: 375–405.

McCormack, P. (1977) Bilingual linguistic memory: The independence–interdependence issue revisited. In P. Hornby (ed.), *Bilingualism: Social, Psychological and Educational Implications*. New York: Academic Press.

Napps, S. (1989) Morphemic relations in the lexicon. Are they distinct from semantic and formal relationships? *Memory and Cognition* 17: 729–39.

—— and Fowler, C. A. (1987) Formal relationships among words and the organization of the mental lexicon. *Journal of Psycholinguistic Research* 16: 257–72.

Norman, D. and Shallice, T. (1986) Attention to action: Willed and automatic control of behaviour. In R. J. Davidson, G. E. Schwartz and D. Shapiro (eds.), *Consciousness and Self-regulation*, vol. 4, pp. 1–18. New York: Plenum Press.

Paradis, M. (1987) Neurolinguistic perspectives on bilingualism. In M. Paradis and G. Libben (eds.), *The Assessment of Bilingual Aphasia*. Hillsdale, NJ: Lawrence Erlbaum.

—— (1978) The stratification of bilingualism. In M. Paradis (ed.), *Aspects of Bilingualism*. Columbia, SC: Hornbeam Press.

Penfield, W. and Roberts, L. (1959) *Speech and Brain Mechanism*. London: Oxford University Press.

Potter, M. C., So, K.-F., Von Eckardt, B. and Feldman, L. B. (1984) Lexical and conceptual representation in beginning and proficient bilinguals. *Journal of Verbal Learning & Verbal Behavior* 23: 23–38.

Schreuder, R. and Baayen, H. (1995) Modeling morphological processing. In L. B. Feldman (ed.), *Morphological aspects of language processing*, pp. 345–64. Hillsdale, NJ: Lawrence Erlbaum.

Shank, R. (1982) *Dynamic Memory: A Theory of Reminding and Learning in Computers and People*. Cambridge: Cambridge University Press.

Tzelgov, J., Henik, A. and Leiser, D. (1990) Controlling Stroop interference: evidence from a bilingual task. *Journal of Experimental Psychology* 16: 760–71.

Van Heuven, W., Dijkstra, A. and Grainger, J. (1998) Orthographic neighborhood effects in bilingual word recognition. *Journal of Memory and Language* 39: 458–83.

Weinreich, U. (1953) *Languages in Contact: Findings and Problems.* New York: Linguistic Circle of New York.

Zwitserlood, P. (1994) The role of semantic transparency in the processing and representation of Dutch compounds. *Language and Cognitive Processes* 9: 341–68.

Index

Major or detailed references are shown in **bold** type. Continuous page references ignore any intervening tables or diagrams.